THE BROTHERHOOD OF THE TOWER RATS

BY GOODWIN TURNER

COVER BY STAR ADAMS

DEDICATION

This book is dedicated to my wife, Star, who without her unconditional love and encouragement, I would never have dedicated the time and effort into writing this book. I also would like to thank my family and friends who, through the years, constantly bombarded me with the words, "You should write a book."

In addition, this book is meant to bring attention to the people who serve their country. Whether it is serving their country in the military, volunteering in their neighborhood, or helping a stranger, it is all service to their country. Anybody who serves in any capacity should be recognized for that effort. One day perhaps nobody will ever have to serve in the military ever again, and instead of declaring war on other nations, we can declare war on hunger and homelessness.

People often left the confines of Miesau Army Depot, MAD for short, in exchange for a padded cell and a straight jacket at Landstuhl Army Medical Center in Germany. Military Policeman stationed at MAD referred to it as Tower Rat Hell. For me, it was the place where I transitioned from a going-nowhere teenager into a functional adult. I did not take any pictures, not even of fellow soldiers, some of whom are my closest friends even to this day, as it was not a place I wanted to remember. Yet, it is a place I can never forget. I was at MAD for fourteen months of the 612 months of my existence, yet it was and still is a big part of who I am. Graduating from high school in 1979, I joined the Army and went to basic training and MP School before flying to Germany for my first duty assignment. I arrived as a naive recruit, fresh out of basic training, feeling I could conquer the world. When I departed, I no longer felt I could conquer the world, but instead knew I could survive in the world. My second duty assignment in Germany was at a Military Police Unit for the 8th Infantry Division where I was in perilous situations, part from my own rebellious attitude and part because of the bullying mentality of a handful of people. This story is a recounting of my time in the military from July 1979 through July 1982. I recall one event in particular more than any other that involved one of my former roommates. When I last saw him in 1981, he was in the psychiatric ward in Landstuhl, Germany. To this day, I wonder what ever happened to him. Did he walk out of the mental ward a free man and return to active duty like I did? Did he suffer permanent mental scars that affected him for the rest of his life? I desire answers to these questions. If he ever reads this book, I hope he is not offended or ashamed by my telling this story. In sharing the details of how I ended up in a mental ward, I am going to start from the beginning of my military career and move forward in chronological order, sharing the events, not only for readers of this book to have insight, but also that I may find answers and make sense of everything that happened.

Tuesday, July 10, 1979:

I arrived at the Processing Center in Denver for enrolling in the Military at 6:30 am on July 10, 1979. I had signed an intent to enlist in December of 1978 for the Delayed Entry Program during my senior year of high school. The enlistment became official on January 31, 1979 when I went to the recruiting office and completed the paperwork to join the military. I had turned 18 during the Fall of 1978, so I did not need my parents' permission to join; otherwise, I suspect my mother would have made a fuss. I thought the day would never arrive. I remember being filled with anticipation of independence and adventure, yet afraid of the unknown events that could occur in the military -- like being killed in a war. The Vietnam War had ended several years before, so at the time no wars were in progress and none seemed to be pending, but you never knew. In addition, the dread of going to boot camp dominated my thoughts. How tough would it be and could I endure it? I was involved in athletics in High School, so I was in fair shape. However, from the time that school ended in June until my enlistment went into effect on July 10, I partied and drank every day. I spent the last night of civilian freedom celebrating at another party where I knew one person. Again, like every night the previous month, I got drunk. This time I awoke in a bathtub, not remembering much of the night before. I had gained about twenty pounds of weight from drinking during the month. My girlfriend took me home in the early pre-dawn hours, pleading with me not to go into the service, but to stay and marry her. I told her I could not. She never spoke to me again after that night.

That morning was somewhat rough. Saying good-bye to my younger brothers, stepfather, and mother was tough. At that moment, I never felt closer to them. My recruiter, Sergeant Jerry Morgan, arrived about 6:30 am to take me down to the processing center. He was a big man at 6'6" tall, weighing about 250 lbs. He was one of the recruiters who came to our high school back in December. The school had an assembly meeting in the theater for all the high school seniors at which two Army recruiters spoke, telling us about the great adventure we would have by joining the

Army. What caught my attention was the chance to go to other parts of the world. Having taken German Language classes throughout high school, I was intrigued at seeing Europe. Being lured into the trap, I picked up some of the brochures and was immediately pounced upon by Sergeant Morgan like a hungry car salesman selling a young rich kid his first car. He introduced himself and asked if any of the programs sounded interesting. Because my father was a policeman in Denver, I always thought a career in law enforcement sounded exciting. I told him that the Military Police sounded interesting. He said that he used to be in the Military Police. He did a couple of tours of duty in Vietnam, stating that he spent most of his time there on the 13th floor of a whore house, getting high and never once seeing enemy action during either tour. I was in a vulnerable time of my life. Not wanting to go to college, yet, not having any career goals in mind and having broken up with a girlfriend about a month before, I was depressed. Going on an adventure was what the doctor ordered. I enlisted in the Delayed Entry program that day.

When Morgan arrived at my house, he already had two other people in his car with him. We had become friends between the time that I enlisted and the time that I graduated from school, as Morgan would drop by and weight lift at our high school because he was a friend with our football coach. Before departing, my family and I all hugged, cried, and said our farewells. The next thing I knew, I was standing in line after line at the processing center, filling out stacks of papers and taking eye exams, hearing tests, psychological evaluations, physical exams, and aptitude tests. I was surprised so many people – about 300 -- were processing in for various branches of the military.

Within an hour of arriving, my recruiter notified me that my birth certificate and social security card had been misplaced and that they needed copies of those items again. I told him my parents had them. He instructed me to stay at the processing center and finish testing while he obtained the documents.

During the aptitude testing and psychological testing, thirty people at a time went into a room full of school desks to test. The physical exam was awkward with two doctors in a room examining thirty people at a time. Everybody lined up against a wall in alphabetical order facing inward towards the doctors who stood in the center of the room. The doctors had us perform various exercises like jumping jacks, push-ups, and jumping on one foot. They also checked for hernias and hemorrhoids.

At the hearing test, six people at a time entered into a sound proof room with six compartments, each containing a chair and table where we sat and put on a headset. Through the headset, we heard a series of beeps in either the left ear or the right ear in a random sequence. If the beep was in the left ear, we pushed the left button on your table; if in the right, we pushed the right button. For the life of me, I could not hear the beeps. All I could hear was the clicking of other people pushing their buttons, but which buttons? As it turned out, I flunked the hearing test. However to rule out an equipment malfunction, they asked if I would test again. Like an idiot, I agreed. After standing in line again for another thirty minutes, I found myself once again sitting in one of those booths in the soundproof room. Once again, I could hear other people's buttons clicking, but I could not hear the beeping tones through my headset. Not wanting to flunk the test, I leaned back and started watching the people around me and whenever they pushed a button, I pushed the same button. What an idiot I was. Had I not passed that test by cheating, I never would have spent the next three years in the military.

As the day progressed, I had no other problems with any of the other tests. It was a long, exhausting day, taking eight hours to be processed. One of the highlights of the day was after all the processing was completed, we were taken into a room -- thirty people at a time -- and sworn into the military.

The Oath of Enlistment was as follows:

"I, Goodwin Turner, do solemnly swear that I will support and defend the Constitution of the United States against all enemies, foreign and domestic; that I will bear true faith and allegiance to the same; and that I will obey the orders of the

President of the United States and the orders of the officers appointed over me, according to regulations and the Uniform Code of Military Justice. So help me God."

It was after this swearing in ceremony that my recruiter told me he was not successful in reaching my parents in time, so they were not going to be able to provide a copy of the birth certificate that day in order for the Army to make the enlistment official. Therefore, I was not able to leave for basic training. "You have two choices," Sergeant Morgan said. "I can take you home tonight and pick you up again tomorrow morning when I pick up your birth certificate, or the Army is willing to put you up at a hotel in downtown Denver for the evening and pay for your dinner." *Heck there was no choice.* It was a thirty-minute ride home to my parent's house.

"I'll stay at the hotel," I said without hesitation, not wanting to go home again for another night and go through another emotional goodbye. Besides, the hotel was one of the premier hotels in Denver.

Eight other people at the processing center were put up at the hotel, too. They were all from out of town and were delayed due to a mix up in paperwork, too. We were driven to the hotel in a van and given vouchers for the restaurant. After getting our rooms, we all took our suitcases to our various rooms and then met back down in the lobby to go to dinner. Before going downstairs, I called my parents to tell them what was going on. They said they had made copies of my birth certificate and SS card and that Sergeant Morgan had picked them up. My mom told me that she had taken off from work a little early to go out to the airport to see me off that day. She thought she had missed me and stood at the airport waving at the plane, thinking I was aboard.

Later that evening during dinner, somebody suggested the idea that we pool our money and buy liquor for a party. A couple of the people went out to a liquor store and bought the booze. Upon returning with the booze, we proceeded to gather ice from the ice machine and loaded it into a bathtub in one of the rooms.

We had a keg of beer and several bottles of whiskey and rum. The evening was a blur and all that I can recall is that at some point we had broken into a supply closet, taken a vacuum to the rooftop - something like 16 stories up -- and heaved it into the swimming pool. *We had to do it.* The swimming pool had black circles within circles painted on its floor, making it look like a giant target.

Wednesday, July 11, 1979:

The next morning we were driven back to the processing center to finish paperwork. Then I was driven out to the airport, where for the first time in my life, I stepped on to an airplane. It was a day I will never forget. Besides flying for the first time in my life, I was, also, leaving home for the first time. I was an adult. The future was wide open and I foresaw all kinds of heroism in my future as a military policeman. But I had doubts. I was heading for six weeks of boot camp, followed by eight weeks of military police training. It was supposed to be brutal but I had confidence I could do it. The flight was a four-hour, non-stop, 747 to Atlanta and left around noon. I did not give boot camp much thought on the plane ride, as I was hypnotized by the view from my window. I was amazed by the blueness of the sky and the illusion of the clouds being solid. I was not at all afraid of flying at that time, though years later I developed a fear of flying while taking private airplane lessons. Once the plane landed in Atlanta, I had to check in at a small military station at the airport where I waited with others for more people to arrive from various parts of the country. At 6 pm, thirty of us were loaded onto a greyhound bus for a long ride to Fort McClellan, Alabama, where we were to train for the next fourteen weeks. The bus ride was somber. Most people were exhausted from traveling and tried to sleep, but four people on the bus were awake and talking most of the trip, and they seemed to be having a good time, keeping the rest of us awake. It was after midnight when we arrived in Fort McClellan.

The bus pulled up next to some three-story tall buildings that looked new. They were all made of cement and steel and had a sterile look to them. The florescent lighting all around the buildings gave an artificial look of daylight to the night. When the bus stopped, a man in a "Smoky-the-Bear" hat boarded. "Ladies and Gentleman," he stated in a calm and pleasant voice. "Welcome to Fort McClellan, Alabama. From this moment onward you belong to the United States Army, but when I give the command to exit this bus, if you are not off this bus within thirty seconds, your ass will belong to me." Without delay several people jumped up from their seats.

"Sit down," the drill Sergeant yelled with his voice echoing throughout the whole bus so loud it hurt my ears. "Did I tell anybody to move? I do not believe I told anybody to move. Why are people moving on my bus? Pay attention to what I tell you and you may live to see another day."

Before the echoing stopped, people were back in their seats with every eye on the drill sergeant. Looks of terror were pasted on faces.

"When I tell you maggots to exit this bus, you will do so as quickly and as quietly as you can. If you have had anything to drink or eat on this bus, you will exit the bus with all of your trash and remaining food and throw it in the garbage can by that pole in the distance. Do not -- I repeat -- do not forget your suitcase as under no circumstances will you be allowed back on the bus. After you exit the bus, I want you to line up in a straight line against that wall to the left underneath that balcony."

People, me included, were looking out the bus windows, to see where the wall and trashcan were.

"Now, I know I've given you detailed instructions on what to do." The drill sergeant said. "Do you know how I know this? I know this because my lips are moving and I hear myself talking. Nonetheless, you mark my words, despite my clear instructions, one of you boneheads is going to mess up. Do not be that person who messes up. But I know somebody is going to mess up. Please somebody mess up because I want to hurt somebody tonight. Please somebody mess up." Fear gripped everybody. "What are you waiting for?" The drill sergeant yelled. "Why are you still sitting on this bus? If you are still sitting on this bus, then you are wrong. Get the hell off of my bus."

Everybody scrambled to their feet, grabbed their belongings and started shuffling to the exit as fast as possible. As each person got off the bus, he was greeted by four other drill sergeants who were yelling at the top of their voices as loud as they could. It was chaotic. People were running in every direction on the compass, trying to dodge the drill sergeants while making their way to either the trash can to throw away their trash and food or to line up against the wall. To make matters worse, the area next to the building where we were to assemble was all cement and it was slippery from the water sprinklers watering the surrounding grass areas. During the chaos, one of the recruits ran into one of the drill sergeants.

"I do not believe you did that," the drill sergeant yelled. "You assaulted me. Your fat ass belongs to me from now on and I am going to make your life a living hell from this moment onward, son. Now, drop and give me 10 pushups. The young man sat his suitcase down and on the cement patio started his 10 pushups. He did 10 pushups and sprung back to his feet.

"Did I dismiss you, recruit?" the drill sergeant yelled.

"No, sir," he replied, shaking in fear. By this time the rest of us were lined up against the wall.

"Sir?" the drill sergeant yelled into the face. If it were not for the "Smoky-the-Bear" hat the drill sergeant was wearing, which prevented him from getting any closer, he would have chewed the recruits nose off while yelling at him. "Did you call me sir?"

"Yes, sir," the recruit yelled back.

"Son, first you physically assaulted me with your fat ass, now, you insult my momma by calling me sir."

"I would not want to be in your shoes right now, son," another drill sergeant yelled in the recruits face, having run up to the side of him.

"Son, I'll have you know, my momma raised me to be an honorable, hard working man, not an officer," the first drill sergeant continued. "Do you see these stripes on my arm? These stripes are earned through hard work and I am damn proud of them. Do not ever call me sir again. You and every one of you sorry ass excuses for human beings here will refer to us as Drill Sergeant. Is that clear?"

"Yes, sir, Drill."

"What did you call me? Drop and give me 25 more pushups."

"You heard him maggots," another one of the five drill sergeants, yelled. All of you drop and give us 25 push-ups."

I felt sorry for this one kid. He had long, scraggly hair and was obese. However, he was not singled out for those reasons, but those things were brought up when they reached his name in the roll call. After we did our push-ups, they had us remain in the "company position," which is in the ready position to do a push-up, while they called each of our names. We had to respond, "Here, Drill Sergeant."

"Abbott, Clarence."

"Here, Drill Sergeant."

"Boyd, Michael."

"Here, Drill Sergeant," Boyd strained to yell out, losing his strength from holding himself up ready to do a push-up

The fat kid with the long, scraggly hair, Robert Butts, was from California. When they got to his name, they could not help but single him out.

"You've got to be fucking kidding me," the drill sergeant with the roster said. "What kind of fairy name is this? Butts, Ronald."

"Here, Drill Sergeant."

"Butts," the drill sergeant said with a tone of disbelief. "Are you telling me that Butts is your name?"

"Yes, drill sergeant," Butts responded, turning a bright red.

"Butts, look at your fat ass," the drill sergeant said. "Stand up so I and the rest of the platoon can have a look at your disgusting ass." Butts stood up.

"I want everybody to have a look at you, Butts," the drill sergeant said. I do not know how in the hell you got in the Army in the first place, but it is obvious they are desperate for recruits if they let you in. You're going to flunk out of basic training aren't you, Butts?"

"No, drill sergeant," Butts protested.

"Are you contradicting me, Butts?"

"No, drill sergeant."

"Sure you are, Butts. Drill Sergeant Leonard did you or did you not hear Private Butts call me a liar?"

"I heard plain as day. He called you a liar."

"Butts, I do not like being called a liar. Do you know why I do not like being called a liar?"

"No, drill sergeant," Butts responded. He was shaking and sweating something awful. I thought he was going to have a heart attack. I was dreading what may happen when they called my name.

"Let me tell you, Butts," the drill sergeant said. "When you call me a liar, you insult my momma. My momma did not raise a liar for a son. So let me ask you one more time, Butts. Are you going to flunk out of basic training?"

"No, drill sergeant."

"Butts, I like your attitude," the drill sergeant said. "I'm going to personally take you under my wing and see to it that you lose all that fat stored on your disgusting body. Would you like to lose fat, Butts?"

"Yes, drill sergeant," Butts said.

"Believe me you will."

During the rest of the role call, no other people were harassed quite to the extent of Butts. When my name was called, I responded, "Here, drill sergeant," and breathed a sigh of relief when they called the next name on the list.

After role call, we were instructed to leave our belongings while we formed columns of four. We were then marched over one column at time to a building where we were given two sheets and a blanket, but not before getting a lecture from the supply clerk who was waiting for us outside the building. This building, unlike the other buildings, looked like it was constructed during World War II. It had that Gomer Pyle barracks look to it.

"When you enter this building to get your linens, you will do so quietly and efficiently," the supply clerk stated. I was impressed with how young he looked; yet, he seemed to be so confident in ordering so many people around. "When you are given your linens, you will be required to sign for them. Make no mistake about it you are responsible for anything that happens to them. If you lose them, if they are stolen, or if you abuse them in any way, shape, or form, you will pay Uncle Sam the cost of replacing these linens. These linens do not belong to you. They belong to Uncle Sam and you are borrowing them from me. You will also be issued a standard lock and key that you will use for your wall locker while on the base. Do not lose it. Are there any questions? Good let's roll."

After the lecture, we filed into the room in a single file line. It took about an hour before we were finished. Next, we marched back to where our belongings were. We then were marched about a half mile away where we found ourselves standing in front of another Gomer Pyle building that was surrounded by several newer buildings that looked like office buildings. Even in the dark, I can remember thinking how spotless and clean everything looked, even the occasional older buildings. The landscaping was immaculate and the concrete walkways, eight feet wide, crisscrossed in perfect North, South, East, West directions, forming a perfect checkerboard look with immaculate-cut, green grass between each walkway. With the sprinklers running, it made for a cool summer evening - or by now early morning as it was well after midnight.

July 12, 1979 through July 19, 1979:

The building we were standing in front of turned out to be our temporary barracks. For the next week we were processed into the base, being issued a duffel bag, army fatigue uniforms, two pairs of boots, army green T-shirts, army green underwear, and army gear. In addition, we had to get shots, and the traditional Army haircut. The Drill Sergeants told us that getting the traditional crew cut was optional and that Army regulations required that we have a standard Army regulation haircut, which meant the hair, was not touching the ears or collar. However, it was implied that it would be in all of our best interests if we chose the traditional crew cut. As it turned out, all but one person, Private Bach, chose the crew cut. Bach had informed anybody who would listen that he had changed his mind about wanting to be in the military and was doing everything he could to hang on to his old civilian life, including keeping as much of his hair as he could. The drill sergeants started harassing Bach from the moment he stepped out of the barber chair, indicating that they were going to send him through basic training with the women. Fort McClellan was a coed basic training facility; however, the women had their own separate platoons.

We were the last of the companies to start basic training that summer and we ended up being the largest with five platoons in the company. We were at the processing center for about a week and, in between doing paper work, eating meals, and being issued gear, we had to do chores, like mowing lawns, cleaning the barracks, and picking up cigarette butts. I had to take an eye exam, too, so I could be issued Army glasses. The Army also issued glasses that fit inside our gas mask.

On the second day, around 8 pm, we were all in the barracks, cleaning it for an early morning inspection, when a drill sergeant walked in. "Attention, drill sergeant on premises," somebody yelled out, so as instructed to jump to attention at the foot of our beds whenever a drill sergeant entered the barracks, I did exactly that. We stood there while the drill sergeant checked on the status of the barracks, letting us know that all the cleaning we were doing up to that point was fruitless as the place looked like hell. While inspecting the barracks, he noticed my foot locker was left open, a violation.

"Private Turner, why is your foot locker unsecured," he barked.

"No excuse, Drill Sergeant."

"Well, it is obvious to me that you do not care about protecting your Army issued supplies," he pointed out. "Drop and give me 10 push-ups. When you are done, you will secure your wall locker and report to the kitchen for Kitchen Patrol (KP) duty for the rest of this week." I dropped to do my push-ups.

"One, Drill Sergeant. Two, Drill Sergeant. Three, Drill Sergeant," I yelled out counting each pushup as we were taught to do. As I did my pushups, he continued going through the barracks finding various violations from five more people. Each person had to do pushups and was assigned to do KP duty for the week. I wrote home to my parents and grandmother about the experience. They all thought it was funny.

KP did not turn out to be too bad. We had to collect the dinner trays, empty the trash, sweep the floors, mop the floors, and help wherever directed to do so. There were no piles of potatoes to be peeled. On the last night of working KP, the six of us who were assigned to the KP were sitting around at a table taking a break during clean up after the final meal. One of the guys asked if he could borrow some money. Everybody told him, "No." He picked up a bottle of Tabasco sauce sitting on the table and offered to drink it for money. We decided it would be worth it, so we all pulled some money together, came up with twelve dollars, and told him he could have it if he drank the whole bottle within thirty seconds and without drinking any water for thirty minutes afterward

Sure enough, he drank that whole bottle of Tabasco sauce down, chugging it straight from the bottle. He turned about six shades of red and looked like he was going to die, but he did it.

Thursday, July 19, 1979:

While waiting in line to get shots, I was pulled from the line and moved ahead to get my shot. I was then directed to report to a room in one of the office buildings adjacent to the clinic. When I arrived I was surprised to find out the reason I was called over there was that the Army wanted me to take a language skills assessment test. They said my 127 score on the Army's Skill Qualification Test (SQT) was high, so they wanted me to take a test to see if I would qualify for the Army's language school and consider switching from Military Police training. I was not as smart as they thought, as I told them, "No, I do not want to do anything other than being in the Military Police." *What a dumb ass.* I did not realize it then, nor knew anything about what Military Police duty consisted of, or else I would have begged to be sent to the Language School. I would have been paid to learn a foreign language at a school for a year. What a plus that would have been in any future career. But, no, I was brainwashed by my recruiter that Military Police was the way to go -- and I believed that with all my heart for about another four months.

Friday, July 20, 1979:

While at the processing center, each person was assigned to a company made up of four platoons with sixty people per platoon. Each platoon was sub-divided into four squads of fifteen people. Each company started their basic training two weeks apart. I was assigned to Company F of the 12th Battalion, otherwise known as Foxtrot. We had five platoons made up of sixty people each. It was the largest company on the base, as the other companies had four platoons. After basic training was over, I felt cheated, as being the largest company on the base we were not given as much training as the companies with four platoons. We spent more time standing in line waiting to eat our three meals per day than anything else - even on the days that we ate out in the field or ate C-rations, it took forever to feed 300 people. That's not to say we were not busy. Sleep was also rare. I was disappointed in the lack of physical training. I had always imagined that basic training would consist of a lot of exercise and physical training. However, as my records would later show, physical training records were forged.

The barracks for Foxtrot were in two brand new buildings. They were each three stories in height and made of masonry. They sat side by side with a huge mess hall in between the two of them. On the ground floor were the drill sergeant's offices, the laundry facility, the mess hall, and the parade area where we fell into formation every morning. The parade area was in an opened-air concrete space that was covered by the second floor of each building. I was assigned to the fourth platoon and our barrack was on the third floor of the first building. Third platoon was on the second floor below us. The first and second platoon occupied the top two floors of the other building. The fifth platoon was made up of the people who, at the last minute, were assigned to our company. They did not even arrive at the base until about a week after we were all supposed to have started basic training. It was a last minute decision to add a fifth platoon to our company in an effort to squeeze as many recruits through training as soon as possible; otherwise, the people in the fifth platoon would have had to wait for six months for another basic training to begin. Five other companies were going through basic training at the time we started. Each company was in a different phase of training. The other companies were Alpha Company, Bravo Company, Charlie Company, Delta Company, and Echo Company.

We were marched over from the processing center to our new barracks where upon our arrival, our platoon was greeted with a lecture by Drill Sergeant Watson. "You maggots belong to me from this point forward," he said while we stood at attention. "From this point onward, I am your mother and your father. However, you will not address me as mother or father. You will address me as Drill Sergeant. Is that clear?"

"Yes, Drill Sergeant," we hollered with the response echoing throughout the cement walls and overhang.

"That was pathetic. Take your right hand," he commanded, "and grab hold between your legs, and see if you have a pair of balls. If you do, let's try that again, and sound off like you have a pair of balls dangling between your legs."

"Yes Drill Sergeant," we hollered collectively even louder than before with the echo hurting my ears. *How dumb is this?* I thought. *What is the purpose of having us yell like idiots?*

Drill Sergeant Watson told us that we had been assigned to squads and that four squad leaders had been chosen from among the platoon. He explained that when we went up to the barracks, we would find our bunk assignments with our wall lockers. The bunks were in rows of four, fifteen to a row, so that each squad had their own row of bunks. Private First Class Tonkell was the squad leader for my squad. He entered the military as a Private First Class (PFC, E-3 pay grade) because he had been in ROTC throughout high school.

One person, Specialist Thompson, was given the assignment of being the platoon Sergeant. He was entering basic training as a Specialist (E-4 pay grade). Most of us were entering the military as Privates (E-1 pay grade). Thompson had served in the Army beforehand in Vietnam. He told us later that he earned a Purple Heart, having lost one of his testicles to grenade shrapnel. He had decided to rejoin the military because he was a newlywed with a newborn baby and he needed the income to support his family. He had been out for seven years. I estimated his age to be between 35 and 40 though I never knew for sure. Not knowing much about military protocol at that point, I found it odd at the time how the drill sergeants treated Thompson as an equal. I learned that other soldiers looked up to the Vietnam vets who had actual combat experience. This was five years after Vietnam ended, so many of the younger Drill Sergeants had not had combat experience either. Of course, even though Thompson had the respect of the drill sergeants, they still had to give the impression that he was subject to their discipline and all the training of basic training.

Drill Sergeant Watson dismissed us from formation so that we could go upstairs to our barracks to unpack our duffel bags. He gave us thirty minutes to unpack and then we were to fall back in for dinner. The stairwell leading up to the third floor was all cement, about 15-feet wide, allowing several people abreast to run up and down the stairs. Carrying our belongings up the stairs was a relief, knowing that I would not have to be lugging that stupid duffel bag around for a while.

I had never been away from home on my own for more than a weekend before joining the army. It seemed strange to be having the responsibilities of an adult; yet, we were told what to do for every waking moment, including when to eat. I was not looking forward to going to dinner. I was hoping we could be released for the day so that we could go to bed. I was tired. During the week that I had been here, we ate three solid meals per day. They were great meals, surpassing many restaurants in taste and variety in menu items. I did not know for sure, but I felt I had gained weight from overeating during the first week I was at the base. Before arriving at Foxtrot Company, it took about an hour from start to finish eating, which included standing in line to get your food, eating it, and clearing your table. The chow hall we ate at while processing in at the base was one of several chow halls on the base, and that was the chow hall were most of the permanent duty stationed personnel ate. The chow hall that we ate at once arriving at Foxtrot Company was shared between our company and Echo Company, feeding 600 people per day, three times per day.

Do you know how long it takes to feed 600 people? A long time. Most of that time was spent standing in line at parade rest, which is a relaxed stance of standing at attention. You stand with your feet about shoulder width apart, hands clasped behind your back with one hand resting in the palm of the other hand facing outward, resting in the small of your back. During parade rest, we were not allowed to talk or move. You look straight ahead. So while standing in line for chow, we were staring at the back of somebody else's head for over an hour. It took every bit of two hours to feed both companies. This was not two hours per day, but two hours per meal, which meant we were standing in line at parade rest for six hours of every day. After a few days of standing at parade rest for hours on end, plus from putting on weight from the frequent, big meals, I soon started dreading mealtime. It was stressful, as the drill sergeants were required to get us through the basic training, which meant we had to have all of the required classes, so they tried to get us through mealtime as fast as possible so training for that day could be completed. The line wrapped around the building like a coiled snake outside the doors of the chow hall entrance. Meanwhile, the drill sergeants policed the line, making sure we stood at parade rest, and kept the line moving as fast as possible. Once inside, we grabbed a tray, silverware, a glass, and a plate. It was a cafeteria style of serving where we moved along the line picking out ready-made items that we wanted to eat while ordering other items like hamburgers from the cooks. Once we had our food, we found a seat and ate without speaking as fast as we could so somebody else could take our seat as soon as we finished. While inside, drill sergeants from each platoon made sure we kept quiet, making us eat as fast as we could because space was limited and they had to have the seat freed so more people could get inside to eat.

Saturday, July 21, 1979:

Basic training lasted six weeks, followed by eight weeks of military police academy training. I was under the false assumption that the six-week basic training started from the day we arrived on the base. I was disappointed to find out it did not. While waiting for the people in the fifth platoon to be processed and assigned to the Company, Drill Sergeant Watson, was teaching us the basics of marching, singing cadence, making our bunks, proper wearing of the uniform, passing inspections, falling into formation, standing at attention, standing at parade rest, standing at ease, saluting, exercising, and cleaning the barracks. All that time, I thought we were doing basic training, thinking the time was blowing by. However, about noon that day, Drill Sergeant Watson lectured us after an inspection, telling us how pathetic we were and that we had better shape up prior to basic training starting on Monday. *Starting on Monday*, I thought, are *we not already two weeks into basic training or what? Who is in charge of this incompetent organization? I want a refund.* What a let down to find out we had not even begun training, yet.

After lunch, Drill Sergeant Watson gave us a marching lesson en route to the base commissary. The commissary was two miles away from our barracks and it was 100 degrees outside, so he let us march over to the commissary in our T-shirts. Marching was cool to do when somebody good at calling out cadence was in charge of the march. The commissary reminded me of the modern day Wal-Mart. It had everything under the sun. I ended up buying a shoeshine kit and a transistor radio, hoping to catch some baseball games on the radio. Upon returning to the barracks that afternoon, Drill Sergeant Watson informed us that tomorrow morning, Sunday, we would be having an inspection of our barracks and that we should budget our time for the rest of the day preparing the barracks. Squad leaders were responsible for assigning clean up duties to each member of the squad. In addition, we were to get our lockers organized and ready for inspection, too.

Thursday, July 26, 1979:

During morning formation, I was ordered to report to sickbay at 8 am with twelve other people from the company. I had a bad feeling they were going to break bad news to me, discharging me from the Army for something to do with the rheumatic fever I had as a kid. Perhaps they discovered some sort of hidden heart problem. However, it turned out to be for a bee-sting allergy condition. The doctors wanted to confirm what type of reactions I had when stung to determine if they should give the drill sergeants a bee-sting prescription in my name should I have a reaction from a sting. I was in and out of the doctor's office by 9 but had to wait for the other twelve people before being marched back to where the rest of the company was training that day. I feared we were missing training and have that result in having to do a make up day later on down the road. As it turned out, by the time we arrived at the classroom, everybody was still outside in a long line standing at parade rest, as usual, waiting to enter the building. That day we received training on the M-16 rifle. We were assigned an M-16 rifle to be used throughout basic training. The armory was on the ground level of our barracks. The entry to the armory was a steel door with a swing window on it made of metal bars and a steel roll-down door that secured the entrance. We had to check out our weapons and check them back in each day. Later during Military Police Training, we would also be issued 45 automatics.

During the class we were seated at tables in a huge auditorium. School cafeteria tables were set up throughout the area. However, some people had to find spots on the floor along the outer walls of the classroom. Each person had a place mat with actual-sized drawings of all the M-16 parts on it. Like a kids mix and match game, we had to take the rifle apart and place the parts on the appropriate drawing. *Real high tech stuff.* The class lasted four hours. We were taught about the parts of the M-16, how to take it apart, how to put it back together, how to clean it, how to use it, how much better it was than the Russian AK-47, how important it was to never lose, drop or damage it, and how to treat it better than your girlfriend, wife, mother, or God. We were warned if we didn't memorize all of the above, to make no bones about it, chances are we would die in combat. Prior to joining the Army, I had never seen a gun or rifle and I knew nothing about them. I did not care to learn about them while in the Army, and I still do not have any desire to know anything about guns, now, but I attempted to pay attention and learn that day, despite the boring topics, thinking it may save my life someday.

Monday, July 30, 1979:

We received word that our drill sergeant was being replaced and that the other drill sergeants from the other platoons would cover our platoon as needed until a replacement was found. Meanwhile Specialist Thompson, the Vietnam vet who rejoined the Army after several years of civilian life, was put in charge of our platoon. We were told that we would have a replacement drill sergeant within days. However, it took two weeks to get a replacement. During that time, our platoon was like the stepchild platoon. We were required to fall in for formation with the other platoons every morning for role call. Specialist Thompson would do our uniform inspection and march us to whatever class or training range we needed to be at for the day. We did not have any training at night except for a drill sergeant stopping by to harass us once. Thompson did a good job and people respected him but he was not trained in playing the mind games that drill sergeants play. He never yelled or raised his voice. He never ordered anybody to do a pushup. He did not act like a drill sergeant. We had it easy, being left on our own; not having consequences to suffer from not living up to a drill sergeant's expectations for uniform and barrack inspections.

What happened to our drill sergeant was not clear but the rumor was that he was at a bar where he sexually assaulted a female recruit who was also at the bar. We never saw him again. Of course, the other drill sergeants would not say what happened, but the rumor about the sexual assault was leaked by them and it appeared to be true.

Thursday, August 2, 1979:

We marched to a firing range where for the first time in my life, I fired a weapon. Before being allowed on the range, the sergeants who operated the facility sat us in bleachers and presented a class on safety procedures, warning us that anybody who knowingly or accidentally violated any of the safety procedures would flunk basic training and have to start again. The safety procedures stated: do not point your weapon except down range, never fire until given the order to fire, aim at the targets in front of us on the range – in other words, do not shoot at anybody else's target, cease firing whenever the order to cease is given, never fire if anybody is down range, and do not leave the firing range unless your weapon has been cleared by one of the sergeants on staff. We were also warned not to wear contact lenses on the range, as a few days before, a recruit who had been wearing contact lenses instead of his Army issued glasses had his eyes burned by the contacts melting from the heat of the weapon. The Sergeants gave a brief demonstration on how to hold the weapon when firing and how to hold it when not firing so that we would not accidentally shoot somebody. Last, we were reminded several times that if we failed to qualify with the M-16 we would flunk out of basic training and have to start all over again with a new unit in several months. Overall, it was a boring day, as we spent most of the day in the bleachers waiting to be able to shoot at the targets.

The firing range was a five-mile march away from most everything else on the post. Twenty-five people with a distance of five yards between each person could be on the range at a time. We were given a magazine clip of rounds, and during the initial time on the range, we were to shoot at a target to see if the rounds were hitting where we aimed. If they did not, the front and back sites on the weapon had some gizmos on them that adjusted the sites up or down.

After two hours of sitting in the bleachers, I was on the firing range, standing in a pre-dug foxhole from which to stand to fire the weapon at the 25-meter target to adjust the sites. Our group was all in our respective foxholes.

"On my command, you will take out a magazine clip and insert it into your M-16," the sergeant in the firing tower commanded over a loud speaker. Three other sergeants were on the ground walking up and down along the firing range, making sure everybody was following instructions and having no problems with their weapons. Each sergeant was responsible for supervising eight people.

"Insert your magazine," the man in the tower ordered. As people inserted their magazines, the sergeants on the firing line confirmed that each had inserted their magazine. Then the sergeants turned and held up a green flag, signaling to the tower that their people were ready.

"Next, on my command, you will chamber a round." The tension was growing.

"Chamber your round." The sergeants checked to make sure each of their people chambered a round and raised their flag once they did.

"Switch off your safety." The sergeants checked their people and raised the flag once the safeties were off. "Clear Down Range," the loud speakers bellowed. At this command, everybody was to check down range and look if anybody was down range of the targets. The sergeants again raised their flags, indicating it was clear.

"After you fire off three rounds at the 25-meter target, place your M-16 on the ground next to your foxhole, and then turn around facing the back of your foxhole," the voice in the tower said. The command we were waiting to hear followed: "Fire at will." Pulling the M-16 close into my shoulder, palms sweating, I tried doing what they said during the demonstration. I held my breath, focused on the target through my sites, and slowly squeezed the trigger. The shot rang out with little kick to the weapon. During the demonstration, they mentioned that we had to tuck the rifle into our shoulder to avoid getting a bruise. I repeated the process a second time and a third time. Afterward I laid my weapon down and turned to face the back of the foxhole as instructed. After everybody had fired their three rounds and was facing backwards, we were instructed to pick up our weapons, eject the magazine clip and pull the firing bolt back while the sergeants on the ground verified that our chambers were clear.

Next, the voice in the tower ordered us to climb out of our foxholes and march down to retrieve our paper targets. We then took them back to the bleachers where we sat, waiting for our drill sergeant to help adjust our sites. If we needed to adjust them, we had to wait to shoot another three rounds and see how the adjustment worked. If we did not need to adjust them, we waited for our first practice round. I needed to have my sites adjusted, as it appeared I hit the target once.

"Were you shooting at the same target for all three shots?" Drill Sergeant Colter asked.

"Yes, Drill Sergeant," I answered, insulted that he would ask.

"You may have hit the target twice as this hole seems quite large," he said. "Perhaps you shot two bullets through the same hole. But where did the third one go? Let me adjust your back site three left and your front site two up and see how that works."

I waited for another hour to fire off another three rounds and again waited for a drill sergeant to assist with adjusting the sites.

"At least all three rounds are on the target this time, but they are on the opposite side," the drill sergeant commented. "Did you aim for the exact same spot as you did the first time?"

"Yes, Drill Sergeant."

"Well, let me adjust them again three right and two down." *That was stupid*, I thought, as that put the sites right back to where they were the first time, but I figured he knew what he was doing. *Apparently not*. My next time on the line the three bullet holes were grouped two in one place near where I had hit the target the first time. The third shot was off by itself on the opposite side of the target. It could have been by shooting technique. After all, it was my first time firing.

"Why don't we go by these two bullets and ignore this one over here," the drill sergeant said, "and move your site back three left and the front site two up."

"Okay," I replied, thinking we were going around in circles, as this was the exact same changes made the first time around that were reversed the last time. After about an hour, I was back on the line again with several other people; however, each time I returned to the firing line, the group of people needing to adjust their sites was getting smaller and smaller. I was in the last group of people needing to get their sites adjusted. The correct terminology used for this procedure of firing three rounds and adjusting your site was called, "*Zeroing In.*" We were attempting to zero in on the target. If your bullet holes were down and to the right of the bulls eye, we raised our back site up or down a little and moved our front site left or right by turning them so many clicks counterclockwise or clockwise. I never did quite grasp the whole concept of how to adjust the sites, and never knew whether I should move them up or down, left or right, clockwise or counterclockwise. Shooting a weapon was not something I found interest in doing. I should had because in combat, it would be to my best interest if I shot the enemy before they shot me. However, I was eighteen and naive in trusting that they would teach us this stuff. They did not. Three hundred recruits needed had to be rushed through qualifications within two days. With all their safety rules, we were moving at a snail's pace. As it turned out, if somebody ended up getting a minimum qualifying score on their first practice round, they were considered qualified and did not get to do the last two practice rounds before doing the live qualification. It took me several attempts to get my sites adjusted. I also needed every attempt to get the minimum score to qualify. I had to go back to the range the next day with everybody else who still had not qualified. They had allotted our platoon two days at the range because they knew it would take that long to get us all qualified. My first two attempts at firing at the targets had me concerned as to whether I would qualify. We had to shoot at each target five times. There was a twenty-five meter target, a fifty-meter target, and a hundred-meter target, all the way up to a four-hundred meter target. We shot five times at each of the eight targets for a total of forty rounds. To qualify, we needed, at minimum, eighteen hits out of those forty shots. On my last attempt on late Friday afternoon, having missed most of the close up targets with a score of three out of twenty, I needed to hit fifteen of my last twenty shots while aiming at the targets at the farthest distances. Thinking I was going to flunk out of basic training, I was desperate. However, something clicked. I realized I was missing the targets because I was squeezing the trigger too hard. Concentrating on holding my breath, I bent my index finger at the knuckle at a ninety-degree angle. Holding it stiffly locked in this position, I slowly squeezed off each round while holding motionless without breathing, sometimes taking five seconds or more to squeeze the trigger. I was ecstatic to learn that I qualified hitting the target fifteen times with the last twenty shots. I hit the four-hundred meter target three out of five times and missed two shots on three of the closer targets. However, the drill sergeant thought that perhaps I may have hit some of those bullet holes in the same place, but he could not confirm that. My final score was eighteen out of forty shots, earning myself a Marksman medal.

Tuesday, August 7, 1979:

The Hand Grenade Qualifications took less skill than the M-16. However, the sergeants who operated the grenade range did show us a certain technique that was supposed to be used for throwing a grenade from a prone position, a standing position, and a squatting position. The technique was to use an overhand lob from any of those positions. I thought a simple overhand throw like throwing a baseball would have worked better and would have left us less exposed as a target while we were throwing the grenade. Even an underhand toss would have been better in some circumstances. However, they required us to use the overhand lob technique from all of the different positions. Prior to throwing the grenade, we had to yell, "Cover me while I throw a grenade."

"You're covered," was the response we waited to hear for before lobbing your grenade.

It was fun in that they had an obstacle course set up allowing us to throw dummy grenades at targets under various simulated circumstances. One circumstance was that we had to lob a grenade from a bunker into an enemy bunker; another was that we had to fire and maneuver up to a half-collapsed building and lob a grenade into the building. Yet another simulation was we had to throw a grenade over a wall at an enemy position. The final test was that we had to throw a grenade from inside a half-collapsed building through the window opening out towards an enemy target.

"Cover me while I throw a grenade," I yelled out.

"You're covered," the range instructor yelled out, watching and scoring me on my technique. Standing next to the window opening, back pressed against the wall, I followed the throwing technique they showed us. It was the perfect form. Standing sideways with my front foot and arm pointing towards the target, I lobbed the perfect overhand toss.

THUD! *What was that loud THUD?* I thought as I turned back to see what landed on the ground behind me. I lobbed the grenade against the wall above the window opening and the grenade bounced back on to the dirt floor behind me.

"BOOM! You're dead," the sergeant who was scoring yelled. "You just blew yourself up with a hand grenade."

I should have followed my instincts and thrown the damned thing like a baseball. I would have had a direct hit. I thought I was in trouble. At the same time, I was relieved we were not using real grenades on the range. They were all duds.

"Let's try it again," the scoring sergeant said. He was not mad at all. In fact, he looked rather amused. The look on his face led me to believe he knew that was going to happen. With the technique they taught for throwing the grenade, it happened to everybody who threw as instructed. It seemed idiotic to me that we had to be scored on how accurate we were at throwing hand grenades, but it taught me a valuable lesson – trust my instincts. At the Hand Grenade Range, I ended up with a final score of 48 out of 60 targets, which earned me a First Class Medal. *Who would have thought they gave medals for throwing grenades.*

Friday, August 10, 1979:

In the Army, somebody is held accountable for everything. The person in Charge is the one who is held accountable, unless the one in charge has high enough rank they are exempt from accountability, meaning a designated person who is lower in rank will be held accountable in their place for any major foul-ups. At night when the drill sergeants were not present, a CQ (Charge of Quarters) was in charge of each platoon. As the name suggests, the CQ was in charge of the quarters and of all the personnel assigned to that unit. A CQ worked at night, weekends, or holidays. During basic training, everybody had to pull several shifts of CQ duty two hours at a time. During my entire time at Basic and Military Police School, I pulled CQ duty seven times, averaging once about every two weeks. Each platoon had to have a CQ at night. The CQ walked through the barracks, did a head count to make sure nobody had gone AWOL, and reported fights or any other problems to the drill sergeant who was working that night. The drill sergeant would be asleep downstairs most of the night in the drill sergeant's office; however, once in a while they would make rounds through the company area, going into each platoon's barracks and make sure the CQ was alert while on duty. One night I had duty from Midnight to 2 am. After my shift, I woke my relief up and went to bed. Fifteen minutes later, the drill sergeant on duty stopped in the barracks and found no CQ. Checking his chart, he found who was supposed to be on duty and woke them up. That person claimed I never woke him up. The drill sergeant summoned me downstairs to his office. Slipping on a pair of pants and tennis shoes, I hurried downstairs. He asked whether I had awakened my relief or not. I informed him that I did wake him, but admitted that I did not see him get out of bed.

He lectured me about the importance of taking Security details like CQ serious and that I was responsible to have not gone to bed until relieved from my shift. He said I would perform many security details and that no matter how small they were, it was important to be serious on each job. He wrote up a warning about the incident that ended up going into my permanent file. He said he was going to write the other person up who was supposed to be on duty. I thought about protesting the whole thing because I did wake the creep up who was supposed to be on duty, and he did wake up; however, since I had dozed off during my own shift that night and on a previous shift, I thought better of it, thinking I should be happy that the punishment was nothing more than a written warning.

How important the CQ was and why they were needed became evident a few days later. Private Bach, the one who refused to get the crew cut during orientation, was pulling a two-hour shift as CQ. Since the day he refused to get the traditional crew cut, he was being harassed without mercy by the drill sergeants. During our four week's at Fort McClellan, Bach had not received another haircut and his hair was close to violating military regulations. He was always getting in trouble, and he had requested that the Army discharge him. He was always complaining, sometimes near the point of tears about how much he missed his girlfriend. Any time we saw him during breaks or free time, he was writing her a letter or talking to her from one of the pay phones in the company area. We had six pay phones in our company area for 240 people to share. Therefore, Bach was also pissing many people off by hogging a phone all the time. He was the most unpopular man in the company, and he was taking a lot of heat. During his CQ shift, Bach decided to go AWOL. He did not get far. He was caught and returned back to our Company, pending charges of some sort and a dishonorable discharge. However, until then, he was put back under the authority of the drill sergeants in our company. He told us that when he left, he made his way to the front gate of the base, but that he was caught by a Military Police patrol car when he tried to scale the fence to get off post.

Three days elapsed from the time he was caught scaling the fence to the time he showed back up in our platoon. He had been held in custody somewhere else on post for two days after being caught. When he was returned to the barracks, he looked haphazard and had a black eye. The black eye was nothing compared to the beating he took a few days later at the hands of some of the guys in the platoon. He received what was called a blanket party, where a group of people sneak up on a sleeping person, throw a blanket over them so they are blinded, pin them down, and beat the crap out of them. The drill sergeants were reminding anybody who screwed up that the whole squad, platoon, or company was, now, going to have to do push-ups, run an extra mile during physical training, have an inspection on Saturday, or miss out on a weekend pass due to that individual.

"I would not want to be in your shoes tonight, son, if you keep fucking up" the drill sergeants would say. "I imagine that if your platoon misses out on getting a weekend pass due to you fucking around, they're not going to be happy with you. In fact, you may find yourself on the receiving end of a blanket party or you may have an accident in the shower."

During basic training Bach was one of two people in our platoon who received a blanket party. I do not know when either person received their respective blanket parties. Both happened during the night and I must have slept through both of them. I was not involved in either one of them. If I had been asked to participate, I would have refused. I thought they were cowards and bullies.

Wednesday, August 15, 1979:

We were assigned a new drill sergeant on this day. He was fresh out of drill sergeant school and never had a platoon before. He was about five-feet, seven inches tall and I would be surprised if he weighed over one-hundred-twenty pounds. He was skinny. *How he had become a drill sergeant?* I wondered. However, it seemed many of the drill sergeants were skinny and it made me think that they became drill sergeants because they had inferiority complexes. After all, by 1979, the Army no longer had the draft, and they were trying to keep people enlisted or to get them to join for the first time. As a result, they could obtain training in about any classification of job by re-enlisting. This is not to say that some of these men and women were not great drill sergeants. Some were. In fact, some drill sergeants seemed super human. For instance, a drill sergeant in another company could do 500 pushups non-stop. He had arms as big as most people's thighs. Others could run marathons in combat boots. Some were known for their extraordinary cadence calling while marching. Of course, many were Vietnam veterans and they had everybody's respect for that.

Our new drill sergeant, Drill Sergeant Conners, seemed to be self-conscious about how skinny he was. The first formation we had he gave us a little pep talk about how we were going to be the best platoon the Army ever had. Then he went on and begged us to help him with a problem he was having with one of the other drill sergeants.

"I have a deal to make with you guys," he said with a pleading look in his eyes. "If somebody can come up with a good cadence song for us to sing while marching about how skinny Drill Sergeant Hammonds is, I'll owe that person big time. I will see to it that you get a weekend pass maybe extended out an extra two days. However, it has to be a song that will eat at him. Keep that in mind, okay fellas?"

This guy was Barney Fife impersonating a drill sergeant. He made Barney Fife look like Superman. It was obvious he was hurt from Drill Sergeant Hammonds poking fun at him for being so skinny, so Conners wanted to get even in the worst way. Drill

Scrgeant Hammonds was skinny, too, but not as skinny as Drill Sergeant Barney Fife. Nobody ever did come up with a song. In fact, nobody even tried.

Thursday, August 16, 1979:

One of the worst days of basic training was the NBC training, which stood for Nuclear, Biological, and Chemical warfare. We received instructions on the use of our gas masks and had to wear our chemical suits all day long in the hot Alabama summer sun. The chemical suit was equivalent to wearing a rubber raincoat. Everything, including our boots, was covered. Once we had our gas mask on, we were covered from head to toe. *Talk about sweating on a hot day in Alabama, this was torture.* During the class, we were instructed on the different types of Biological and Chemical hazards we might encounter during warfare. Nerve gas, being the most common, had an antidote. We were shown how to self inject the antidote into our thighs and how to administer a dose into the thigh of somebody else. We did not inject ourselves or anybody else; we went through the motions without unwrapping the injector pin. We were shown pictures of how the chemicals and biological weapons affect a person. Who these poor people were in the pictures I do not know, but they looked like they had suffered. When they told us the symptoms and reactions if exposed, we knew they had suffered.

We were also shown how to change the filters in our gas masks and how to clean them. To gain confidence in the use of our gas mask, we had to practice putting it on several times throughout the day when the drill sergeants threw tear gas canisters at us. Whoever detected gas first was supposed to yell out, "Gas," as loud as they could as a warning. You were then to hold your breath, yank out your gas mask, which was carried in a canvas bag on your hip, balance your steel pot helmet on your M-16, and slip the mask on over your head. Once on, we adjusted the straps to a tight fit, covered both side filters of the mask with each hand, and blew to clear the airways. Then we covered the filters in front of the mask and blew. This was done to insure a proper seal. The mask would suction itself on to your face. They were impossible to see out of the lenses. The clear eye coverings were all scratched and they fogged my eyeglasses as I breathed. They had special eyeglasses that were Army issued and custom made to fit inside your gas mask. The Army did not issue me the special eyeglasses until after basic training ended and never showed me how to fit them into the gas mask. In fact, I did not even know what they were until about a month before I left the military. I found it easier to remove my own glasses and put them in my shirt pocket while wearing the gas mask. However, without my glasses on, my vision sucked. Wearing the gas mask was the pits. Once we had our own gas mask on, we were to yell, "Gas," as loud as we could and then assist others with getting their masks on. The drill sergeants would time us to see how fast the entire company took to get their masks on; the faster the better. However, even if we put our masks on in record time, it was still not fast enough. We had to keep our masks on until one of the drill sergeants gave us the "all clear" approval to remove our masks. Early on in the day, we found out that it had to be the specific words, "All Clear," before we were allowed to remove our masks.

"Go ahead and remove your masks," one of the drill sergeants said as he removed his mask about fifteen minutes after one of our first practice drills. Following his lead, everyone -- except for the other drill sergeants -- removed their gas masks.

"What the hell is the matter with you people?" the other drill sergeants started yelling at everybody. "Are you stupid? Who told that you could remove your gas masks? You, you, and you, you're all dead," they said tapping people on the shoulders as they said it. "Never remove your gas masks unless the 'all clear' signal is given. Put those masks back on, then drop, and give us twenty-five pushups. What are you waiting for? Hurry up, put them on, or do you want to try for fifty pushups?"

Everybody scrambled to put their mask back on. In the process, somebody dropped their M-16 on the ground.

"Please, God, let that be what I think it was," Drill Sergeant Brown yelled out, looking like a lunatic ready to pounce. Out of all the drill sergeants, he was the one everybody seemed to fear the most. He was a large, muscular black man with large biceps about the size of a football. He had served in Vietnam and was always stating how he hoped somebody would screw up because it had been a while since he killed somebody. "Who is that who dropped their M-16? Whoever it is, your ass belongs to me, now."

Sergeant Brown ran to the recruit who had dropped it. As a result, he still did not have his gas mask on quite right, yet, either. I was glad that I was not in his shoes.

"Soldier, what are you trying to do to me?" Sergeant Brown screamed in his ear. "Are you trying to kill me by dropping a loaded weapon on the ground?"

"No Drill, Sergeant," he screamed.

"What are the rest of you mother-fucking maggots doing?" the company's Senior Drill Sergeant yelled. "You're supposed to be doing pushups, not watching Drill Sergeant Brown. Do you like Drill Sergeant Brown?"

"No, Senior, Drill Sergeant," several people yelled out.

"I better hear you counting off those push-ups loud and clear," he said. Everybody was doing push-ups at various speeds and people were haphazardly counting. Some people seemed to do twenty-five push-ups much faster than was humanly possible, and I suspected that, as often was the case, they did not really do the required number of push-ups. Most people, myself included, were about half done with the push-ups when the Senior Drill Sergeant blew a gasket.

"I can't hear you," he yelled. "You sound like a bunch of little girls. We are going to do these push-ups right." The people who had completed their push-ups moaned, as they knew they were now going to have to do them again – this time for real. "Assume the ready position," the senior drill sergeant commanded. The ready position for push-ups was with your body raised in the air, ready to lower yourself to the ground with your arms locked, body slanted, and back rigid. The senior drill sergeant was a stickler for keeping us in the ready position for a long time before giving the command to go down for the first push-up. Then once we lowered our self, he waited a long time before letting us rise to the ready position. Upon rising, we counted off each push-up, "One, Drill Sergeant," and so forth. After completing the first push-up if he was satisfied we did it right and we sounded off loud enough, he would give the up and down commands at regular intervals; If he were not, he would repeat the process and the first push-up would not count. After what seemed like an eternity of doing push-ups in our nuclear suits and feeling close to heat stroke, he allowed us to remove our gas masks.

"May I have your attention, please," Drill Sergeant Brown yelled. "Please observe that Private Gomez has volunteered to show us the proper way to put on your gas mask and to take off your gas mask without dropping your M-16. It is my hope that after watching this demonstration that somebody else will fuck up the way Private Gomez did and drop their M-16, too. Believe me; you do not want to be that person. Private Gomez will demonstrate for the rest of the day on how to do this. If you would like to join him in the demonstration, then be stupid enough to drop your weapon. Watch and learn. Private Gomez, when I yell 'Gas,' you will demonstrate for the entire company the proper way to put your gas mask on without dropping your M-16."

"Yes, Drill S--," Private Gomez responded.

"Gas," the drill sergeant yelled without giving him a chance to finish his sentence. Private Gomez placed his M-16 between his legs, removed his steel pot, and placed it on top of his M-16 rifle barrel. He then opened his gas mask carrier and put his mask on. After clearing his gas mask and adjusting the straps and hood, he put his steel pot back on and slung his M-16 back over his shoulder and stood at attention.

"Out fucking standing," Sergeant Brown said, grinning from ear to ear. "Now, on my command of 'all clear,' you will demonstrate for the entire company on how to remove your gas mask without dropping your M-16. Is that clear?"

"Yes, Drill Sergeant," Private Gomez said, sounding like Darth Vader.

"Excellent," Sergeant Brown said pacing back and forth. He then stopped. "All clear," he barked. Private Gomez un-slung his M-16, placing it back between his thighs, removed his steel pot and rested it on his rifle barrel, removed his gas mask, folding the cover up nice and neat and placed it back inside his carrier. He then placed his steel pot back on his head, re-slung his M-16 over his shoulder, and stood at attention.

"I am disappointed in you, Private Gomez," Sergeant Brown said. "I was so hoping you would drop your weapon again.

I do not believe you can go the rest of the day without dropping your weapon. I also do not believe that the rest of these screw-ups quite have the hang of it themselves, do you Private Gomez?"

"No, drill sergeant," Private Gomez said.

"Good, we think alike," Sergeant Brown said. "Being that you and I are so concerned about them understanding how to do this, for the rest of the day, you will demonstrate over and over again how to properly put on your gas mask and how to properly take it off. Starting now, you will put your gas mask on as you demonstrated. Then you will immediately take it off as demonstrated. Then you will put it back on. Then you will take it off. You will do this repeatedly until I tell you to stop. You may begin, now." For the rest of the day during breaks, lunch, or whenever we had a spare minute in between classes, Private Gomez did as Sergeant Brown had ordered. He did it without dropping his M-16 again.

We had a break for lunch. It was the first day that we were served C-rations. We ate at the NBC training range. C-rations came in a cardboard box and included canned meat or spaghetti, dessert, and canned fruit. It had all the essential items for a well-balanced meal. I liked them. I preferred the ones that came with a chocolate bar. Most people seemed to hate the C-rations and some chose to go hungry rather than eat. So from those who did not eat, it was possible to pick up a lot of extra food to pack away to eat at a later break. Some people complained that eating C-rations and the mess hall food caused constipation and reduced your sexual drive due to the saltpeter they put in the food. I did not notice any changes. I was still full of shit and needed to do my business on a regular basis. After lunch, people were bitching and moaning about having bellyaches from the C-rations. I was fine. Within a couple of hours a bellyache was going to be the least of their problems. Not a single person would be spared. Up until this day, we had heard rumors throughout basic training that the gas chamber did not exist any more and we would not have to go through it. Those rumors turned out to be false. The drill sergeants must have started the rumors, so people would not go AWOL prior to going into the gas chamber. The gas chamber was a small square building big enough to hold about twenty people. So, twenty people at a time were sent in to the building. A few of the drill sergeants were waiting inside and were already wearing their gas mask along with an instructor from the NBC range who was not wearing his mask.

"The purpose of this exercise, gentleman" the instructor said, "is for you to gain confidence in the use of your gas mask. In a few minutes, we will release tear gas into this room. When instructed to do so, you will place your gas mask on, adjust the straps, clear the airways, and breathe normal to show you that the gas mask does work. Are there any questions? Good, let's get started." He walked over to a contraption that looked like a gas barbecue grill, adjusted some knobs and tear gas began flowing out of it. Within seconds, everybody was feeling the effects -- burning eyes and skin.

"Gas," the instructor yelled. "Let's get those masks on." As practiced, I had my mask on in a matter of seconds. However, I was still feeling the gas. My mask did not seem to be working. I noticed several other people seemed to be struggling, too. One person bolted for the door. The drill sergeant grabbed him and ordered him to stand his ground, pushing him up against the wall.

"One at a time, starting right here," the instructor said, placing his hand on somebody's shoulder standing next to him, "remove your gas mask, state your name, rank, and serial number. Then, and only then, you may exit the gas chamber, if I dismiss you. Go ahead, Private." By this time I was coughing, wheezing, burning, and wanting to bolt, too. The instructor was standing in the midst of all the tear gas without a mask on. He had mentioned earlier in the day while igniting a tear gas canister that after a while people build up a tolerance to it. He was immune to the effects of tear gas. Meanwhile the first soldier took his mask off and blurted out his name, rank, and serial number so fast we could not tell what he said.

"What was that, Private?" the drill sergeant asked. "Slow down and repeat yourself clearly." With snot bubbling out his nose, tears streaming down his face, the red-faced private repeated his information louder and slower.

"That's more like it," the drill sergeant said. "Go on get out of here.

"Drill Sergeant, my mask isn't working," somebody cried out, hacking, and coughing under their mask.

"Bullshit, son," the instructor said. "You have to learn to trust your mask. Three people bolted for the door and made it out before the drill sergeants could grab them. One of the drill sergeants followed them out the door to get them.

"Anybody else want to leave?" the drill sergeant asked. "Be my guest. But if you do leave, you will have to repeat this part of the course."

"When I give the order to do so, everybody will take their mask off at the same time and state their name, rank and serial number," the instructor said, pausing for effect and then hollered, "Remove your masks."

We all removed our masks. My mask must have been working somewhat as when I removed my mask, the effects of the gas increased ten fold. I was coughing and snorting snot and my eyes were burning so bad I thought I was going to die. I felt I was going to vomit.

"State your name, rank, and serial number," the instructor said. We all did so. I stated my information so fast in between coughs that it was unintelligible even to me." The drill sergeant pointed to several people.

"You, you, and you can go," he said, pointing to a few of the recruits who had stated their name, rank, and serial number to their satisfaction.

"Again, state your name, rank, and serial number and sound off this time," the drill sergeant said. We repeated the information again. My effort did not improve. If anything, my effort and condition degenerated to the point that I was convinced I was going to die any second. I made the decision to bolt.

"All right, the rest of you get out of here," the drill sergeant said at the exact second I bolted. I could not get to the door fast enough. Neither could anybody else as we all stampeded to the door. Upon getting outside to fresh air, I noticed through teary eyes that some of the people who had already gone through the chamber were standing around outside waiting for their buddies to come out so they could have a good laugh at their expense. For every single person who was standing around laughing and joking, three or four people were lying around dying. I stumbled about twenty-five yards over to a tree, barely able to see and breathe and proceeded to puke my guts out all over the ground beside the tree. I laid down, convinced I would never recover. The rest of the day was spent waiting for the entire company of 300 people to go through the gas chamber. After everybody went through the chamber, as was typical of most days after training was complete, we marched back to the barracks, arriving in time for dinner. This was my favorite time of the day, looking forward to eating a cheeseburger, fries, and Pepsi after a long hard day of training. Nights were spent shining boots, writing letters, doing laundry, and sometimes cleaning for an inspection. It was mandatory lights out by ten. Sometimes, I might hit the cot earlier than that if it was an extra hard day of training or if I had to pull CQ duty.

Saturday, August 18, 1979:

We had an early morning inspection of our barracks. The drill sergeant went through and inspected everything in detail, ranting and raving how things were sub-standard and how it appeared we had not cleaned anything prior to inspection. He postponed giving us a pass for that evening. Instead, he rescheduled another inspection for later that evening. He said we had better pull together, working together to whip the barracks into shape or else we would flunk out of basic training and have to start all over again with the next class. When he left, the squad leaders assigned everybody duties and for the next six hours, everybody busted their butt, getting the barracks spic and span clean. We had a buffer, so we melted car wax with a lighter and poured it on the floor and then buffed the floor to a high glass shine. In the bathrooms, we scrubbed the grout in between the tiles with toothbrushes. Our boots were spit shined and all of our uniforms were cleaned and pressed. We washed windows, mopped the stairwells both front and back, and scrubbed the walls. Not a single person slacked. About three that afternoon, the drill sergeant came back and re-inspected the barracks. He acted stunned.

"Holy shit," he said, glancing around the room. "This place looks incredible. I'm proud of the way you all pulled together as one unit and came through." Any idiot could see, at least I could, that it was all psychological games. He could have cared shit as to how the barracks looked. We could have had the floors ready to eat off when he came in the first time and he still would have flipped a lid in order to break us. Then when he came back, he rebuilt us back up with praise. It worked. The platoon was happy, as indicated by high-fiving, hooting, and hollering. "At ease," the drill sergeant yelled out. "I'm not through. You have earned yourself your first passes. The rest of the day is yours. You have to be back at midnight or else you will be considered AWOL. Is that understood?"

"Yes, drill sergeant," we hollered. I was excited about having some free time.

"You must come downstairs to our office to sign out of the company in order to get your pass."

Several of us changed into our civilian clothes, went downstairs, and obtained a pass. Then we caught a shuttle into downtown Anniston, Alabama, the town right outside of Fort McClellan, Alabama. The shuttle dropped us off at the USO office in Anniston. They had pool tables, books, and television. It was a boring place to hang out. I could not wait to get back to the base, as I wanted to catch up on some letter writing. I caught the shuttle back at 8 pm and spent the rest of the evening writing letters to family and friends. At 11 pm, I went to the chow hall. They were serving a late night breakfast for those who were stationed on the base and had to work. After eating, it was time to turn in our passes. We had to form a line outside of the drill sergeants' office and sign back in to the company. Many people returned drunk. Three drill sergeants were on duty, and they were having a hard time keeping the drunks under control. Private Bach was calling attention to himself again. He was plastered and babbling on how screwed up the Army was. After being told to shut up for the third time, our platoon's new replacement drill sergeant decided to handle the situation.

"Private Bach," he yelled, strutting over to him, trying to look tough, but at the same time, he was hesitant. "This is the last time I am going to —" Wham! Bach clobbered him with a clenched fist right in the nose, sending him sprawling backwards to the ground with blood spurting all over the place. He looked up at Bach with a look of shock. Meanwhile, Bach was stumbling around, so drunk he was barely able to stand, trying to act cocky from decking the drill sergeant. Everybody was looking at him as if his life was over. I remember thinking he was going to be killed. I expected the drill sergeant, despite looking like a 98-pound weakling, to jump up and beat his ass to a pulp. Instead, he laid on the ground, leaning on his elbows with one hand over his bloody nose, staring up a Bach with fear in his eyes. *What about the other drill sergeants? Aren't they going to beat the shit out of Bach? After all, you do not hit a drill sergeant. All the movies you see, all the hype you hear, a drill sergeant would kill you if you hit them.* However, none of this happened. Instead, the other drill sergeants physically restrained Bach, mainly to keep him from falling down, and then escorted him back to their office where they kept him until the military police arrived to arrest him for assault and battery. He also had a few other military charges added on top of those like disrespect to a Non-Commissioned Officer and Conduct Unbecoming a soldier. Bach was already waiting for a general discharge for going AWOL, but these charges were enough to have them change that to a dishonorable discharge. Discharges did not happen over night. Paper work took weeks, sometimes months, to prepare. Perhaps they delayed the discharge as revenge for hitting a drill sergeant. Bach was still at Fort McClellan when I left two months later, still waiting for his discharge to be finalized. While waiting for his discharge, he was still expected to fall in for formations, participate in all the training, and go through all of the basic training as if he was not being discharged. Who knows, maybe they made him go through all that then gave him the option of changing his mind about the discharge. Bach was already at the lowest rank possible, so they could not bust him down in rank. However, he was restricted to base, had to forfeit his pay, and was assigned extra duty. From that point on, he was the model soldier, participating in all the training as required and doing all of his extra duties. Heck, he even got a traditional military haircut.

Monday, August 20, 1979:

On this day, one half of the company was doing defensive training while the other half did offensive training because the facilities they had were not large enough for us all to train at the same time on one subject. I was in the half that was partaking in defensive training. It took place in a huge gymnasium. We were allowed to wear our tennis shoes for the training instead of our combat boots so that we would not scuff up the floor. The training consisted of being trained in hand-to-hand combat, self-defense using hand-to-hand techniques, and self-defense using our M-16 rifles. However, for the actual training we did not use our M-16's, we used padded poles. It was a fun day. With each move, they first demonstrated it. Then we had to pair up. One person would act as the aggressor while the other practiced using the self-defense move. Then we would switch roles. The day started with role call. After role call, the other companies would do exercises, which consisted of sit-ups, push-ups, mountain climbing lunges, trunk twists, arm twirls, and more. Then they jogged anywhere from one to five miles. However, our company was so large and it took so long to get us through the morning meal, we seldom did physical training in the morning except when the Senior Drill Sergeant came in early, which was once per week. He liked to lead physical training and then take us on a five-mile jog. The Senior Drill Sergeant seemed to be under the impression that we had been doing physical training every morning. However, we had not been. He enjoyed when somebody fell out of the jog. He would brag about how he could run all of us into the ground. I thought he was full of bull, as I did not think he could run too many people into the ground. Hell, he ran as slow as a rock, barely shuffling his feet forward with each step. At that pace, I could have run three or four back-to-back marathons without breaking a sweat. After role call, the drill sergeants would march us over to the chow hall so we were eating before any other company. That way we could be on our way to our training for the day. While training, if we were near a chow hall, we would break for lunch anywhere between 11:30 am and 1:00 pm for lunch. Of course, if we were near our own chow hall, we would eat there with no problem. However, if the training was taking place near some other company's chow hall, the drill sergeants would obtain permission for us to eat there and schedule our lunch around the schedule of the other company's lunch. On those days, they would stress how we had to make great impressions by being at our military best when marching to and from the chow hall so that the other companies would know we were the Foxtrot Company. The other names of the companies were Alpha, Bravo, Charlie, Delta, and Echo.

Wednesday, August 22, 1979:

We marched to a wooded area about a mile away from our barracks. The gymnasium was about the size of half a football field with bleachers that accommodated three-hundred people. The bleachers faced a grassy area surrounded by woods on all sides except the front where the bleachers were. The grassy area also included shrubs, bushes, and some trees. However, for the most part it was cleared of trees. The grassy area was the size of a football field. Once we were seated, one of the instructors stood at a podium with a microphone. His face was painted with camouflage. He started his lecture about the importance of camouflage, describing how it could save your life in battle. The objective was not to be seen. If the enemy cannot see you, they cannot hit you. Of course, proper cover like a foxhole, wearing all of your issued equipment, and keeping your weapon clean were also great safeguards. He talked to us for an hour, giving a demonstration on how to apply camouflage makeup and how to add natural elements of the surrounding countryside to your equipment by stuffing branches under the straps of your backpack, ammunition belt, or through the top of your boots. Then he pointed out that during the entire class, several people were in front of us in the grassy area. He asked if we could spot them. He said that one of them would soon be moving from the far end of the grassy area up towards the bleacher area and we were directed to try to observe and spot him or any of the other four people.

"If these four people were the enemy and you could not spot them, we would all be dead," he said. "They could wipe us out while we sat here. Likewise, if you are out in combat and the enemy cannot see you, the chances of survival have greatly increased. Camouflage techniques are the best way to survive; they are one of your most important but most overlooked things to do when preparing for field duty. Do not make that mistake and overlook it." For the next fifteen minutes we all stared out into the grassy area, looking for the four people. I thought for sure the person moving towards us would be easy to spot, but I could not spot them. "One of the people out there is so close," the instructor said, "he could lob a grenade right into the bleachers, and kill us all. Can anybody spot him?"

We all shook our heads or responded, "No."

"Specialist, Adams," the instructor shouted. "Come out here and show yourself."

At that moment a man no more than 25-feet to the front right of the bleachers came out from behind a two-foot shrub. In fact, he was the majority of the shrub. The bush itself was a foot tall. However, with all the shrubs he had tucked into his back pack straps, his belt, his M-16, and his boots, along with his camouflage makeup, I could not tell he was human. He looked like a bush. Hiding in plain sight behind a one-foot tall bush, he looked like a two-foot tall bush as he lay prone on the ground with his M-16 rifle pointed right at us. Everybody was in awe as he moved from where he was. Not a single person saw him before he revealed himself.

The instructor in turn had each person in hiding reveal themselves one at time. The final person who revealed himself had started moving from the back of the grassy area when the class began. He moved from one-hundred yards away towards the bleachers. He was twenty-five feet away by the time he revealed himself.

Next, the instructor had two people give a demonstration on advancing from the end of the grassy area towards the bleachers. Except this time they were not going to be wearing any camouflage.

"While they advance," he said, "notice how they communicate back and forth where one person does not advance forward until the other one provides cover fire." Without the camouflage, their movements were noticeable. By the time they got to the bleacher area, everybody knew where they were. It took them about five minutes to advance the whole one-hundred yards. "So, you can see, without camouflage, the enemy can easily spot you. Now we have two more people who are going to do the exact same thing. They are going to advance on to our position. However, they are going to be properly camouflaged. If you can see them, notice how instead of verbally communicating, they use hand signals."

Even looking for movement we could not see them. It was not until they were within about twenty-five yards that we could detect their movements, but even then, they were hard to see. It was an impressive demonstration. I vowed that if I was ever in combat, I would be camouflaging myself like crazy. After the demonstration was finished, we all had to put on camouflage makeup, were critiqued as to how we did, and were given pointers on how to improve. After c-rations for lunch, we broke up into four-man teams and were able to practice our fire and maneuvering skills in a team where one to two people advanced at a given time while the others laid ground fire down. We were allowed to use blanks for the practice to make it more realistic.

After going through the fire and maneuvering skills a few times, we were evaluated and graded. At the end of the day, we had to crawl through a rope course on our bellies through mud while live machine gun rounds were fired from a tower over our heads. I do not think they fired within 20 yards of our heads and they may have been using blanks, too, but it was still scary. It was great to get back to the barracks that night and wash the camouflage and mud off.

Thursday, August 23, 1979 through Sunday, August 26, 1979:

As basic training neared completion, we had Bivouac in which we went out into the field and played soldier and war games. After being issued equipment, blanks for the M-16, tents, and sleeping bags, we were instructed on how to pack it all on our backpacks. The most important piece of equipment was the shovel, used for digging foxholes and holes for burying our poop. At 3 am Thursday morning, we had to fall into formation with all of our gear, packed and ready to go. After formation, we were instructed to leave our gear with one member of each squad to stay and stand guard over it while the rest of us went to eat at the chow hall, as the drill sergeants had arranged for the chow hall to open up extra early that morning.

"Eat hardy, ladies," the Senior Drill Sergeant said. "This is going to be the last real meal you're going to get all week long. It is C-rats for every meal hereafter. Do not expect any time for sleep either." After the first people were done eating, they were to come and relieve the people who were standing guard over the equipment. I volunteered to stay behind for our squad, figuring that the later in the morning I ate, the longer the meal would last.

The first thing we did when we arrived was set up our tents. Each person had half a tent and had to pair up with somebody else who would be carrying another half of the tent. Combining the two we were able to make a two-man tent. If we were out on our own, we could use our Poncho for the other half of the tent. However, if we had the two halves and it was raining, a poncho could be placed over the tent to waterproof it. I shared a tent with Gonzales, as we had to pair up with the person on our left within our squad.

We did not get to rest. After getting our tents up, we marched over to a firing range where we spent the rest of the day getting instruction on how to fire the M-60 machine gun. It seemed to jamb a lot. However, part of the course was how to un-jamb the M-60. What a scary weapon. The bullets are huge and could rip a person to pieces. We also saw a demonstration on the M-50 machine gun, which shoots even larger bullets and was mounted on a jeep in order to control the kickback. That night we still did not get any rest. We had to do night firing at the range where we fired live tracer bullets from our M-16 at down range targets. Tracer bullets glow in the dark as they are fired. We were given clips of ammunition that had a tracer bullet about every third bullet. By seeing where the bullet is going from the glow of it, we could see how close or how far away we were from hitting our target. After the night firing, we had two hours of sleep prior to starting another day of training.

We marched over to another range where we were able to shoot the M-72, Light Anti-Tank Weapon (The Law). This is like a mini-bazooka that shoots a rocket. We were given a demonstration of how to hold it, pull it apart, and ready it for firing. Then five people at a time were taken to the firing range and we each had an opportunity to fire it. On the range, they had several old tanks set up as targets. After firing the pre-packaged rocket, the launcher could then be thrown away. The LAW is capable of penetrating a foot of armor at a range between 170 to 220 meters. The launcher, which consists of two tubes, one inside the other, serves as a watertight packing container for the rocket. By the time it was my turn to fire the weapon, I was excited.

"Pick up the weapon," the drill sergeant said. I picked it up. "To cock the weapon, the inner tube must be pulled out, locking it in the extended position. All this must occur before the weapon can be fired. Upon doing this, point the weapon down range towards the target you want to hit. Now place one hand on the outer tube of the weapon, grab the inner tube with the other hand and pull it outward, locking it into place. *When you do this, do not let go of the outer tube. Otherwise, the weapon will swing like a pendulum and scare the shit out of the drill sergeant.* "What the hell are you trying to do?" the drill sergeant screamed as the weapon swung back and forth like a pendulum. He then grabbed the front of the weapon as it swung back and forth. His eyes were big as golf balls and he had little beads of sweat pouring from his forehead. "You're damned lucky that rocket did not fall out of there and explode, killing the both of us."

He is lucky, too, I was thinking. *He should have done a better job of supervising and explaining the procedure for firing the damn thing.* After he regained his composure, he guided me through firing the weapon.

"Fire when ready," he said. I fired, having a direct hit on a tank 150 yards away.

"Excellent shot," he said. "Go back and send the next person in line. Don't say anything about what happened."

Getting back to the campsite close to dinnertime, our squad was told that each of us throughout the night would be responsible for pulling a two-hour security shift somewhere on post. We had a brief class on what was expected from us as we walked our post.

My shift was from 2 am to 4 am. Our drill sergeant took our squad out in a deuce-and-a-half truck and dropped us off one at a time at various sites. I was the second to last to be dropped off. He checked each of our weapons to make sure we had live ammunition. We were given live ammunition for our guard duty. I was dropped off on the side of a long warehouse. What I was guarding and what I was watching for I do not know. I was tired and it was cold, so I paced back and forth within about a twenty-five meter radius of where I was dropped off in order to stay awake and warm. I did not know if I was supposed to walk around the building or stand in one position and look for bad guys. We were not given any instructions at all. As I paced, I counted my steps, trying to calculate how much time had elapsed. I was bored stiff; however, at the same time I was alert, wondering if we were going to be tested by the drill sergeant to see how well we guarded our posts and performed our duties. We had been instructed to challenge anybody we did not recognize by yelling, "Halt. Who goes there? Identify yourself and state your business." What seemed like four hours later, I saw the deuce-and-a-half approaching. We arrived back at the campsite about 4:30 am. We had to be up at 5 am to begin training. Not much chance for sleep, yet, again.

We spent the majority of the day in classroom being instructed on various things, like the use of Claiborne Mines. "These mines," the range instructor said as he held one up in the air, "can be your best friend or your worst enemy. They are triggered by a trip wire. The explosion is like a huge shotgun blast, killing everybody or everything in front of it within about a twenty-five yard radius. However, a kickback blast will also kill anybody behind it within fifty feet. In Vietnam, more of our own soldiers were killed or wounded by these things than by any other activity. These things, due to carelessness killed more of our own men than the enemy did. Due to improper training on how to use them, they would not clear far enough away from them. So, when an enemy soldier tripped the wire, our own men would be killed in the kickback blast. Other times they would clear more than fifty feet away, but still be killed because they set them up backwards. So, if you learn nothing else today, learn that you have to pay extreme attention when handling any weapon. Do not become a statistic and die by 'friendly fire."

In addition, we were shown how to use night flares to illuminate the sky. The flares had two purposes. First they lit up the battlefield so that we could see the enemy. Second, when they went off, they would temporarily ruin the night vision of the enemy. Different types of flares could be triggered manually, or they could be set up to trigger by a trip wire.

The rest of the day, we spent digging two-man foxholes. We were going to have a mock battle that night. One of the platoons was going to play the part of the enemy while the rest of us defended our campsite. We were issued blanks, no mines were to be used, but flares would be fired to illuminate the night. It took hours to dig the foxholes. When we thought we had it deep enough, a drill sergeant would come and tell us to keep digging. We had to have the foxholes about chest deep and about three feet wide. Once they were big enough, we had sandbags around the perimeter for extra protection, allowing for gun ports where we could aim and fire our weapons. Then the most important part was to camouflage them so they would blend in with the surrounding environment. We were working on the foxholes until 10 pm. Then we had to climb into the foxholes and wait for the attack. When it would happen or from what direction it would happen we did not know. Even though it was not a real battle, it was still tense. During the alert, we watched out into the woods for any possible sign of an attack. Hours dragged by. It was 2 am in the morning when the attack began. People started firing their blanks. Flares were firing off, illuminating the woods in front of our bunkers. It was fun. Had it been real, I could imagine shitting my pants if in a life or death situation like that.

The whole thing lasted about fifteen minutes. Afterward we were instructed to stay in our bunkers and stay alert for another attack. Being tired, the guy I was with in the bunker, Private Addison, and I decided to watch in shifts while one of us at a time would take an hour of sleep in the foxhole. No other attacks occurred and as soon as sunrise started, we were allowed to get out of our foxholes.

Bivouac was finished, and we were going back to the barracks. First thing out of the foxholes, we spent an hour cleaning up the shell casings from the blanks and picking up trash and cigarette butts. We spent a lot of time in Basic having to police the grounds and picking up cigarette butts. After picking up the grounds, we disassembled our tents, rolled up our sleeping bags, and packed up our gear.

Upon arriving back at the barracks, I was hoping we could turn in our equipment, be dismissed for the day, and allowed to sleep. Instead, we were issued cleaning kits to clean our M-16s. The kits consisted of wire brushes used to clean inside the barrel and a series of metal tubes that screwed together on which we screwed the various brushes on to in order to get inside the barrel. We had to disassemble the whole rifle and clean each part. Inside the kit was oil used to oil the parts down to prevent rust. When we thought it was clean, we took it to a drill sergeant for inspection. They looked it over thoroughly.

"Are you sure you even cleaned this thing?" Drill Sergeant Hammonds said to me, as he looked down the tube.

"Yes, drill sergeant," I replied with enthusiasm, hoping he would give me permission to turn it in.

"I think you better give it a little more effort than this," he said. At noon, anybody who was still cleaning their weapon could stack it in the gun rack and go eat lunch as long as one person was standing guard over the weapons. My third attempt at getting a drill sergeant to inspect my M-16 was successful. I turned it in and hauled my equipment upstairs to the barracks. We did not turn in our equipment, yet, as we would be using all the gear the following week for our twelve mile march that was required to graduate basic training. We were to clean the equipment and have it ready for inspection the next day, storing it on top of our wall lockers. In addition, the chores of shining boots and attending to laundry had to be done. Each building had its own laundry facility to share. Four washers and four dryers were available in the laundry room to use for free, but two platoons in each building meant that 120 men had to share all the machines, so sometimes it was hard to get your laundry finished. More than one time, I found myself doing laundry in the middle of the night so I would have a clean uniform to pass inspection during the morning formation. Then we had to iron our uniform. I was never good at getting a high gloss spit shine on my boots. Some people had a knack for shining their boots so good, they reflected better than a mirror. I shined and shined my boots, yet I barely passed inspection. Writing letters home or calling home on occasion always seemed to take a back seat to doing some personal chore. In short, we did not have much time for rest that weekend, going into the last week of basic training.

Monday, August 27, 1979:

In preparation for graduation from Basic, we had two days of review of everything we were supposed to have learned in basic training; however, some of the material that they reviewed was presented to us for the first time. In addition, we also had to take a First Aid class on Tuesday. During breaks, the drill sergeants would drill on different questions that we might be asked during the testing. To graduate we would be tested on some basic skills and knowledge by a couple of officers.

The testing took place on Wednesday, August 29. Wearing our dress green uniform, one at a time, we entered the room where the officers were sitting. Removing our military hat as we entered, we were to place it neatly on our left forearm, which was bent at the elbow at a ninety degree angle, palm up. If wearing our fatigue uniform or khaki uniform, the hat would be tucked into the back of our pants between the belt. I approached the table where the officers were sitting, stood at attention, saluted them, and sounded off, "Sirs, Private Turner reporting for testing, sirs."

"Stand at Ease," they responded. At that point, the officers may ask anything they wanted concerning anything we were to have learned in basic training. For example, what are your General Orders? What information are you allowed to give to the enemy if you are a Prisoner of War? What is the proper method for responding to a Nerve gas attack? While answering their questions, they graded us on our military appearance. Was our uniform ironed and cleaned? Were our shoes shined? Were we properly displaying our rank and medals? When we saluted, did we salute properly?

Overall, it was a pressure-filled week leading up to this test. When it came down to the actual test, it lasted less than a minute. The testing took place on the parade grounds where they had five tents set up. In each tent were two officers and we were to pretend the tents were offices. In this way, they were able to move all three hundred of us through the testing at a fast pace. I do not even recall the question I was asked, but it turned out to be one I knew the answer to and they dismissed me.

"Sir, thank you, sir," I responded as taught as I returned to the position of attention. Then doing an about face, I walked to the tent entrance, removed my hat from my belt, and put it on as I exited the tent.

Thursday, August 30, 1979:

Now that the testing was finished, we had a twelve-mile march in full gear. Anybody who dropped out would flunk basic training. We had to wear full gear for the march, which included backpack, tent, sleeping bag, shovel, gas mask, M-16, ammunition, extra boots, and extra clothing. We marched in formation out to some dirt road far away from the main part of the base. The march to the dirt road was two miles by itself.

"We are going to march in single file formation on both sides of the road," the senior drill sergeant instructed us. "We are simulating an actual march in which along the way, you may encounter attacks from the enemy. In a large march like this, you want to distance yourself far enough apart so that if attacked, a single grenade is not going to kill a bunch of people. You want to maintain a distance of ten yards from the person in front of you. Those of you up front need to march at the same pace. If you vary your pace, going from slow to fast, we are going to have an accordion effect at the back of the line, and it is going to cause delays. We will march on both sides of the road. However, one person will start down the middle of the road as the point and will be responsible for watching for signs of possible ambushes. We will rotate the point man about every half hour. If we are ambushed, take cover immediately. During the march, there will be no talking at all. Is that clear?"

"Yes, Senior Drill Sergeant."

"What's that? I don't think I heard you."

"Yes, Senior Drill Sergeant," everybody roared.

"All of the drill sergeant's will be in contact with one another through their radio men," the senior drill sergeant continued. Six people had portable radios that they were carrying with their gear. The portable radios with the battery pack were not so portable. The combined weight was twenty pounds and was in a pack about a foot square. Coming out of the pack was a microphone that attached to the shoulder strap of your backpack. The radioman had to go everywhere the drill sergeants went so that the drill sergeants could hear incoming messages and relay orders or to communicate any problems.

"Once the point starts out, then the man on the right side of the road will start off about ten yards after him," the senior drill sergeant said. "Then the man on the left side of the road will start about five yards after that. Remember to maintain your distance and pace on both sides of the road. Remember, if anybody drops out of the march, you do not pass basic training." He paused and looked around. "I know that at least one person is going to drop out of the march. You do not want to be that person because you will deal directly with me. Are there any questions?" Without giving anybody a chance to ask a question, he turned and started walking away. "Good I did not think so. "Let's get started, ladies. We will march in order of the platoons. First platoon will take the front, followed by second, third, fourth and fifth. Sergeants, take your men."

Each drill sergeant then took control of their platoons with their radiomen at their side. We stood in platoon formation of four lines of fifteen men per line as each of the first three platoons started off on the march, one person at a time, one platoon at a time, staggered on each side of the road. It took quite a while before it was the fourth platoon's turn to join the march. The distance between the first person in line and the last person in line was about a mile. Plus, the pace at which we were marching seemed to be a snail's crawl. I wanted to get the march going and over with as fast as possible. Of course, the Army was hurry and wait. We were always standing in line for something, like food or shots. We had to get a series of shots two times during basic training. We were all given a shot record that we had to keep and each time we got shots we had to get it stamped at the clinic as to the type of shot and the date it was given. I never knew, nor asked what they were for as I assumed it was all for our benefit. Who knows maybe we were guinea pigs and given experimental dosages for germ warfare experiments. Thinking that we could march twelve miles in three or four hours was not a wild expectation. However, it took most of the day. We had to stop and wait and allow the people at the front of the march to spread out farther apart because about every fifteen minutes, the distances between each man would get closer and closer. The line was like an accordion, bunching up one minute, being stretched back out the next minute.

Once in a while a drill sergeant reprimanded somebody in line for talking, or could be heard communicating on the radio. We were about an hour into the march when the silence was broken with a shout of "Gas. Take cover." Everybody ran into the woods that lined the narrow dirt road.

"Put your gas masks on," the drill sergeants yelled out. "Put your gas masks on." Lying on the ground in the woods, I donned my mask. From my vantage point, I could see a tear gas canister in the middle of the road a little distance ahead from where I was positioned. The gas was dissipating into the air. About five minutes later, one of the drill sergeants yelled, "All clear," and we resumed our positions on the dirt road, taking off our gas masks.

"Ladies," our drill sergeant yelled, pacing back and forth in the middle of the road. "That was a piss poor response to an attack. When somebody yells gas, the first thing you do is put on your gas mask. Then seek cover. What good is it going to do you to take cover first if you have been exposed to nerve gas? You want to take cover first if you are being fired upon, but when you hear the word gas, always put your gas mask on first. We are going to have some more attacks throughout the day, so be prepared."

We resumed marching again, having to wait several minutes until the proper distances were re-established up front again. Every so often, the senior drill sergeant would drive by as a passenger in a jeep going either to the back of the line or to the front of the line to check on the spacing of the troops. He had a radio in his jeep to communicate with all of the drill sergeants.

As promised, several more attacks did occur throughout the day. One of the attacks was a simulated ambush from a squad from one of the platoons that were stationed on the base. They played the part of the enemy and attacked us with blanks. The rest of the attacks were of tear gas. It was starting to get quite old. After our sixth tear gas attack, I was quite irritated. It had ceased from being training and was turning into stupidity. It was a hundred degrees, so wearing full combat gear, we all wanted to finish the march.

In the afternoon we had another tear gas attack. I dove for cover in the forest behind a log lying on the ground. Unfortunately, next to that log was trash and left over junk food that had attracted a bunch of wasps. Within seconds, one of the wasps stung me on the left arm. Then another stung me on the right arm. Being allergic to bees and not having seen the wasps, I did not know if it was a bee sting or what. I was furious. I pushed myself off the ground to where I was kneeling on my knees. I looked at both arms. I had a sting on each forearm. As I stood up, I yanked my gas mask off and flung my M-16 into the middle of the dirt road. "Fuck this shit," I yelled out. "I'm sick and tired of this crap." I picked my gas mask up off the ground, picked my M-16 up, went out into the middle of the road, and yelled, "All clear. Let's get this fucking thing over with. The next time somebody throws tear gas, I'm going to kick their fucking ass." Everybody started coming back out on to the road and looked at me as if I was crazy. Then it hit me that I was in deep trouble. However, I saw our drill sergeant was looking at me funny, too. He was not yelling and screaming in my face. Instead, he was radioing a message to somebody else.

"All right," he yelled out after finishing his radio message. "Let's move out." Without delay we began marching without having to wait for the front of the line to establish proper distance. We did not stop during the rest of the march and we had no further tear gas attacks. In fact, within the hour the senior drill sergeant drove by and told everybody as he passed that we would be double-timing it the last mile of the march.

I never was reprimanded for what I did. I suspected the drill sergeants were not authorized to be throwing tear gas canisters at us, so if they busted me, they would have been busting themselves, too.

We jogged the last mile of the march at a slow pace and every part of my body ached. My feet hurt the most, but it felt great to be finishing the march and completing basic training. Upon getting back to the barracks, we had to clean our M-16's once again. We were told that we would be having an inspection of our equipment the next morning before we turned it all back to supply. We were then dismissed for the day so that we could clean our equipment, getting it ready for the inspection.

Friday, August 31, 1979:

After inspection, we marched over and turned in our equipment. Next, we marched over to the parade grounds and practiced the march for the graduation ceremony for basic training. We marched in unison, one platoon after another. As a platoon passed in front of the bleachers, where guests of the ceremony watched, their drill sergeant gave the command of "eyes right." Everybody, except for the people in the row nearest to the bleachers, would turn their eyes right and look at the people in the bleachers as we passed. The people in the row nearest the spectators would keep their eyes and head focused straight ahead. We practiced the whole thing twice, including the rifle drills where, in unison and perfect timing, each man, one after the other, performed a move with the rifle, giving the illusion of a domino effect as they fall down, one at a time.

Saturday, September 1, 1979:

During the real ceremony the next day, we wore our dress green uniforms and had an inspection at eight in the morning where the drill sergeant inspected everything from head to toe, including how shiny the brass on our uniform was, whether or not our ties were straight, whether our belt buckle lined up with the buttons on our shirts, the shine on our boots, how we had our hats tilted and so forth. Everything had to be perfect. The ceremony began at 10 am. It was magnificent with the Army marching band playing marching tunes and all the people watching. I did not realize it until after the ceremony that we were allowed to invite our family to the graduation ceremony. The first I knew we could do that was after the ceremony when I saw several people from my squad rush out to greet their family and loved ones who had been sitting in the bleachers. If I had known, I would have invited my parents. I do not know if they would have been able to make it or not, but I bet they would have found a way.

After the graduation ceremony, we were given our first full weekend pass. It started at noon. Because Monday was the Labor Day Holiday, we did not have to be back until 10 pm on Monday night. Four of us decided to go into Anniston, the town located outside the base. After changing out of our dress greens into civilian clothes, we called a taxi, going straight to a motel and rented two adjoining rooms. Each room had two beds. When we arrived, we each contributed $10 per person for booze and went to a liquor store across the street from the motel. It was 3 pm by the time we arrived back at the motel with the booze. One of the guys got out the phone book and started paging through it, calling different escort services and arranged for some female escorts to come over to the hotel to party with us. The evening turned into a wild night. My night did not last long, as I passed out on the bed and awoke later that night when the other guys came into the room. They had gone out to a bar, drinking some more after the escorts had left. They were all excited about the evening and talked about how hot those women were and what a great lay they were. We slept late into the morning, right up until check out time, and caught a taxi back to the base. I was glad to be back and was able to get lunch right before they closed the cafeteria down for the afternoon.   Then as was my custom, I went out and bought a newspaper and tried to find out how the Denver Broncos were doing.

Tuesday, September 4, 1979:

By the time we graduated from basic training, we were cocky, thinking we were the meanest, toughest, leanest, fighting machines that ever existed because they drilled that into our heads during training. First, they tore us down, and then they built us up to where we thought we could kick any ass on anybody and everybody. However, it was nothing compared to the build up we were going to get during Military Police Training. The Military Police Corps Code of Ethics reads like this:

> I am a soldier in the United States army. I am of the troops and for the troops. I hold allegiance to my country and devotion to duty above all else. I proudly recognize my obligation to perform my duty with integrity, loyalty, and honesty. I will assist and protect my fellow soldiers in a manner that is fair, courteous, and impartial. I will promote, by personal example, the highest standards of soldiering, stressing performance and professionalism. I will strive to merit the respect of others; seeking no favor because of position but instead, the satisfaction of a mission accomplished and a job well done.

We spent most of this day being issued our military police gear; such as, a military police arm band, a lanyard for the forty-five automatic pistol, a holster for the pistol, an extra liner for a steel pot that we had to spray paint with a high gloss paint and then decorate with MP stickers, and military police insignia. We also had to sign up to be issued a forty-five automatic to be used during training. As with the M-16's, we had to keep those in the armory and we were not allowed to have live ammunition except on the firing range while qualifying.

Wednesday, September 5, 1979:

The entire company marched back over to the building where we did our indoor training with the M-16 where we had to learn to break it apart and put it back together again while blindfolded. Today, however, they had chairs and wooden tables throughout the whole room. The class subject was Military Law.

We were told how military law differs from civilian law and, when on duty, how Military Policeman out rank the highest-ranking general where military jurisdiction is valid. What stuck in my mind the most was the use of deadly force. A military policeman is allowed to use the force necessary to apprehend a criminal, including the use of deadly force when justified. The instructor then gave us an example of the use of force.

"A few years back," he said, "right here on this base, a gas station was robbed. The robbers were armed and dangerous and had shot the gas station attendant during the robbery. A military policeman arrived at the scene seconds after the clerk was killed. The robbers fired at the military policeman. He exchanged fire, wounding one of the suspects and killing the other with a bullet to the head. Did the military policeman use reasonable force? Was he justified in using deadly force? How many people feel he was not justified in using deadly force?" the instructor asked. "Raise your hand if you think he was not." Nobody raised their hand. "Well, today that military policeman is serving time in Leavenworth. He was court-martialed. The suspects in the robbery were stationed right here on the base. The judge ruled that the military policeman used excessive force in shooting the suspect in the head. It was determined that he could have wounded him and that shooting him in the head was excessive force." Everybody let out a collective groan all at once. "Gentleman, I can't stress to you enough how important it is to use minimum force in each situation. In a situation like the one I described, you will have seconds to decide what the proper amount of force should be. The rule of thumb for deadly force is never pulling your weapon out unless you plan to kill. If the situation does not warrant killing somebody, then a lesser force to apprehend a suspect should be considered."

I could not help but thinking that if ever in a situation like that, I might find myself getting court-martialed, too, because I misjudged how much deadly force to use. I was wondering if I had made the right choice to become a military policeman.

Thursday, September 6, 1979:

I considered this my finest day in the Military Police Academy. We went to the firing range to qualify with the 45 automatic. After having had experience with the M-16 and learning to hold my breath while squeezing the trigger with the tip of my index finger, I could not wait to see how well that technique worked using a pistol. Having never fired a pistol before, I was a little nervous about whether I would qualify and whether my technique for firing would work. I did not know whether I got lucky qualifying with the M-16 or whether I had learned to aim and fire with accuracy.

As it turned out, during the practice rounds, I could not seem to miss the target. From fifty-yards, we shot seven rounds from the prone position, lying flat on our stomachs. From thirty-five yards, we shot seven rounds from a standing crouch position and then we shot seven more rounds with one knee on the ground. From twenty-five yards, we repeated the previous two positions. From fifteen-yards, we fired seven rounds from behind a partition, simulating that the partition was a wall and that we were shooting around a corner. Finally, from seven-yards, we fired eight rounds from a standing crouch position. We had to fire all eight shots in less than ten seconds in rapid fire.

When it was time to test, I was excited, thinking I would do well. I did. My score was forty-eight out of fifty. The instructor thought that I scored fifty out of fifty, thinking two of my rounds went through the same hole twice, as two of the holes on the target were larger than the normal bullet holes, but he could not tell for sure, so I was not given credit for a perfect score.

Saturday, September 8, 1979

We had an early morning inspection of our barracks, wall lockers, and equipment while wearing our Khaki uniforms. We passed the inspection and were given a weekend pass. Private Addison, Private Butts, and I shared a taxi to Birmingham, Alabama. When we arrived, we played pool at a pool hall for a couple of hours. Addison had his own pool stick and was a damned good player. After playing pool, the three of us shared another taxi back to the base, where I spent the rest of the weekend doing laundry, shining boots, and writing letters home. That night one of the guys in our platoon told me that after the morning inspection we had earlier that day, he saw Private Gonzales from my squad take my lanyard from my bed while we had our military gear on display. The lanyard was a white rope that we looped around our shoulder and then attached the other end to our gun. It was to be worn with your military police gear. We were all issued one earlier in the week. I went over and checked my wall locker and, sure enough, it was gone. I had not noticed it missing when I put my gear away after the inspection. Chances are if it were not for this guy telling me that he had seen Gonzales taking it, I would not have noticed it missing until I needed it. I could not believe that Gonzales would do such a thing. We both arrived on the base on the same bus, had been assigned to the same company, the same platoon, and the same squad. We had become good friends. He was from New Mexico and I was from Colorado, so we had a little in common in that he had visited Colorado many times. I went over to Gonzales and asked him if he knew anything about my missing lanyard. He denied knowing anything about it. I told him – without mentioning names – that somebody said they had seen him taking mine.

"I was afraid something like this might happen," he said. "I brought my own personal lanyard with me from home when I came to basic training and because somebody saw me with two of them, they've used that as an excuse to steal yours and blame me for it."

"So you have two lanyards" I said, repeating his statement, "and somebody other than you stole my lanyard?"

"I do not know if somebody else stole your lanyard, all I know is that I did not steal it."

"What are the odds of that?

"I do not know, but I'm telling you the truth."

"I do not think you are," I said. "I bet if we searched this entire barracks from top to bottom, we would not find another person with two lanyards as you are saying.

"Somebody is trying to set me up," he said.

"I do not think so. I think you ripped me off. I would never do anything like that to you. I have considered you a close friend, but you stabbed me in the back. You're a thief and a liar."

"You better take those words back or be willing to pay the price," Gonzales threatened.

"Let's step out on to the back stairwell where there are no witnesses," I suggested. By this time our voices had become loud enough so that a dozen or so people heard us arguing.

"Let's go," he said and started walking toward the back door leading to the rear stairwell. I followed him. However, thinking there would be no witnesses was incorrect, as, now, the people who had overheard us were alerting everybody that there was going to be a fight. The stairwell was narrow, being wide enough for two people standing shoulder to shoulder to ascend or descend at the same time. It was made of concrete and steel. The lights were dim. By the time we got to the stairwell, so many people were following us, we had to move to the landing between the second and third floor. It looked like all 60 people from our platoon had gathered on the stairs above us. Meanwhile, all the noise had alerted the people in the third platoon that something was going on and they all gathered on the stairs and landing below us. It was nuts. About 120 people crammed on to the stairwell, all jockeying for a position to see the fight that was about to take place.

"I don't want to fight you or hurt you," Gonzales said. "All you have to do is apologize for what you said."

"If you don't want to fight, you should have thought of that before you stole my lanyard."

"I did not steal you're lanyard, but if it will make you happy, I'll give you one of mine."

"How did you get more than one lanyard, Gonzales?" somebody yelled out.

"He stole one from me," I said.

"Beat the crap out of him," somebody yelled.

"I don't want to fight you," Gonzales said.

"You should have thought of that before stealing my lanyard," I said. "What are you chicken like everybody else from New Mexico? Everybody in New Mexico is a thief and a liar like you." I could tell I was beginning to rub him the wrong way. "Your girlfriend is a bigger liar than you. She is probably out stealing right this minute." Those last words pushed him over the edge. He grabbed me in a bear hug, slamming me against the concrete wall. The back of my head hit the wall and I was seeing stars. *What was I thinking picking a fight with Gonzales?* He outweighed me by about fifty pounds. He was several inches shorter than I was and I assumed his extra weight was from fat, but by the way he picked me up like a rag doll and slammed me into the wall, it was obvious he had some muscle packed on, too. However, I was pissed and angry that he stole from me. I felt betrayed. Though shaken, I freed my arm and repeatedly hit him in the side of the head until he let me out of his bear hug. By this time, he was dazed and was about ready to fall to the floor when somebody yelled out that the Drill Sergeant was coming. Several people pulled us apart while everybody else scattered like flies.

Everybody rushed back to their bunk and wall locker areas, acting as if nothing had happened. Within seconds, the drill sergeant for the second platoon entered the room. He was in charge that night. The drill sergeants rotated on who was in charge of babysitting us each night. "I heard a rumor about a fight going on up here this evening, Gentlemen," he said strolling up and down the isle ways between the bunks staring intently into the eyes of each person he passed. "I know that was a rumor, but I thought I better check it out anyway because I would love to catch recruits fighting. In fact, I would like nothing better than to court martial their asses. So please, somebody be stupid and let me catch them fighting tonight. Please, oh, please somebody be stupid." He continued strolling through the barracks for a few more minutes, staring at people as he passed them, as if he expected somebody to confess to a crime.

After the drill sergeant left, I was not done being stupid that night. Ricardo bunked across from Gonzales. He was from Puerto Rico and was always practicing karate in his spare time. He loved to do roundhouse kicks. When basic training first started, we got along okay. He was in the fourth squad and I was in the third squad. His was a friend with Gonzales, 25-years old, married, had two kids, and was always pulling practical jokes on people. One of his favorite practical jokes was to stick his index finger and his middle finger out through his underwear opening, and then when your back was to him, he would sneak up behind a person and stick his fingers in their hand or poke them in the rear, pretending his fingers were his penis. He did it to me several times. It was funny once or twice, but he did it all throughout basic training. It was getting annoying and after telling him repeatedly to stop, he continued to do it, thinking it was funny. The day before I got in the fight with Gonzales, I decided to pay him back by doing the same to him. He was in the bathroom. Having showered, he was putting his robe on when I sneaked up behind him with my fingers sticking out of my underwear and poked him in the hand with them. He was furious and told me never to do that again.

"It does not feel so good, does it?" I asked. He stormed out of the bathroom, cussing up a storm in Spanish and giving me dirty looks.

About an hour after my fight with Gonzales, I went to the bathroom. When I came out of the bathroom stall, Ricardo came rushing towards me from the other side of the bathroom, and wearing his boots, gave me a roundhouse kick square on the mouth. I fell backward about ten feet, biting my tongue as I stumbled. He rushed towards me and tried to kick me in the face again. I caught his boot in midair, inches from my mouth. I flipped his leg way up over my head, causing him to fall backwards, hitting the back of his head on the hard stone tiled floor. Furious and hurting from the first kick, I then jumped on top of him and began choking him. I was choking him as hard as I could when several people yanked me off him. Ricardo laid on the floor, gasping for air. His attack on me was provoked by my practical joke that I played on him the day before, combined with him being angry about me getting in a fight with Gonzales, who was also his friend. When I left the bathroom and returned to my bunk, Gonzales handed me a lanyard.

"I did not steal your lanyard," he said, "but I'm going to give you my personal lanyard and hope we can be friends." I took the lanyard without saying a word, not because I did not want to, but because I could not. My lips and tongue were swollen from the kick that Ricardo had given me to my face and my jaw hurt, so I could not even speak. I thought my jaw was broken. For the next two days, I could not eat any solid food. I could slurp soup and drink fluids through a straw. By the third day, I was recovered enough that I knew my jaw was not broken. Despite Gonzales' gesture to become friends again by giving me his lanyard, we did not speak two words to each other -- not even good-bye.

Monday, September 10, 1979:

This day was set aside for learning to drive the Army's jeep, otherwise known as a Utility Truck M-151A1 or one-quarter ton. We had to also test for our license. We had a whole week to learn how to drive, study for the written test, and take the driving test. From this point on, Military Police Training was self-paced. As soon as we obtained our license, we could move on to the next self-paced class. We had to take each class, be tested, and get a stamp on our training card from the instructor, showing we passed. We could then move on to the next class. Driving the jeep was easy for me, as I learned how to drive in my mother's five-speed Toyota Corolla. After spending a couple of hours practicing on the course, where they had various driving situations set up, like starting off while going uphill, left and right turns and other simple stuff, I took my written test and driving exam, passing them both on the first try on the first day.

I expected to be released so that I could go on to the next phase of the training, thinking I was going to be one of the first people done with the Military Police Training if I stayed on schedule the rest of the time. However, instead of being released to go on to my next class, I was drafted by the driving instructors to stay on at the driving school to teach others how to operate a manual transmission. I ended up being stuck at the driving school through Wednesday teaching others how to stop and start and how to down shift a manual transmission. Meanwhile, people that I was helping to pass the class were released to go on to other classes and got ahead of me. I did not like the situation. Though I felt honored to have been picked to assist the instructors, I felt wronged in that people I had helped pass their driving tests were getting singled out with praise at how fast they were moving through the rest of the self-paced training, and I did not even get so much as a thank you. I would not have been released that week if I had not brought it up to one of the instructors that I wanted to move on to the next course. So late Wednesday afternoon they told me that the next person that I helped to pass the test would be my replacement for Thursday.

Thursday, September 13, 1979:

Now that I had my military driver's license, I was able to take the next class, "Operating a Law Enforcement Vehicle." We were shown videos, which included instruction on defensive driving, responding to emergency calls, high speed chases, radio operating procedures, using a seat belt, and securing the vehicle while leaving it unattended on a call. After the classroom material was covered we went out on to the obstacle course where we had to drive a patrol car without knocking down any of the orange cones that outlined the course. We had to drive through the course in less than two minutes and had time added to our score for each cone we knocked down. The course had a series of tight turns to maneuver, which is hard enough to do at slow speeds, let alone at high speeds in order to make it through the course within the allotted time frame. Then at the end of the course, we had a straightaway to build up speed to do a reverse turn at the end of the road. Upon completing the turn, the clocked stopped. It was a fun course to drive.

Friday, September 14, 1979:

The class this day, "Traffic Accident Investigation" was mostly done in the classroom, on subjects of how to fill out forms used in investigations of traffic accidents, how to secure the scene, what to look for at the scene -- like skid marks on the road -- and how to gather information from witnesses. First secure the scene, using the patrol car with lights running to keep other cars from becoming part of the accident. Next, get help and provide help for anybody who is injured. Then further secure the scene by putting up flares and orange cones to direct traffic away from the accident. Then separate witnesses from each other and have each one fill out a sworn affidavit, detailing what they witnessed. Taking photographs of the vehicles, of skid marks, of the surrounding area were also important. Then, drawing a diagram of the scene, including such details as directions of travel, traffic lights, roadway signs, weather conditions, road conditions, the lighting, and the position of cars was also discussed. This class took three days, as we filled out forms and practiced conducting investigations at several mock accidents.

Thursday, September 20, 1979:

The next phase of training was for the entire company to participate in together. So no matter what stage of the training we were in at this point, we had to postpone it to participate in Physical Security Combat Operations. In this training, we were trained on setting up Prisoner of War Camps. We were trained on how to treat prisoners of war. It was stressed that at all times we were to treat POW's with respect and dignity, keeping in mind that how we treat our enemies prisoners would determine how the enemy treated our soldiers being held prisoner. The rule of thumb was that the enemy would treat our soldiers ten times worse than how we treated their soldiers who were POW's. During the training, we set up a mock POW camp and some of the company members played the part of the prisoners while most of us played the part of Military Police. Some general rules were to forbid prisoners from talking to one another and keeping them isolated, so escape attempts would be minimal.

Thursday, September 27, 1979:

On this day, I participated in Unarmed Self Defense. It was a class on how to use your baton to defend yourself and how to control a prisoner during an arrest, using your baton. The baton could be used in a number of obvious ways to control an unruly suspect. At no time were we ever to hit them in a joint with the baton. Hitting somebody in the back of the knee was an effective way to knock them off their feet. One police officer would be in the front of the suspect, drawing their attention. Meanwhile, another police officer approach unnoticed from behind and hit them in the back of the knee to knock them off their feet and get them handcuffed. Another way to gain control was to come from behind with our baton out in front of us in our left hand, palm facing upward, and then hit the suspect in the side of the neck with our left hand for a momentary shock. While the baton is still in front of their neck, we crossed over with the right hand, grabbed the other side of the baton and forced the suspect to the ground without ever hitting them with the baton. If a baton is not available, the same technique was used to control a suspect by using our arm in place of the baton, locking our hand around the inside of our elbow of our free arm while our free hand forced their head forward. I had to use this technique a few times in making an arrest. It takes little effort to push their head forward, choking the suspect. In no time, they become compliant. We had to team up in pairs and practice using these techniques on each other. We also learned how to search suspects and how to handcuff without injuring or cutting off the circulation in their wrists. We practiced searching and handcuffing each other, as if making a real arrest.

Monday, October 1, 1979:

Next on the agenda, "Crime Scene Investigation," was one of the toughest courses in Military Police School. It took a full five days to complete the class. The classroom had a set of mock crime scenes, where we secured them without disturbing any of the evidence. In addition, we had to fill out the required forms and file a report about each crime scene, get sworn statements from the witnesses, draw a diagram of the scene, and take photographs. In reality, as military police officers, we would secure the crime scene until higher ranked military investigators from Central Intelligence would arrive to do the other type of work.

At each crime scene, instructors at the school or other pupils would play the parts of victims, witnesses, or suspects. Although it might seem obvious who had what part, each crime scene included a wrinkle where the person who looked like the victim may have really been the suspect. Also, we had our hands full trying to secure the scene, as an instructor who was playing the part of a drunk witness would do anything to stumble through each crime scene, ruining evidence. Therefore, in some scenes, arresting a witness was our best option to preserve a crime scene.

For the next four days, I went through each crime scene, practicing for the test on Friday, which was another mock crime scene with instructors or other students playing the parts like in the practice crime scenes.

Monday, October 8, 1979:

"Patrol Incidents," was the class I started this week. It, too, had staged scenes and events. This class was different, however, in that instead of being crime scenes where the event was already over, the events in this class were in progress when we arrive on the scene of an event or crime already in progress.

It was the same type of setup where instructors and other students played the roles of suspects, victims, and witnesses of different events, like a domestic disturbance, a grocery store robbery, or a bar fight. Upon arriving on the scene, one person played the part of the senior military policeman in charge and the other provided support as directed by the senior military policeman. Then we switched roles and did it again.

The senior police officer was to take control of the situation, arrest suspects, separate and question witnesses, secure the scene, and keep everybody safe. In domestic disturbances that can be hard to do, as it was never known if the abused spouse would turn on us for arresting his or her spouse. One thing they taught us in all of the incidents was never allowing our self to be left alone in a room with a member of the opposite sex. We had to always make sure we had a witness to anything we did in regards to questioning or arresting a member of the opposite sex because they may seek revenge by accusing you of sexually assaulted them while alone with them. I saw it happen to a co-worker. He was lucky that unknown to the woman who accused him that I had witnessed the whole thing and he was cleared of all allegations. I tested out of this class, first as the junior patrol officer in a mock domestic dispute, and then as the senior patrol officer in a mock arrest of two drunks causing a disturbance on the street.

Thursday, October 11, 1979:

My next class was "Traffic Control." It is not as easy as it sounds. Standing in the middle of a busy intersection with cars driving all around is one of the most dangerous jobs as a police officer. People are idiots behind the wheel of a car. In the class, they taught us the hand signals to use for signaling a driver to stop, turn left, turn right, or come forward. With each change of hand signals, we had to blow our whistle loud enough to signal the drivers that we were going to halt traffic one way and start traffic up from another direction. We wanted to over exaggerate all of our movements so that a driver we were signaling to stop would not somehow mistake the fact that we were holding our palm up as a signal to bolt through the intersection. Later on in my military career, I had ample opportunity to do traffic control and I experienced first hand how stupid people are behind the wheel of a car. Drivers would see us signal them to stop, go, turn, or whatever, and then ignore us. At times I felt like stopping their vehicle, demanding their driver's license and tearing it up on the spot while having their car towed away so that they would have to walk.

Friday, October 12, 1979

We were taken out to various intersections around the post and had to do fifteen minutes of traffic control at an intersection. There was not much traffic and it was simple, so I moved on to another weekend, having passed the test for traffic control.

Monday, October 15, 1979:

This was the last required exercise and training in order to graduate from Military Police School. It was a nighttime exercise, so during the day, I began all the necessary legwork for checking off the base and getting my new orders. The legwork consisted of a lot of paperwork that required walking to many different places. In addition, everything had to be turned in to supply. I turned everything in, except for my linen, on Tuesday.

Meanwhile the nighttime exercise started at 10 pm Monday night. I had to ride along for half a shift with an on-duty Military Policeman who was stationed at the base. I was assigned to ride with Specialist Anderson. He had been stationed at the base for almost a year, having re-enlisted for a second term in the military, and requesting that base. The other half of the shift I was required to spend at the MP Station to see how it operated, and how the shift commander and Desk Sergeant assigned patrol areas and supervised the dispatcher, who kept track of the MP units on patrol and determined which ones should respond to various calls. The Desk Sergeant also was responsible for checking over all of the forms that the MPs turned in during their shift, making sure they were completed correctly and legible.

Riding along with the on-duty MP was rather boring and I was feeling tired. We did not have any calls to respond to and all we did during the entire four hours was drive from building to building on the base, making sure they were secure. After checking each building, we had to log the time we checked it into our shift report. The one thing that left the biggest impression was the radio chatter. Everything was in code and it was hard to tell who was talking to whom. I could never tell when our car unit was called, but Anderson could. All the radio chatter sounded the same to me. He assured me that with little time, I would have no trouble remembering all of the codes and would get used to the radio chatter, being able to distinguish one call from another.

After a couple of hours of security checks, we stopped by a chow hall and had a midnight dinner, then it was back out doing more routine security checks for another hour before returning to the MP station. At the MP station, I spent time with the dispatcher, the shift commander, and the desk sergeant. I had to do one final thing before completing the Military Police Academy which was at 3 am when the desk sergeant had another Private and I clean the MP station and then sweep and mop the floors. What a moving graduation ceremony. After we cleaned, the desk sergeant signed our cards showing we had completed the last exercise and dismissed us. A patrol unit gave us a ride back to the barracks.

Back at the barracks, I laid down to sleep but I had so many things going through my mind, planning on what I was going to do first for out-processing. I had to turn in my equipment, go to the clinic with my shot record and have them verify I had all the required shots, and go to personnel and get my orders for my next duty assignment. I had found out a few weeks earlier that I was going to be sent to Germany, as I had requested when I enlisted. However, that was all I knew. Personnel would have to schedule me a flight to Germany.

Since it was cleaned many times before that, I did a half-ass job of cleaning my equipment, as I packed it in my duffel bag. I then hauled it to supply half a mile away. The supply clerk took out a checklist that showed everything I had been issued, and checked things off.

"Did you change the filters in your gas mask?" he asked when he got to that item.

"I did," I responded, lying to him, as I had no idea that we were supposed to do that, and I did not have any filters for it. It hit me that maybe that is why the tear gas seemed to affect me so much in the gas chamber. Perhaps my filters were bad and needed to be changed. I felt a twinge of anger that we were not even shown how to change filters or even given filters in the first place other than those in the gas mask. I would not learn how to change filters in a gas mask until much later at my next duty assignment.

"Some of this equipment does not look like it has been cleaned," he remarked. "Did you clean it?"

Noticing him staring at me as if he was studying me, I answered, "Yes, sir, I cleaned it inside and out."

"Do not call me, sir, I work for a living," he said. I had the feeling he did not like me and was going to be a jerk and have me clean the equipment again before he would accept it. However, he did not, he continued to check everything off on the list and had me sign the form and stamped it with a date and gave me a copy of the form. I hustled out before he changed his mind

My next stop, I went to the medical clinic. It was 9:30 am. Heck at that rate, I thought I would be finished before days end and on my way to Germany before I knew it.

The clinic was over a mile away. I hoofed it over there, hoping I would be able to get in and out right away. However, the waiting room was packed with a long waiting line at the desk to see the receptionist. It was not until the afternoon that I was able to have them review my shot records and verify that I had all the required shots.

Still having time to go to headquarters and meet with personnel, I returned to the barracks, spiffed up a little bit and grabbed all of my records, thinking that I would be on my way out of Alabama real soon. However, I hit a snag. When I got to personnel and they were looking over all the paperwork, verifying that I turned in all my equipment, that my shots were in order and that I had completed all of the classes, the personnel clerk noticed a missing stamp.

"I do not see that you have a stamp for having completed the crime scene investigation class," he said, looking at me over the top of his glasses. "You can't leave training until you have completed all of the classes."

"I did complete that class," I responded, trying to control my horror. "I must not have had the card stamped. Do I have to take the class over again?"

"Perhaps," he said. "Go talk to the instructor and see how they want to handle it." Devastated, I left headquarters thinking I was screwed. I did not want to have to take the class again. By that time, it was too late to do anything about it, as by the time I walked over to the class, it was after 5 pm. I did not get much sleep that night, tossing and turning while worrying about what I was going to do the next day. Up at the call of reveille, which was played over the loudspeaker system in the barracks each morning from a stereo system inside the drill sergeant's office, I dressed, ate breakfast, went to role call, and headed over to the training center. It did not open until 8 am and I wanted to arrive before that to talk to the instructors. I approached the head instructor at the class and told him the situation about the missing stamp that was needed to prove I took the class. He took my card from me and looked it over.

"Are you sure you took the class?" he asked, looking me in the eye.

"Positive," I answered without hesitation. "In fact you were the one who did my evaluations on the last day of the class."

"And how did you do?" he asked, not remembering me.

"You passed me on both of the evaluations when I played the junior patrolman and the senior patrolman," I said, trying to sound as convincing as possible while fearing he would not believe me.

"Okay, I'll go ahead and stamp it," he said. "Good luck to you." He stamped my card and handed it back to me.

"Thank you, sergeant," I said feeling for some reason as if I had conned him into something, but the fact of the matter was, I did take the class. I departed before he had the chance to change his mind and somehow remove the stamp from my card.

Once back at the barracks, I decided to grab my linens and turn them in, thinking I would be leaving the base that day.

Next, I went over to headquarters. I had to wait thirty minutes to see the clerk I spoke with the first time. He still had a few more surprises for me.

"All your papers are in order," he said. "Congratulations on completing your training. It looks like you are going to be going to Germany, but before that you've been approved for thirty days as a recruiter aide back in your home town."

"What is that?" I asked.

"You don't know?"

"No," I said, "I have no idea."

"Your recruiter must have put in the request on your behalf," he said, looking surprised. "That is unusual as most people want to be a recruiter aide and are denied the opportunity. However, you have been accepted. It means you will be stationed in your hometown for thirty days assisting your recruiter. It is easy duty."

"Then will I be going to Germany?" I asked, feeling like I was being tricked.

"You will," he said. "I have scheduled you a flight from Anniston airport to Atlanta on Friday morning. Then you will fly back to Denver. We will have a shuttle that leaves from headquarters at 8 am Friday morning that will take you to the airport. I'm going to issue you a payment voucher where you can stop by any military base and pick up pay while you're in Denver."

"That's it?" I asked. "I'm done?"

"Not quite," he said, "you have to do one other thing before leaving. You have to go get a dental examination before you can leave the base."

"Where do I do that?"

"The dental clinic is right across the court yard from our building," he said. "You should be able to get right in and right out if you tell them you have orders to leave on Friday." As it turned out, I went to the dentist office where they took X-rays to put in my records. They also discovered that I had two minor cavities and since I was not leaving until Friday, scheduled me an appointment for Thursday afternoon to get the cavities fixed. Therefore, I spent my last full day on the post, saying my goodbyes and getting two cavities filled.

Friday, October 19, 1979:

Having everything I owned packed into my duffel bag. I was shuffled from Fort McClellan to a tiny airport in Anniston, Alabama. It seemed so long ago that I had been on the bus from Atlanta arriving for basic training. Yet, the time flew by fast. I felt proud, strong, and invincible. I still wondered what it was going to be like in Germany and was excited about being a Military Policeman. I would have to wait thirty days to find out.

Monday, October 22, 1979:

I started my assignment as a recruiter aide for thirty days. It was a thirty day vacation. The duty was easy and it was in my hometown. I did not ask for it and did not even know such an assignment existed. My recruiter put in the request to have me be an aide. They asked me if I would need temporary housing while there. I declined, knowing that my parents would let me stay at their house and their house was a short twenty-minute drive to the recruiting station. I had to show up at 8 am every morning and act as gopher, going for donuts and coffee, running errands, accompanying the recruiters to various high schools for recruiting campaigns to answer questions from prospective recruits. Most of the time, they had little for me to do and I was allowed to leave early. Weekends were free to do as I wanted.

Monday, October 29, 1979:

Before I left Fort McClellan, I was told that I should report to the payroll department at Fort Fitzsimmons in Denver to be paid. I had lived all my life in Denver and the surrounding area and had never been on that base. It was right smack dab in Denver, east of downtown. When I got to the payroll office, they gave me two-thousand dollars in cash and had me sign a paper for it. I was shocked. I questioned them why I was getting so much money, as the pay of a Private E-1 was peanuts. I had never seen so much money in my life. I was told it was a bonus for being selected as a recruiter aide to use as spending cash while on special duty. What a crack of crock that was. If you could sue idiots, I would sue the idiot who told me that garbage. Of course, I was the bigger idiot for having believed him and not investigating that information. As it turned out it was not a bonus, but an advance on future pay. This misinformation would come back to bite me in the ass about a month later when I got to my permanent duty station and was told I was going to have to start paying back all of that money. The government kept the majority of my paychecks until the "bonus" was paid back in full, so I had little money to spend each month.

During my time as an aide, I spent a lot of time partying with my old friends, getting drunk and working out at the gym with Jerry, my recruiter. A few times after our workouts, we went back to his house. He had a home in Arvada, Colorado. He introduced me to his wife. She was a nice person. Whenever, she was not around, he offered me a joint. I was not into smoking marijuana, as I had tried it a few times and it did not do anything for me. However, not wanting to appear un-cool, I took a few puffs. I was a little shocked that a former Military Policeman was smoking a joint. I was naive. I would soon find out how wide spread the use of drugs was throughout the military. I hardly saw my family at all while there. I was home for Thanksgiving though and it would be the last one for a few years. I had to go down to the main recruiting station several times during the month, assisting Jerry with getting other enlistees enrolled in the military. On several days, Jerry had me accompany him to local high schools. We were all decked out in our best uniforms. I put on my MP gear and was looking sharp; however, I did not have a forty-five automatic to put into my holster. That was not a problem. I went to a children's toy store and picked up a plastic sword that had a look of being a King's sword. It looked real enough and had a fake, gold-plated handle with a fake, plastic, red ruby embedded in the handle. Jerry signed three or four people up into the military police based on dumb high school kids seeing that sword and thinking it was real. It was almost a year ago that I was that dumb high school kid who was duped into joining the Army based on the fancy talk of the recruiters in our high school gymnasium.

After Thanksgiving, I received my orders for Germany. I was scheduled to fly from Denver to Charleston, South Carolina on December 2, 1979. Then, I needed to catch a military transport to Germany. The time flew by, and before I knew it, my thirty days elapsed.

Saturday, December 1, 1979:

The night before I was to take off, I went to a party with my old girlfriend. If not for her, I would have been AWOL. I drank so much at the party I blacked out. When Lois woke me up, I was lying fully clothed in the bathtub. She got me steady enough to travel. I had a massive hangover. Jerry, my recruiter, was going to take me to the airport, so she dropped me off at his house. On the way, we said our goodbyes. She asked me to stay behind and not go. I declined her invitation. She never spoke to me again after that.

As Jerry drove me to the airport, we made small talk. "Do you regret joining the military," he asked.

"Not at all," I said. "I'm looking forward to finding out what Germany is like."

"I bought you a going away present," he said. "It is in the glove box." I opened the glove box and inside was a bag of weed, a dime bag, apparently called so because it cost $10. "That's for when you get to Germany. I hope you enjoy it."

"Thanks," I said, feeling uncomfortable about taking it. I put it into my coat pocket. Later on at the airport, I stuffed it into my duffel bag.

The plane ride to Charleston, South Carolina was uneventful except for the massive hangover that I could not shake. It was a beautiful day; however, it hurt my eyes to look out the window. The pressure in the plane felt as if it was crushing my skull. Halfway through the flight, I ordered a beer from the flight attendant and that relieved my headache. I felt shaky the rest of the day.

When the plane arrived in Charleston, I caught a shuttle to the location of where the military transports took off. I did not have to leave that day. My actual flight from Charleston was an early morning flight on Monday. However, Jerry told me if I arrived a day early and was able to get aboard a plane, I could have a day of sightseeing once I arrived in Germany. When I went inside the terminal, the place was jam-packed. It was noisy. People and luggage were strewn about all over the place. Feeling as if I was pushing my luck by trying to make the early connection,

I panicked, turned around, and went back outside. Somehow, I felt that if I tried to board a plane right now, I would regret it, thinking they would search my luggage and find that marijuana. I hopped in a taxi and asked the driver to take me to a nearby, cheap motel. On the drive there, while stopped in a long line of cars at a red light, a man in the car in front of us exited his car and approached the car in front of him, yelling at the driver. Meanwhile the driver of the car in front of him got out of his car, too, and they got in a fistfight in the middle of the street. When the light changed, they returned to their cars, drove to the next light and repeated the scene. The cab driver did not even blink an eye.

"Does that sort of thing happen all the time?" I asked.

"Oh, yeah," he replied, giving his shoulders a slight shrug. "You have to ignore it and not get involved."

I arrived at the motel at 4 pm. It was $39.99 per night. *Why not call it what it is, forty dollars per night.* It was worth every penny of it. I was starving, but still feeling a little shaky from the drinking binge the night before. Instead of going to a restaurant, I ate junk food from the vending machines and watched television all night.

Monday, December 3, 1979:

The next morning, at 6 am, I called for a taxi. As soon as I got off the phone, I went to my duffel bag, grabbed the marijuana, and flushed it down the toilet. I did not want that crap anywhere near me when I went to board a military transport.

At the terminal, a long line of people were waiting to check in. Other people were sleeping in the terminal waiting to get a flight on a standby basis. There was a couple in front of me who checked in and were over the twelve-hundred pound weight limit allowed for luggage, so they were told to step aside and they would try to add some of their luggage on with another passenger who had less weight. I was the other customer. I had no idea we were allowed to bring personal items with us; otherwise, I would have brought more than two changes of civilian clothes with me.

The plane departed at 9 am, flying from Charleston, South Carolina to Nova Scotia where we refueled. It was a twenty-two hour flight. The flight was long and boring and most of it took place during darkness. Everybody tried to sleep during the flight.

Tuesday, December 4, 1979:

By the time the plane landed in Frankfurt, Germany, it was 7:30 am. It was still dark and cloudy. It was December and it was supposed to be cold and cloudy. However, over the next two years, I would come to hate the weather. I tell people it rained twice while I was over there, once for 11 months and once for nine months. It rained most of the time. When it did not rain, it snowed or was dark and cloudy. The sun poked through for a total of two days the whole two years I was there.

The processing station was surrounded by a brick fence. Inside the compound were three old buildings. One was an office building where people worked processing people in and out of Germany. One building was a barracks with several rooms filled with single beds. It reminded me of a hospital. I am not sure where families of military personnel were processed or whether the families themselves stayed there or at a separate facility, as I did not see anybody but non-commissioned military personnel buzzing about, as no officers had spent the night in the barrack room that I was assigned. The last building was a chow hall. The first thing we were allowed to do was put our luggage in a storage room and go eat breakfast.

After breakfast, everybody went to an orientation class. There were fifteen people in the class. We were told what to expect life in Germany to be like and what was expected of us. Another topic covered in the class was what to do if we encountered Russian diplomats in a restricted area. They showed us a picture of a Russian Diplomatic License Plate. Like the diplomats the United States had in East Germany, the Russian Diplomats could go almost anywhere they wanted; however, some places were restricted, like military bases and the immediate perimeter around a military base. If you saw a Russian Diplomat's car on a road outside a military base, you were authorized to detain them. However, in doing so, you had to treat them with the highest esteem and respect, keeping in mind that if we treated them with disrespect, they, in turn, would treat our diplomats in East Germany ten fold worse. If you could not detain them, then you were to obtain the license plate number of the vehicle.

The rest of the day was spent doing paperwork, going from one desk to another desk where our records were checked. Where you were going to be assigned depended on where you were needed the most. Towards the end of the day, I was told that I would be going to Miesau, Germany, a physical security site. Not knowing what that meant, but having heard talk about it in basic training as being crappy duty, I did not want to go there. I wanted what was known as "White Hat" duty where you perform the duties of a military policeman, wearing a fancy military police uniform with a white officer style hat. That was considered prime duty and it was what everybody envisioned when they joined. It is what their recruiters' told them being a military policeman meant. I was not too keen on the idea of physical security. I remembered the night in basic training where I had to spend two hours walking a post, guarding a building. I did not want to do that for the next three years.

"Going to Miesau involves getting a top secret clearance and they can take up to a year to come through," the desk clerk told me. "However, it looks like your Top Secret Clearance was approved while you were in basic training."

"How did they do that?" I asked.

"It is done by the FBI," he said. "They ask questions and check references of your family, friends, neighbors, schoolmates, stuff like that."

"I had no idea," I said. "Did they find anything wrong?"

"You have been given a Top Secret Clearance to work at sensitive areas," he answered. "We need to ask you a few questions, however." He paused, and then slowly stood up from his chair. As he rose, he said, "I'll be right back." He left the office, leaving me sitting in my chair, wondering what was going on. In a few minutes, he returned with another person, a sergeant, who introduced himself.

"I've got a few questions to ask, and we need you to be honest. What is said here stays here in this room," he said.

"No problem," I answered, suspecting he was lying about it staying in the room.

"First," he paused, looking me in the eye. "Have you ever used illegal drugs?" I was caught off guard and was not sure how to answer. If I told him the truth, I may be busted. If I did not tell him the truth, I still may be busted for lying because they already knew the truth based on information they gathered from friends during the Top Secret investigation. I pictured Jerry in my mind as having informed on me. Perhaps they even knew about the marijuana I flushed down the toilet back in Charleston.

"I have smoked marijuana a few times," I said, thinking I would admit to it and face the consequences, hoping that at worst they would revoke my Top Secret Clearance and assign me duty at a White Hat Unit.

"How many times," the sergeant asked.

"Two or three times," I lied. In reality, it had been about six times in which I took no more than a puff from a shared joint.

"When was the last time?" he questioned, as if trying to obtain a confession.

"Back in High School," I lied, not revealing that my recruiter and I had shared a few joints within the past month. I put all my cards on the table, hoping that I was not being set up for a bust.

"That's typical," the sergeant said. "So, you do not have a drug addiction problem. That's good."

"Is this going to affect my Top Secret Clearance?" I asked, trying to sound disappointed.

"Not at all," he said. "We appreciate your honesty." Then the sergeant left the room, leaving me alone with the desk clerk again.

"Well, we'll be busing you to your unit tomorrow. They are in need of immediate replacements and seem to have the greatest shortage of personnel over all the other units."

"I heard rumors that if you do a year of duty at a physical security site, you can then put in for a transfer anywhere you want, correct?"

"It is," he said. "You will be spending the night in the building across the courtyard. There are some free bunks in the sleeping area on the second floor. Your bus will leave tomorrow at

10 am, so you will have time to dress and eat breakfast and report back here about 9:30 am. Any questions?"

"I guess not," I replied.

Wednesday, December 5, 1979:

At 6 am in the morning, loud music blared from a radio in the barracks. The room accommodated twelve people and was full. Simultaneously when the music started blaring at an ear-deafening volume, eleven of those people, myself included, shot up in bed, holding our ears and cussing. The one person who did not wake up was the person to whom the radio alarm clock belonged. He continued to sleep right through it. I had my own alarm clock set for 8 am and was mad that the idiot had set his alarm so early and did not even wake up. The guy next to the bunk of the sleeping idiot got up and unplugged his radio, putting an end to the pain. Most people went back to bed at that point. I decided to get out of bed. It was then that I noticed my own alarm clock had melted into a twisted, warped box. I had to throw it away, learning that the 110 electrical appliances made for American households are not compatible in Europe's 220 electrical plugs without an adapter.

The bus ride from Frankfurt to Miesau was on a German Greyhound bus. We left Frankfurt at 10 am. There were twenty people on board the bus being transported to various military bases throughout Germany. Three other people were going to Miesau. There was Roscoe, a short, redheaded, freckled-faced, chubby kid who looked sixteen; Cowboy was a tall, lanky kid from Oklahoma. Then there was Riggs. He was five feet five inches tall and equally as wide as he was tall, weighing about two-hundred-fifty pounds. He was a black man of 18 out of Los Angeles. Riggs boarded the bus with a boom box that was half as long as he was tall. Within minutes of the bus departing, he started playing it, turning it up louder each time his cassette tape came to another song he liked. Thirty minutes into the bus ride, we were on the highway, traveling at seventy miles per hour, maybe faster. By this time, the volume was unbearable and annoying to everybody, including the German bus driver. So, does he ask him to turn it down? No. He stopped the bus in the middle lane of the highway, opened the bus door, and told Riggs to get off the bus.

"Aussen," he yelled in a heavy German accent, which means out. He pointed first at Riggs and then to the door. "Aussen."

"What?" Riggs shouted, looking at him in disbelief. "Are you crazy?"

"Aussen," he repeats. "Aussen." He then picks up the microphone of his radio and begins speaking into it.

"I'll turn it off," Riggs said with a slight twinge of fear in his voice. Meanwhile cars are speeding by the bus at incredible speeds.

"Bring radio here," the driver said. "Kommen." Riggs turned off the radio and took it to the front of the bus, handing it over to the driver. Riggs was the single person on the bus who was not happy. He grumbled the rest of the way to Miesau. We did not arrive until about 8 pm, as along the way, we made several stops at other bases, dropping people off at their new duty stations. When we arrived at Miesau, we were dropped off at the recreation building. We were told we would be sleeping there for about two weeks while they found room for us at the 164th MP barracks. Since the chow hall was already closed, we were given vouchers to go to the cafeteria that was across the street from the chow hall. Across from the cafeteria was a 4-lane bowling alley on one side. On the other side was a one-screen movie theater that played movies that were two years old. After eating, the four of us returned to the recreation center. It was dark and none of us knew anything about the base, so we did not have anything to do but hit the sack. We were given clean linens and bunks to sleep on. It was not hard to get to sleep, as it had been a long day of traveling.

Miesau Army Depot, known as MAD for short, lived up to its name. I knew what Miesau was like from the day I arrived until the day I left. However, on the Internet I found many websites about the history of it and similar Physical Security sites. Knowing the history, now, rather than when I first arrived, does not change things a bit. In fact, if I had known the history before I arrived and had any glimpse of what life was going to be like for the next year, I might have gone AWOL. However, because ignorance is bliss, I went there with an open mind.

One of the many Internet sites I found was at the web address: http://www.usfava.com/USAREUR/Histories/Weapons%20Depot%20Chapter.pdf.

Here is a summarized composite of the history and description of Miesau and other bases as well as the typical living conditions experienced by the people assigned to these bases as described on the above website, all in line with my own recollections, experiences, and observations of my time at Miesau:

The U.S. Army activated the Military Police units that provided the security forces for the "special weapons" depots of Europe, such as Miesau, for service during the Cold War (from 1946 to 1991), to provide security to facilities that were rapidly converting from standard ammunition dumps to Special Weapons Depots. These weapons sites, defined as the facilities that held nuclear, biological and chemical (NBC) weapons, were the Army Ordnance Corps posts that assembled, maintained, repaired and stockpiled the atomic, thermonuclear, neutron and chemical warheads as well as the armament system designed to deliver them. The MP units provided the security guards needed to protect the sites.

In order to meet the mandated requirement that military police guard special weapons sites, commanders created "temporary" MP Companies as guard units for both facilities and transportation of the weapons. By March of 1962, AWSCOM (the 71st Ordnance Battalion) was re-designated as the 59th Ordnance Group, and it was under this organization that most of the MP units would serve in Europe; many until the end of the Cold War.

All of the depots, and the MP Companies that guarded them were similar in facility, mission, and working conditions. The Special Weapons Depot was an Army post. Often located in rural, isolated areas, one section of the installation was a typical army post containing billets, mess hall, company administrative offices, and a motor pool. Most depots had a singular entrance point known as either A-Gate or Main Gate and this position was an MP post. The second "restricted" section contained the weapons facility. These more secure areas, referred to in official documents as either "limited" or "controlled," consisted of several acres of earth-covered bunkers or igloo's. The storage bunkers, which were known technically as "Yurt igloos," were constructed during 1957 after plans to use existing underground facilities were canceled The Yurt igloos were concrete buildings large enough to admit either a truck or forklift, were covered with several feet of earth and contained a double steel access door. Generally, one large bunker was an assembly or maintenance building where Ordnance soldiers worked on warheads and the remaining bunkers were storage igloos. A guardhouse, used to control access to the limited area, was located on the roadway leading beyond the perimeter and this post was manned by the MP Sergeant of the Guard (SOG). A motorized MP patrol stationed at the "SOG Shack" patrolled the bunkers and troopers were required to sign a check sheet every hour attesting that each igloo door was secure.

The restricted area of the depot was encircled with several guard towers and it was in the towers that the MP's performed guard duty. Site size dictated the number of towers. During the 1960's and early 1970's, the towers consisted of a sheltered wooden shanty measuring six feet square with a three-foot wide catwalk around the outside. The towers were approximately twenty feet high and spaced to allow visual coverage to the adjacent tower. The perimeter of the weapons section was protected by a lighted, double fence, while the remainder of the installation was encircled with a single fence. Most of the depots were fenced during the early 1950's and the original guard towers were erected in 1955 when nuclear warheads began arriving in Europe.

While on guard duty, the MP's watched for unlawful entry and unauthorized behavior. The MP's were armed with either an M-14 or an M-16 rifle and they were authorized to use deadly force for the failure to obey the command of "halt." Equipment in the original towers consisted of a chair, a field phone, and a Standard Operation Procedure (SOP) Manual. During the Cold War, the MP guard units provided two of the most paramount security functions required by USAREUR; that of keeping intruders out of the weapons sites; and, that of keeping secret weapons, secret. To accomplish these objectives, the MP's controlled complete and continuous access to the secure areas, maintained perimeter security from the infamous towers that encircled the sites, and provided guards for both airborne and road convoys when warheads were either moved or relocated.

The sound of an alarm or the opening of a bunker also received special attention. When entering an igloo, Ordnance personnel had to connect a field phone to the front of the structure and give the proper code to the alarm center. The alarm center, originally located outside the inner perimeter, was staffed by MP's around-the-clock and alarms sounded when bunker doors were tripped without the proper codes. Violations or questionable practices brought out first, the Security Alert Team (SAT) and then the Back-up Alert Force(BAF), both of which were on-call MP's who had minutes to respond to a problem area. Motion alarms located on the fence-lines brought similar responses.

Mission mandates required that the Special Weapons Depots, because of their importance, be inspected and evaluated on a regular basis. As such, the MP units that secured these facilities became some of the most inspected units of the US Army. Security inspections were scheduled for weapons sites approximately three times a year. These were conducted by USAREUR commanders and resulted in a certification of the facility and its personnel as a secure site. The inspections were of two types.

Command alerts and dignitary visits were also a common occurrence at the weapons depots. AWSCOM commanders would frequently initiate alerts to test both the MP and Ordnance personnel responses to a variety of predetermined circumstances. Dignitary visits to the sites by both NATO officials and Allied Commanders were not as frequent, but did require additional allocation of resources.

Living and working in mostly sub-standard and isolated surroundings, the MP's endured boredom, loneliness, and during the winter months, frigid conditions. As the years progressed, conditions improved somewhat but mission mandates required monotonous guard duty as the backbone of site security. Technological upgrades involving motion alarms, better communications and improved facilities helped make the job of security guard more palatable, but these improvements did little to alleviate the constant boredom, monotony, and low morale. Morale problems originated from a variety of sources.

First, the MP's suffered from a feeling of subservience to the Ordnance staff. This subordinate status was inherent in the "need to know" security requirement, but resulted in many MP's never knowing exactly what they guarded or why it was important. Also, the MP's manned their posts around the clock while

Ordnance personnel generally worked day shift with weekends off.

Second, duty at a Special Weapons Depot was monotonous and boring. MP's watched a fence-line where nothing happened. Potential intruders knew deadly force was authorized and seldom challenged that consequence. Many MP's picked out either a tree or a deer family and watched them grow. Some of the more enterprising troopers were able to tame hedgehogs and squirrels and make "tower pets" of them. This practice probably led to the eventual use of the term "tower rat," which MP's called themselves. Work schedules were constantly being changed in an effort to relieve boredom. Company Commanders would alter work cycles and/or hours in an effort to reduce boredom. However, in the long term, the changes had little effect on the monotonous routine.

Third, tower duty during winter months was cold. The original wooden towers did not get heaters until after the bitter winters of 1965 and 1966 after many MP's suffered freeze related injuries.

Fourth, any activity other than watching the fence-line was prohibited while in a tower. Both reading and writing within the confines of the "inner perimeter" was verboten. Similarly, radios were also prohibited during guard duty. However, these restrictions were violated wholesale. Although done en masse, the MP's who were caught by their Lieutenants either reading or listening to a radio were assured a weeks worth of walking post as punishment. Thankfully, most squad leaders, the Sergeants, turned a blind eye on these restrictions.

Fifth, recreation and diversions from poor working conditions was also limited during off-duty hours. Recreation was available at either the post movie theater, the Enlisted Men's (EM) Club or a local civilian nightclub. However, overindulgence in alcohol and, later, drugs had tragic consequences. On many nights after the clubs closed, the post facilities suffered either property damage or arsons. On more than one occasion, an intoxicated MP was the victim of either a fatal pedestrian or an automobile accident.

Throughout the 1960's and 1970's numerous organizational problems existed at the depots. Some were eventually corrected but some were beyond the solution capacity of either the MP or Ordnance Commanders.

Administratively, the MP Company Commander was in charge of his unit. However, operational control of the unit was vested with the Commanding Officer of the on-site Ordnance Company, usually a major. This duplicity of command created friction between the officer cadre and on occasion, it would percolate down the chain of command. On more than one occasion ordnance procedures conflicted with that of the MP's. For example, the Ordnance Commander would frequently initiate alerts during weekends to test the reaction time of the SAT and BAF units without the knowledge of the MP Commanders. The result was a less than ideal working relationship between soldiers of the different units.

Also, incoming troopers, both enlisted men and officers, had to endure a special "security clearance" background investigation prior to being allowed to work in the weapons portion of the depots. In many instances, this process, later referred to as a "personnel reliability program" or PRP, took over four months, and frustrated everyone. Commanders were prohibited from proper utilization of MP's until they were "cleared," and the MP's working tower duty viewed assignment pending PRP as "busywork."

Finally, all enlisted personnel who were unmarried were required to live in the post barracks. This rule made garrison troopers susceptible to call-up for alerts and extra duty. The requirement also resulted in overcrowding at the post and another contributor to low morale.

During the early 1970's, both radical group activity and protest demonstrations in Europe drastically increased the Army's concern about potential attacks on the weapons sites. Following several years of planning, in 1976 major renovations of the weapons depots began. Some sites were abandoned but most were completely rebuilt. In addition, Ordnance Corps reorganization resulted in the restructuring of the type of nuclear weapons held at each site. From 1977 through 1980, as the changes were nearing completion, the greatest threat was from terrorist groups. From the 1972 terrorist attack at the Munich Olympics to the rise of attacks throughout Europe, there was a great concern that terrorist would attack a nuclear weapons site in an effort to get a nuclear weapon. The increased threat and emphasis on security had a significant and positive effect on the MP units and the storage sites. Everyone finally got attention and money.

From 1976 to 1980, the weapons depots were completely rebuilt with security buildings constructed within the inner perimeter. They had new alarm systems, sensors, communication devices, and a large concrete central tower. In addition, new fence lines were erected with new steel towers replacing the old wooden structures. The new towers had bulletproof glass.

The depot security units went co-ed in 1976. The first female MP's graduated from Fort Gordon in late 1973 and within four years women were assigned to most MP Companies. By 1980, all platoons had women MP's assigned and in some units, the Company Commander was a woman. Separate and "off-limits" areas had to be created to house and assimilate female MP's into the workforce. These separate facilities, notwithstanding, many marriages between the MP's at weapons depots were the result of women working at the sites.

Finally, by the early 1980's, Military Working Dog (MWD) sections had become operational at most of the depots. The K-9 teams aided security by performing vehicle searches, package checks, and perimeter patrols.

Despite all the changes, for most soldiers, either enlistee or the earlier draftee, the real problem was always boredom and monotony. The endless duty as a tower guard was debilitating. Many professional and well-qualified soldiers left both the military after the experience.

During the 1960's, scores of MP's requested transfer to Vietnam in order to escape security duty. The re-enlistment rate for E-4 and below became almost non-existent. During the 1970's a drug problem also became pervasive. However, the majority of the MP's were both conscientious and diligent. As guardians of the most devastating weapons known to humankind, they helped in some small measure to win the Cold War. The end for the depots, the weapons, and the units stationed at the sites began in 1991 with the implementation of the Intermediate Range Nuclear Weapons (INF) Treaty of 1987. The INF treaty had been under negotiation between the US and USSR for several years but languished until the US announcement of the "star-wars" defense system convinced the Soviets that economically they could not remain in the arms race. By 1994, the last weapons depot closed and the units were retired.

The 164th Military Police Company was activated at Miesau Army Depot in early 1962 and deactivated in 1992. It was at NATO Site 104. The depot, operated by the 9th Ordnance Company, became the largest and most active Army ammunition facility outside the United States. Miesau was both a general depot supporting conventional ammunition as well as a nuclear warhead maintenance facility. The 164th MP Company was responsible for security of the special weapons portion of the depot and remained on station for thirty years.

By 1973, the last draftees were assigned to the unit, and by that time, a drug and alcohol problem had become rampant. Several veterans from that time period reported that the barracks, the Battalion Headquarters, and the Commander's jeep were either set on fire or vandalized, as inebriated soldiers made the facilities the target of their frustration. Continued acts of defiance eventually drove three Company Commanders from office and resulted in a Congressional inquiry investigating problems and deficiencies at all the Special Weapons facilities.

The 164th MP Company continued to increase in personnel allotment throughout the late 1970's and 1980's. In 1977, as both site and mission expanded, the unit was re-designated as a "heavy" nuclear surety unit and allotted six Officers and 264 Enlisted Men. Part of the personnel increase was used to staff the K-9 unit that began operations at the site in 1975.

The 164th had the additional mission of securing Special Weapons in and out of Ramstein. The Air Force gave the 164th a couple of bunkers in their storage area. Likewise, the 164th had a similar mission at Hahn AFB. In addition to the nuclear storage area, Site 104 was a huge conventional ammo storage area.

Throughout the decades of the Cold War, MP's lived and worked under the threat of immediate annihilation, many of them without even knowing that the Warsaw Pact targeted missiles to eliminate each weapons site. Regardless of any deficiency, not one site was ever penetrated where MP security units were on station. In all those years, the sites and the material contained in them remained secure.

Promised by recruiters, indoctrinated by the MP School, desirous of law enforcement experience, the coveted "white-hat" duty evaporated on the catwalk of an isolated, lonely tower. Most troopers never got over the damage to their psyche. They made the best of a bad situation, adapted to their environment, left the Army, and began a career with a civilian law enforcement agency. It was a preventable loss for the Corps. Had motivational, reward and retention techniques been applied, conscientious and dedicated soldiers could have been retained.

Thursday, December 6, 1979:

After breakfast, we were escorted over to the barracks of the 164th MP Company. All the buildings looked identical, three stories in height, about sixty feet wide and double that in length. The chow hall building was the second building on the left once inside the main gate. The cafeteria was on the first floor. The cooks had rooms on the second and third floors. Fifty yards further on to the base on the left hand side was the barracks for the 164th MP Company, the largest MP Company anywhere three-hundred people. The building was three stories tall. On the first floor, one-fourth was reserved office space for the Captain and the Lieutenants for each of the three platoons. I do not know if the dog handler platoon had a lieutenant or not. On the North end of the building, past the office space, was where formations were held for a change of shift between platoons and where the radio communication room was located. Shift changes occurred every twelve hours at 6 am and 6 pm. This room was where the Alert Force conducted their operations. On the opposite side of the first floor on the South end of the building were the rooms for all of the dog handlers and all of the women, including the women's bathroom and showers.

The Armory was in the basement. All of the ammunition and weapons were locked up in a room that resembled a bank vault. The basement also housed the supply room. On the second and third floors were the rooms for all of the male personnel in the First, Second, and Third platoons. Each room was large enough to house three people with their three separate bunks and wall lockers. Each room was about twenty square feet and was equipped with a community wall locker for everybody to share for storing supplies. A mini-refrigerator was in each room for everybody to share, too. In addition, enough room existed for people to set up their own personal stuff like a stereo, desk, television, a chair, or things of that nature. Each floor also had a laundry room and a large bathroom with ten stalls and ten urinals, and a big shower area within the bathroom with ten showers. There were twenty rooms on each side of the hallway. The First platoon occupied the South end of the second floor and the Second platoon occupied the North end.

Going up to the third floor where the Third platoon was barracked, the set up was identical except right next to the laundry room was a large recreation room that had a pool table, foosball table, a ping-pong table, and a television. Of course, I did not learn all of this until later. When we first arrived, we were introduced to the Captain who welcomed us to the company. He said they would do their best to find us room at the barracks as soon as possible. We spent the majority of the day filling out papers. At 3 pm we were informed they already had found open rooms for us. After dinner we went back to the Recreation building where we had stayed the previous night and a pickup truck with a canvas shell on the back arrived to pick us up with our luggage. We threw the luggage in the back of the truck and climbed aboard. We were then driven back over to the barracks.

Riggs and I were both assigned to the First Platoon. Cowboy was assigned to the Second Platoon, and the other kid, Morgan, was assigned to the Third Platoon. About six months later, he was discharged from the Army. Rumor had it that his roommate was passed out drunk on his bed and awoke to find Morgan performing oral sex on him. I did not know if it was true or not.

Our squad leaders that we were assigned to each came downstairs to the first floor to introduce themselves and show us to our rooms. "My name is Specialist Payne," my squad leader said, "follow me, and I'll take you to your room." On the way there, he gave a little advice. "If you have any problems about anything, do not hesitate to come to me. Always follow the chain of command. If I cannot help you out, we will go to the platoon sergeant and so forth and so forth."

My room was on the second floor, the second from the South end of the building. When we arrived, Payne knocked on the door. A tall lanky fellow with a mustache and a tanned, wrinkled face, which made him look much older than his twenty-eight years, opened the door. He stepped aside to let us in. His name was Specialist Saber. Another man, PFC Seeley, was sitting on a bunk. He was a short, stocky black man. He was muscular with a mean look to him. Saber, as I would find out within the month, was a burnt out alcoholic; Seeley was either the biggest drug pusher on the base or working undercover for narcotics. I was one of about ten new arrivals during the next few weeks. We were all referred to as a newbie.

For all newbies, an initiation into the unit existed. It was not an organized initiation that was based on tradition. It was people being drunk and stupid. During my time at Miesau, some of the initiations I witnessed were such things as newbies being dragged out of their rooms and taken to the laundry room where their head would be held underwater in the utility sink until they passed out. Some newbies were hung upside down by their ankles from a third floor window until they pissed their pants. Once I saw a newbie get knocked unconscious by a cold cock fist to his face, which broke his jaw.

My first night in the room did not generate any feelings of trust or endearment for my roommates. In one evening -- one moment -- all the feelings of pride and respect that flourished during basic training and Military Police Training, all the pride I had for joining the Army, the comradeship developed with fellow soldiers all disappeared. As soon as introductions were complete, Payne, Reeder, and Seeley left the room having pointed out the obvious fact that the empty bunk without linen and the wall locker next to it belonged to me.

My initiation was not anything like what the majority of newbies experienced, and at that time, I did not know that initiations existed. I started unpacking my gear into the wall locker and making my bunk. About the time I finished and sat down on my bunk to take my boots off, Reeder, Seeley and a person named Blair came back into the room, closing and locking the door behind them. They surrounded my bunk area. "Let's make one thing perfectly clear," Reeder said, leaning against my wall locker. Seeley had taken up a position against the wall between my bunk and the door while Blair sat down on the opposite side of my bunk. "If you are a nark, we're going to kill you."

"We do not like narcs and we do not take kindly to them," Seeley added.

"What are you talking about," I asked, assuming they were talking about drugs. "I don't use drugs and I do not like it when people try to entice me to use drugs, so you better keep that shit to yourselves." I did not know if this was some sort of test or what, but I felt I had breached some sort of Military Police Honor code by not standing up and saying that if you use drugs, I will do whatever I can to bust you. At the same time, I was not stupid either. Saying something like that could have gotten me killed. I did not know how serious they were with their threats.

"That's cool," Reeder said. "I think he sounds cool about it."

"We're not asking you to use drugs," Seeley said. "That's your business. Of course, if you ever need to score some, I can set you up. We are telling you to mind your own business and we'll mind ours."

"At the same time, being roommates, we watch out for each other," Reeder said. "We'll watch your back and cover for you, and you do the same for us. Deal?" He extended his hand for a shake.

"Deal," I said, shaking his hand.

"Welcome to Miesau," Seeley said, extending his hand, for a shake, too.

"Thanks," I said, shaking his hand.

They spread the word around that I was not to be harassed or initiated into the unit like the other newbies unless they wanted a fight on their hands. I felt anger and bitter resentment towards them, feeling that they were disgraces to the Military Police, threatening me to compromise the values and sense of duty and honor instilled during Military Police Training. Of course, my recruiter did not do so hot in living up to those ideals either. I guess the difference was that with my recruiter, I considered him more of a friend and he never threatened to kill me. In this situation, I was not being offered a choice. At the same time, it was my first day in the unit. I did not know jack shit about anybody. I did not know whom to trust. Even if I wanted to take a stance and say, hell no, if you are doing drugs, I am going to bust you or at least nark on you, I would not have known where to turn to do such a thing. As far as I knew, everybody in the entire company could have been corrupt.

I never achieved any sort of bond or lasting friendship with them, let alone any respect. As time went on, I came to think of Reeder as a loser. He was always getting into trouble for missing formations because he would get so drunk all the time that he could not get out of bed. He had been busted in rank, I heard, at least once and while we were roommates, he was busted in rank for dereliction of duty. Before coming to Miesau, Reeder was stationed at Fort Ord in California and was in love with a woman back there. During his second three-year term in the Army when he was transferred to Germany, the relationship ended and he became an alcoholic. About six months after my arrival, Reeder re-enlisted for a third term on the condition he was assigned to Fort Ord. He got his wish. It seemed to pick him up a little. When he left, I did not bother to say goodbye.

Seeley ended up re-enlisting about three months after Reeder re-enlisted and was assigned to do undercover work in narcotics at his new unit. I had to suspect that he was already doing undercover work at Miesau because he sold more drugs to people while at Miesau than anybody I knew. He never tried to sell them to me and I never witnessed him using any drugs. I had to wonder where he got the drugs from in the first place. If he was not working undercover at Miesau, then re-enlisting and being assigned to work undercover narcotics was asinine.

That first night, the first platoon was finishing the last of three days off, getting ready to start four days of a 12-hour night shift that went from 6 pm to 6 am. After our talk, I showered and went to bed.

Friday, December 7 1979:

The next day we finished processing into the company, being assigned an M-16, gas mask, flak jacket, steel pot, canteen, ammunition packets, web gear, and other field equipment.

At 6 pm the first platoon started the first of four, twelve-hour night shifts. After the fourth night shift, we would get 24 hours off, and then would pull four, twelve-hour day shifts. The last day shift was followed by three days off, and then the cycle began over again. Since Riggs and I were still processing into the company and had not completed orientation, we did not have to fall in for formation. We did have to report downstairs at 6 pm to the first floor where the formations were held. By that time, the formation was already over with and the change of shift had already begun. This area housed a foosball table, vending machines, a television set with a VCR, a couch, a lazyboy chair, and several other chairs. Also, a cubicle with four-foot high wooden walls, four inches thick, housed the radio communications area where the Sergeant in charge monitored radio transmissions with the people out at the nuclear site. Sergeant Compton was in charge that night. Specialist Becker was monitoring the radio with him. Since the schedule had been made in advance, Sergeant Compton assigned me to work at the command station where they monitored the radio. He explained what they were doing along with the normal procedures. He also had me read through the company's Standard Operation Procedure (SOP) Manual. It was required that once an hour they do a radio check with the main tower and the main security building at the nuclear site. If an attack at the nuclear site took place, the X-Area would reach us by radio. At that point, we would be required to sound the base alarm over loud speakers, alerting everybody that the nuclear site was being attacked. It meant that everybody in the entire company who was available would be sent out to set up a perimeter in the woods around the site, to prevent anybody who may have made it into the site from getting out alive with a nuclear weapon. Everybody who was in the first platoon who was not at the nuclear site was required to be on active alert during that time. About a dozen people were on active alert that night. The rest of the platoon went out to the nuclear site to work. The people in the Second and Third Platoons were off duty, which meant they were on the Standby Alert Force. They could go to bed, the movie theater, bowling, or drink themselves into a drunken rage, but if something went down, they had to report to the Sergeant in charge in full uniform, get their weapons, and be ready to be trucked out to the site to provide additional security in less than thirty minutes. They would set up a wider perimeter than the people who responded first. According to Compton, a real incident in which terrorists attempted to attack the nuclear site never had taken place. However, at any given time, the major in charge of the base, our own company commander, or the Sergeant in charge at the site could call a practice alert to test the response times. Of course, they would not tell anybody it was a practice alert. As far as anybody knew, it was the real thing. It was rumored that if we shot a terrorist or anybody attempting to break into the nuclear site, we would be rewarded with a transfer back to the States or anywhere we wanted to go. Compton showed me a book that contained wanted posters of known or suspected terrorists. Bombings and kidnappings happened at least monthly. In fact, many times we had to evacuate our own barracks building because of phoned in bomb threats. The dog handlers would search the building with their dogs. A bomb was never found, but the terrorists met their goal in that they disrupted our lives and routines.

At midnight, we were allowed to go to the chow hall and get a midnight meal that consisted of scrambled eggs, toast, hash browns, and coffee. After returning from midnight meal, Compton asked me questions about my personal life, about where I was from and how I ended up at Miesau.

On Monday a week long orientation class was to begin in which we were to be taught a little of the German language. Since I had two years of German in High School, I did not see the relevance of taking a short course on German, now. I brought it up with Compton, asking if there was any possibility I could get an exemption from having to attend the class. His reaction was the first clue that I had that I had made a mistake. He about fell over backwards in his chair.

"So, you want to opt out of taking the week long class and be put on the duty roster?" he asked suspiciously. Duty could not be that bad, I thought to myself, but by his reaction, I was wondering. However, I felt it was too late to change the situation, now.

"Sure," I said, trying to sound positive. "What could I learn by attending this class? I've had two years of German already." He must have heard the concern and a slight hesitation in my answer.

"I'll get you added to the duty roster right away," he said before I changed my mind. "How do you feel about pulling tower duty tomorrow night?"

"Why not," I said, wondering what tower duty was. Unfortunately, I was going to find out soon.

At 4 am, Compton had us start on cleaning the Command Room and the lobby area of the building where the CQ was. The CQ was like the Captain's secretary and sat at a desk in the lobby where he or she monitored the whole building. The person on CQ duty rotated every twelve hours and always had an assistant. They were required to do a physical inspection of the building every hour, keep everybody in line, and when the Captain was not there, inform him of any problems that arose that he should know about. The people who pulled CQ duty were people who for whatever reason were not able to perform any of the regular duty; for instance, a broken foot or their security clearance had not been approved, yet, so they were not allowed to go into the secure area at all. Some people's security clearance took up to a year to come back. Mine took a couple of days. The clearance for Riggs, one of the three other people who arrived at Miesau the same time I did, took eight months to come back. In the meantime, he was assigned to work as a CQ assistant. A CQ had to be at least an E4 in rank. The rank of the assistant did not matter.

After emptying all the trash, sweeping, mopping, and buffering the floors downstairs, we had to go do the same on the second floor for our side of the barracks. In addition, we had to clean the latrines on each floor. It took the twelve of us the whole two hours to do it. I was sweating like a pig, working my butt off and putting some hard effort into it, still having that basic training mentality. Compton commented that I was working harder than the others, stating that they did not seem to care whether dirt remained on the floor after they completed sweeping. Everybody was going through the motions of cleaning without cleaning. After change of shift at 6 am, we were dismissed from duty, free to go to bed or do whatever we wanted. I chose to go eat breakfast at the chow hall before going to bed.

Saturday, December 8, 1979:

I slept off and on until noon. I got out of bed feeling as if I had little or no sleep, but I found sleeping during the day to be difficult. Quietly, I left the room so as not to disturb Reeder or Seeley, as they were still sleeping. I did the three S's, shit, shower, and shave, not necessarily in that order, and not at the same time. Then, I went and ate lunch. The rest of the afternoon, I spent shining my boots and trying to make my fatigues presentable for my first night of tower duty.

The formation started at 5:30 pm, as the platoon coming on duty was required to relieve the other platoon by 6 pm in the X-Area. My routine was to get out of bed sixty to ninety minutes before the formation so that I could be showered, shaved, dressed in combat fatigues, boots shined, and wearing full gear, which consisted of flak jacket, steel pot, web gear, gas mask, and ammunition pouches. Then I went to the armory and signed out my M-16 and 100 rounds of ammunition that were already loaded in magazines, but sealed in foil wraps. We were also given another magazine, loaded with ammunition that was not sealed in foil. However, we were not allowed to put it in our M-16 until it was time to pull our shift inside the X-Area. The shift change did not always happen without incident. Sometimes we had sergeants from various platoons pissed at each other, so they would screw them by arriving at the X-Area as late as possible.

The formation room was small, so the platoon formation was rather tight. Each person was assigned to one of four squads. I was in the first squad, so we stood at the front of the formation. Important information was relayed, such as upcoming training, upcoming inspections, problems at the X-Area, promotions, and anything else of importance. The formations here were nothing like what we had in basic training. Some people did not bother to shine their boots and their uniforms looked ragged and dirty. Others, on the other hand – like in Basic – had a spit shine on their boots, with a reflection that put mirrors to shame; their uniforms were starched solid, their equipment was perfectly arranged and they looked sharp. Sergeant Ryan called out everybody's last name and we were to answer, "Here, Sergeant." However, the responses varied depending on the person's attitude.

"Adams."

"Here, Sergeant."

"Adair."

"Ninety days and counting, Sergeant," which I later learned that Adair had ninety days left in the military.

"Buell."

"F.T.A.," Buell shouted, which stood for "Fuck The Army." In fact, I noticed several people had "FTA" written on the front of their stretch bands that held the camouflage covering on their steel pot.

"Davis."

"Short-timer," Davis screamed out. I later learned that this, too, meant he had a short amount of time left in the military. Of course, some people considered themselves to be short-timers with less than two years to go; while others did not consider themselves short until they had less than thirty days.

"Evans."

"I'm so short an ant pissed on me today." Everybody laughed at that remark.

"Jones."

"Here, Sergeant," Jones shouted in a way that a drill sergeant in basic training would love to hear. As I came to know everybody in the platoon, I found out that Jones was a kiss ass. He was also a "lifer," somebody who stays in the military as a career.

"Mitchell."

"Here, Sergeant."

"Reeder." No answer. "Reeder," Sergeant Ryan shouted out.

"Huh?" Reeder said, as if he woke up that moment, but was experiencing a hangover.

"Nice of you to join us," Sergeant Ryan said.

"Seeley."

"Present, Sergeant," Seeley bellowed out, always the professional while on duty, but behind, closed doors, always the drug dealer.

"Turner."

"Here, Sergeant," I answered. After role call was finished, Lieutenant Barge, Sergeant Ryan, and our respective squad leaders inspected all of us, making sure we had all of our equipment, that our M-16's were clean, and our uniforms looked presentable. I was warned for my boots. I had shined them for over an hour, but no matter how much effort I put into it, they always looked dull.

"Take a look at the shine on Specialist Miller's boots, Private," Lieutenant Barge said. "It is outstanding. Isn't that right, Specialist Miller?" Miller was one of the squad leaders and came over to us.

"Out fucking standing, sir," Miller said with a stupid ass grin on his face. He was one of the kiss asses, rumored to be a lifer who was one of the lucky few who lived off post with his wife. His uniform was always ironed to perfection; creases were crisp and pockets laid flat and his uniform was stiff as cardboard from the starch that was added to it. His boot shine reflected like a mirror. It turns out his wife would prepare his uniforms and shine his store bought boots for him. "If you need any help with how to shine your boots, do not hesitate to ask."

"I expect you to do better by tomorrow night's inspection," Barge said and moved on. Miller went back to wait with the other squad leaders in front of the formation until his squad was being inspected.

After the inspection was completed we were given a briefing on terrorist activity and told to be alert and do not get caught sleeping on duty. We then loaded up into the back of a couple dodge pickup trucks with canvas shell coverings on them. The backs were equipped with wooden benches.

The drive to the X-Area was a ten-minute drive if doing the posted fifteen-mile-per-hour speed limit. When we arrived at the X-Area, we all disembarked at a one-and-a-half-story building made of masonry-concrete with a four-story tower on the side of it. The building served as a gate between the outer perimeter fence and the inner perimeter of the storage area. The area between the two fences was known as "No Man's Land" and we were authorized to use deadly force to stop anybody who crossed or attempted to cross the outer fence. To get into the X-Area, a large swing gate existed for vehicles to pass. For people to enter the building, a metal turnstile gate allowed one person to enter at a time. Right before the turnstile gate was a large bulletproof window behind which sat a person who monitored who was coming in to the facility. That person had the ability to shut down the gate electronically at any time. At the base of the window was a speaker box so that the person behind the window could communicate to people coming in and out. On both sides of the gate were two guards who, if they chose, could search us or anything we were bringing into the area. Anybody entering the area had to pass by the window and the guards. If somebody – like a terrorist disguised in an Army uniform was forcing us to get them into the area by gunpoint, or blackmail, or some other method, we could alert the guards at the gate or the man behind the glass by addressing them by the wrong rank. For instance, the man behind the glass was required to be an E-4 rank or higher. If the person was a Specialist, which is what most E-4s were, we could alert him or her that something was wrong by saying, "How are you today, Lieutenant Smith?" Upon being addressed by the wrong rank, he would know something was wrong, shut down the gates and call for SAT, the Security Alert Team. The gate guards would then force everybody to lie face down on the ground. Each person who entered the premises was supposed to sign in and sign out, but the sergeant in charge of the shift would sign in and out for everybody. The building was about two or three years old and looked out of place with everything else in the area. It looked new in contrast to all the other buildings in Germany, which all seemed to be old and falling apart. Our barracks was built before World War II and looked every bit that old. Not to mention, the X-Area was out in a wooded forest area surrounded by trees, but here was this clear area surrounded by two ten foot tall fences with razor wire on the top. The perimeter of the area was about two miles. Every fifty feet around the outer fence line, facing outward, were tall lights that gave off a yellow, eerie glow. Inside the perimeter of the two fences were metal towers, four in all. There was also a concrete tower attached to the main building we had entered. That was

Tower Two. There was no Tower One. They were numbered this way in case terrorists were monitoring the radio frequency. They would not be able to figure out which tower was which because Tower One did not exist. When we talked on our field phones or walkie-talkies, we identified our self by our tower number. For example "Tower Four, this is Tower Two, come in, over."

I was scheduled to pull duty in Tower Three from 8 pm to 10 pm and then again from 2 am to 4 am. The five people scheduled to pull the first shift up in their towers were whisked away, walking down the tower line with the Sergeant of the Guard towards a tower in a southeasterly direction five-hundred yards away. Being winter, it was already dark outside before we arrived at the X-Area, so I could not see much of the area that night or the next two nights to follow. The rest of us went into the building through a three-foot wide steel door. The front of the building was jammed full of electronic equipment, such as sensors for alarms along the fence lines and storage bunkers, radios, and phones. To the left was the person who controlled the electronic equipment to let people in and out of the X-Area. To the right were a desk and a little office area for the site commander. Farther into the building on the right was an alarm panel where a person of at least E-4 rank or higher sat 24 hours a day, watching the alarms. That person had to do electronic checking of the alarms once an hour to make sure they were all working. If an alarm did not respond or if one sounded at any time, then all hell broke loose. I would have my first experience with responding to an alarm within the week. Past the alarm panel was a small room to the left with three bunks in it. That was the sleeping room for members of SAT. A bathroom was off to the right. Beyond that the building opened up into a large spacious room. This room had couches, a TV, a foosball table, some folding chairs, and some folding tables like what are in elementary school gyms during lunch period. This room was where meetings were held and served as a combination dining area and recreation area. On the far side of the room was another steel door, providing access to the upstairs and to another set of stairs that led up to the top of Tower Two. At the top of the stairs more rooms existed. One room was full of cots; another was a storage area; and, another was a gathering place for the escort guards who worked day shifts, Monday through Friday. They were responsible for escorting people who needed to enter inside of the X-Area for various jobs of servicing alarms, locks, or to get access to weapons for maintenance or moving.

Meanwhile, the people we were relieving stood by while Sergeant Sampson inspected the building. If he did not find it clean, he could refuse to relieve the other platoon until they cleaned whatever was found unsatisfactory. That seldom happened except when personal arguments raged up among the sergeants of the three platoons. As soon as Sergeant Sampson signed in, the other platoon exited out the same door we entered. The same trucks that brought us out to the X-Area took them back to the barracks. One of the trucks would have to return to pick up the people who were still in their towers waiting to be relieved by people from our platoon who were at the moment walking the tower line en route to each tower to pull their first of a double, two-hour shift.

The first thing we did was to place our M-16's into a storage rack in the Meeting room, and then we removed our gear. We were called together to have seats in the room, as Sergeant Ryan was going to give us a class on procedures in the X-Area. "Specialist Moran," he said, "I know you are dying to share your wisdom with some of the new guys in the platoon, so why don't you come up here and explain the duties and response times of the various teams that provide Security for the X-Area." Moran was twenty-four years old and had been at Miesau for two years. Still wearing his flak jacket, Moran strutted up to the chalkboard with a wise guy grin on his face, hanging his thumbs from the armholes of his flak jacket.

"I'd be out-fucking delighted," Moran said. "I'll start with SAT, which stands for Security Alert Team and is a three man team that is first to respond in the X-Area to any situation," he said, writing the words SAT on top of the flip chart with the numeral sixty next to it, followed by the word seconds. "SAT has exactly one minute to respond anywhere in the X-Area. SAT is otherwise known as Suicide Alert Team because if somebody has broken into the X-Area to steal a nuclear weapon, you can bet your sweet ass, they are going to be heavily armed.

"After SAT comes BAF, the Backup Alert Force. BAF is made up of the ten tower rats who were not in their towers. The Sergeant of the Guard is in charge of BAF and his second in command is the sergeant in charge of the Tower Rats, making it a twelve-man team that has five minutes to respond to an incident as Backup to SAT.

"Basically your first responsibility is to set up a perimeter around SAT's location and not let anybody outside of that perimeter. He wrote 'BAF – 5 Minutes' on the flip chart.

"Who do you suppose comes next? Well, I'm going to tell you. The Alert Force responds next and is composed of every MP on this base with or without a dick. They have exactly thirty minutes to respond," he said writing 'Alert Force – thirty minutes' on the flip chart directly below BAF. "Their responsibility is to set up a perimeter around the entire X-Area and see to it that nothing living, nor a nuclear weapon, gets outside that perimeter.

"Suppose after all that we still need help?" He asked, pausing to wait for a response. "Anybody?"

"Eighth Infantry Division," somebody yelled out.

"Anybody?" Moran asked again, ignoring the first response.

"Eighth Infantry Division," the same person said louder and with more confidence.

"Well, I'll tell you," Moran said with a cocky smile on his face. "The entire Eighth Infantry Division of twenty-thousand people out of Baumholder has two hours to move their asses down here and set up a perimeter around the entire base. Their job is to make sure nothing living gets outside of the base with a nuclear weapon." He wrote '8th Infantry Division – 2 hours' on the flip chart.

"Finally, if that still isn't enough," he said turning back around to face everybody, "kiss your ass's goodbye because if the Eighth Infantry Division cannot keep containment of the area, you'll hear a five minute blast of the alarm system. What does that blast mean?

"You have five minutes to clear the area before your ass is toast," somebody said.

"Anybody?" Moran asked. "Anybody at all know? Well, I'll tell you again," he said with that same cocky smile smeared across his face. "If you hear a five minute blast of the alarm system, that means you have five minutes from the time that the alarm stops sounding to clear the area before your ass is toast because at that point Ramstein Air Force Base is going to obliterate the entire area, wiping this place off the face of the earth."

"Hoorah," somebody yelled out, setting off a chain of Hoorahs.

"You're damned right, Hoorah," Moran said. "Any questions? Anybody?"

"Thanks, Moran," Sergeant Ryan said, exchanging places with Moran in front of the room. Sergeant Ryan then began to quiz us on everything Moran had covered, picking people at random to answer each question. It seemed simple enough. I could not help but wonder how I would react if that situation played out and in the end what would I do upon hearing the five minute alarm, announcing I had five minutes to live before a big ass bomb was dropped on my head. *How far away would I have to be in order to survive the bomb from Ramstein Air Force Base? Could I clear away far enough to survive? Would taking shelter somewhere allow me to survive?* This was serious stuff to ponder. We were no longer playing with blanks like in basic training. We had live ammunition, daily briefings about terrorist attacks, and procedures on how long we had to live if certain events occurred.

The class lasted an hour, so I had one more hour before my first shift in a tower. After the class people broke up into various groups and played cards, while some went upstairs to sleep on one of the cots, meanwhile a few others popped a tape into a VCR and watched a movie. I sat in the main room downstairs and read the Stars and Stripes trying to catch up on some of the NFL football games. The hour went fast.

Thirty minutes before it was time for the change of shift, Sergeant Ryan told us to get our gear on, grab our weapons, and muster by the main gate. In all, six people – one person for each tower -- plus Sergeant Ryan gathered together. Sergeant Ryan had us insert our magazine clips into our M-16's, then the person who was working in Tower Two went back the other way as the access to Tower Two was up the stairs on the other side of the building. Wearing our steel potted helmets, flak jackets, full web gear and carrying our M-16's, we were let out of the building by Specialist Jones, who was the person for our platoon who manned the gate and all of the electronic gadgets that controlled entry into and out of the X-Area. Jones worked the gate every shift that First platoon was scheduled to work. He pushed a button that popped the lock on the door that allowed us to go out into the tower line between the two fences. I was working Tower Three, which was the next tower down the Tower Line. The Tower Line was about twenty yards wide. On the outer fence were light poles with square cases containing yellow lights that glowed eerily away from the X-Area, towards the woods. A light pole was positioned every fifty feet. Tower Three was five-hundred yards away at a forty-five degree angle from the Security Building. I was working the second shift, which went from 8 pm to 10 pm, and the fifth shift, which was from 2 am to 4 am. As we were walking to the towers, we all walked at different paces and were, for the most part, silent. I had a million questions I wanted to blurt out. I was scared that I would mess up. The night before I had read in the procedure manual that the tower guard was required to challenge people as they approached by yelling, "Halt. Senior person in charge, state your name, rank and purpose and the password for the day." The password changed every twenty-four hours and we were given the password during our role call meeting at the start of the shift. We did not want to forget it. Once the tower guard was satisfied everything was in order, the people would be permitted to proceed. If the tower guard, for any reason, suspected foul play, they were to have everybody lay face down on the ground and call Tower Two on the field phone and notify them of the problem. This would trigger SAT to respond, followed by BAF. If necessary, the tower guard was authorized to use deadly force on anybody who was within the perimeter of the outer-most fence. As we approached the first tower, I expected the tower guard to challenge us as we approached. He did not. I was confused. How strict were they on having us follow procedures? Was I correct in what I read about being authorized to use deadly force? I wanted to ask all these questions, but I did not want to appear to be afraid. Instead, as we got to the tower, I followed Sergeant Ryan up the hundred or so stairs to the little, metal box that sat forty feet in the air. I stepped inside the tower and Sergeant Ryan gave me a quick run down on how to use the field phone to call Tower Two should any thing happen. Then he and the person I was relieving descended down the stairs en route to Tower Four, which was barely visible about five hundred yards away. From my Tower, looking inward into the X-Area, I could see the Security Building off to the left. Inside the X-Area were rows and rows of bunkers each with a yellow light centered at the top of the steel doors on the front side of each bunker. Cement driveways rolled up to each one. A one-lane road snaked around inside the X-Area, giving paved access to the three rows of bunkers. Between the Security Building and my tower was a large building about fifty feet by fifty feet wide that sat inside of the X-Area. I later learned that this was where the Ordinance Battalion people worked on the Nuclear weapons. I had learned in the short time since being at Miesau that all the MP's referred to the Ordinance Battalion people as maggots and it was not an affectionate pet name. Our MP unit had no respect for the Ordinance Battalion. They felt the same about us, referring to us as Tower Rats. The term Tower Rats was a name of pride and honor among the MP's. In fact, back at the base on the third floor of the barracks in the recreation room was a mural almost the full length of the wall. The mural was about twenty feet long and ten feet high. It showed a cartoon rat wearing a flak vest, steel pot, web gear, and an MP arm Band. The rat was dragging an M-16 behind him down the tower line -- the same tower line that I had finished walking to my tower. Despite looking dirty and tired, the Rat stood there flipping off a bald eagle about ten times the size of the rat. The eagle, with its razor sharp talons about ready to gorge into the rat wore a ribbon that said, "Uncle Sam's U.S. Army" on it in big bold letters. The picture had a caption that said

"FTA." That mural represented the way that every MP who I knew to pull tower duty felt in a short period of working the towers. My transformation had begun. Fresh out of basic training, I was full of pride, loyalty, and self esteem for the Army, the Military Police and the United States. Tower Rat duty, the fake sense of honor that the Army Recruiters and the Drill Sergeants led myself and others to believe that Military Police duty and Army life beheld and all the daily crap that took place transformed me from an honorable, proud soldier, willing to die for Country, into a bitter and sarcastic soldier. The transformation started that second night when my roommates threatened to kill me, and it continued during my first shift in the tower.

I saw other people come and go who also transformed the same way, some faster than others. Some had nervous breakdowns, some were given Article 15's, and some were dishonorably discharged. For the most part, I survived Miesau due to several factors. One, my overall time spent doing tower duty was not as long as some other people, and two, after about eight months at Miesau, I hit rock bottom. Feeling my life was spiraling out of control, I took action to change it as best as possible under those conditions. My first two hours of tower duty are forever burned into my memory. Thinking back to those two hours – even my first few months at Miesau, I wonder how I could have been so naive. Once I was in the tower, I paced back and forth, going from window to window and monitoring all four directions of the compass. It was pitch black up in the tower above the lights. We were not allowed to read, eat, drink, smoke, sleep, sit, or do anything except watch for breaches in security, challenging anyone we saw. I still was confused as to why we were not challenged as we approached the tower, so I watched the others proceed on to Tower Four and strained to listen to see whether the person in the other tower would challenge them as they approached. I heard nothing. I did not have a watch on so I tried to keep a count, by counting in my head as to how much time had elapsed. I was convinced that somebody of authority was watching me from the main tower, or some other location, using an infrared telescope to make sure I did not slack while on duty. Convinced that if I had been caught slacking, I would be court-martialed, I did not cease from pacing back and forth to each window in regular intervals, making a point to move my head about as if I was observing and checking out everything within eyesight. The tower box could not have been more than five feet by five feet and about eight feet tall. Each wall, except for the wall with the doorway had metal siding about four-feet high. From the top of the siding to the ceiling were bulletproof panes of glass. One corner had a shelf with a field phone lying on top of it. The field phone connected to Tower Two. Hanging from the ceiling of the tower was a piece of metal about two feet long. Hinged to that was another piece of metal about the same length with a rubber gripped handle on the end of it. That metal arm controlled a large spot light that was mounted outside on top of the tower. The spotlight was eighteen inches in diameter. I was told never to turn it on unless needed -- like in the event of a real attack -- as turning it on could blind the dog handlers or their dogs who patrolled the woods. During the fourteen months I worked towers, we never were allowed to turn on the overhead spotlight, not even to check it to see if it was functioning. I pointed out numerous times during my later months at Miesau that it would be a good idea to turn them on to see if it worked before a terrorist attack, as that would not be the time to find out that the light bulb was burned out. "Go ahead and turn it on if you want an Article 15," was the standard reply. I never did turn it on, feeling it was not worth being busted in rank over a spotlight.

Four to five dog handlers were on duty throughout the night. They were the K-9 unit. They were Military Policeman who were in our company but in a separate platoon of their own. Their rooms were on the first floor of our barracks and in all there were fifteen dog handlers. To become a dog handler, they had to attend dog handler's schooling. The dogs were trained to attack at command in case of attack and to sniff out suspects, bombs, and drugs. At least once a month, a terrorist organization would call the barracks or somewhere on post and announce that a bomb was in our barracks. We would have to evacuate while the dog handlers went through the building with their dogs searching for bombs. It never seemed to fail that the bomb threats always seemed to happen during my off time. Looking back on it now, I doubt that any terrorists phoned in any bomb threats to us. I could be wrong, but why would a terrorist plant a bomb and then phone in to announce it? Of course, it could have been a terrorist phoning in the bomb threat to disrupt our routines and to destroy morale. However, the truth of the matter is I suspected it was our company commander and our leaders who staged the bomb threats in order to give valuable training to the dog handlers to allow the dogs to practice searching out bombs and to also search for illegal drugs in the barracks.

The tower was cold, as it had no heat, so pacing helped to keep warm. The time dragged by, and long after I had estimated two hours had elapsed, I was still pacing back and forth. At one point, the field phone rang. "Hello," I answered, not sure who would be calling.

"Who is this?" the voice on the other end asked, sounding angry.

"Private Turner here," I answered, thinking the people with the infrared spyglasses were calling because I had done something wrong.

"What Tower are you in?"

"Tower Three."

"Then that is how you answer the phone. State your name and location, understood?"

"Yes, sir."

"It is Sergeant East in Tower Two. I'm not a sir. Comm check."

"What?"

"Comm check."

"Can you say that again?"

"Hasn't anybody told you the proper procedures for doing a comm check?" the voice said.

"No, Sergeant."

"When I call and say comm check, if you can hear me okay you say loud and clear, unless you can't hear me, then you tell me that. Let's try it again. Hang up the phone and I'll ring you again." *What I was supposed to say if I could not hear him and how would I know I could not hear him if I could not hear him*, I wondered. He called back within seconds.

"This is Private Turner, Tower Three, I answered with confidence

"Comm check."

"Loud and clear."

"Is this your first time in a tower?"

"It is."

"I better not catch you sleeping out there. Stay alert."

Now, more than ever I was convinced that I was being observed every minute. I would later learn that Sergeant East was an alcoholic and the more drunk he was at work, the more serious he took his job. A few months later, he was drunk and driving down a narrow cobblestone street in a small village in Germany, not far from Miesau. It was 3 am in the morning when he lost control of his car and crashed through the front window of a bakery. When the German Police, the Polizei, arrived, they found his car inside the bakery with him standing next to it eating a banana from the bakery's produce department.

By the time my two-hour shift was up, my legs were tired, I was craving sleep and wanted nothing more than to go to bed. After what seemed like four hours, I saw the next shift walking down the tower line towards the tower. I was afraid. Should I yell for them to halt and to identify themselves? I was told we had to challenge everybody even if we recognized them. That was stupid. Why challenge somebody we recognized, having them identify themselves and to state their business if we already recognized them? I knew their business; they were coming to relieve us in our towers. I chose not to challenge them, thinking I would roll the dice. If I got in trouble, I could do nothing about that. The person whom I relieved had not challenged us. I was glad that I had not challenged them because as I found out, it was not a procedure that was practiced except during inspections of security. As it turned out, we never challenged anybody unless VIP Congressman, NATO officials, or high-ranking Army officers were inspecting. The single time I had to challenge anybody was ten months later while working in that same Tower Three. It was during the day and the commander of the Ordinance Battalion, Miesau's Base Commander, was escorting a colonel around who was visiting all of the Weapon Storage facilities throughout Germany. While they were out at the X-Area, the major had pre-arranged for a fake attack to take place, so that the colonel could observe first hand how all the security teams responded. I had started my shift in the tower at noon. Thirty minutes before the end of my shift is when the phony attack started. Three hours after my shift began, after the colonel was satisfied with the whole event, having watched SAT, BAF, and the Alert Force Team back at the barracks all respond and play out their various roles in response to the phony attack, my field phone rang. It was Sergeant Spencer in Tower Two calling to say that the major and the colonel were both coming down the Tower Line with the relief team for the change of shift in the towers, so be ready to challenge them. "I'll be listening," Spencer said. "I want to hear you all the way over here."

Oh, God, I thought. *What is the procedure for challenging somebody?* By that time, it had been over a year since learning that crap at basic training. I started going over in my mind what the whole procedures were. "What if they do not know what the password is," I asked Spencer.

"Well, then, you better not hesitate to drop them face down on the ground." *Oh geez, please let them know what the password is*, I thought to myself.

"Alright, thanks for the heads up," I said, hanging up the phone. I could see them exiting the building and starting their walk down the tower line. It would be about five minutes before they got to the tower. They were walking in a staggered formation. Procedures called for the relief team to walk at ten-meter intervals so that in the event of an attack, they would not all be shot or bombed at the same time. The theory was that if we were spaced apart and a sniper shot a person, the rest would have the opportunity to take cover and return fire. In reality, during the changing of the shifts, people dragged themselves down the tower line, as if they were going to their own funeral and paid no attention to spacing. Sometimes people bunched together. Other times one person may be way ahead of the group or way behind. Meanwhile, others may be off walking at their own pace, shooting the breeze about something they did not want others to hear. Procedures were not followed.

I began rehearsing the whole thing in my mind as they approached. I saw that Lieutenant Hill was coming down the tower line with the group. He was a no-nonsense, by- the-book officer. He was about 25 years old and as second lieutenant, he acted as if he was General Patton. However, he always seemed to have a kind word to say about everybody, so I did not dislike him, but I never wanted to get on his shit list either. By the time they were within a reasonable distance of where I thought they could hear me, I stepped outside on to the catwalk of the tower.

"Halt. Who goes there?" I screamed, thinking how stupid that was, as I knew who they were.

"Lieutenant Hill."

"Place your hands on your head and State the nature of your business and the password for the day?"

"We are posting the relief guards and the password is Jungle Fever," he said, as they all started to place their hands on their heads.

"You may proceed," I yelled back. *How stupid and dorky did all that sound*, I thought, yet, hoping I did it right. The whole exchange of conversation took about five seconds. They did not even finish putting their hands on their heads before I was telling them to proceed. The group then walked the remaining one hundred yards to the tower. When they arrived at the tower, they continued to use proper procedures. During a normal shift change, our relief person came up the stairs; then we departed down the stairs. Proper procedures, however, called for both the relief person and the person in charge of the relief team to both walk up the stairs to the top of the tower. Sergeant Pritchard was the sergeant in charge of the relief team. His job was to inspect the tower for damage and to give the new guard any special instructions pertinent for the day. If he noted in his book that no damage existed to the tower and that all the equipment was functioning, then the new guard would be held accountable if damage to the tower was found or if the equipment was malfunctioning at the end of their shift.

Once relieved from duty, our shift was not over until we walked around the entire Tower Line with the rest of the group, circling back around to the backside of the Security building. From Tower Two this took thirty minutes. Then we had to have somebody in charge clear our weapon before entering the building. Five-gallon barrels lying on their side, half buried in the ground were at every entrance. The tops were cut open and they were filled with sand. First we ejected our magazine full of rounds from the M-16, pointing the muzzle into the barrel, pulling back the chamber, and tilting the weapon so that the person in charge could look into the chamber and see if a round was in it. If there was and we released that chamber bolt, it would fire that round.

"Chamber clear," is what the person in charge would say, if the chamber were clear. God help us if we did not clear our weapon and fired off a round and shot somebody. We would be court martialed. In addition, the person in charge of clearing the weapon would be in for an ass chewing, too. Somebody accidentally fired off a round at the clearing barrel once. Nobody was hurt and the person who fired it was busted down two ranks, paid a huge fine, was restricted to barracks, and assigned extra duty. Sergeant East, the drunk, was the person in charge of clearing the weapon. I heard he was barred from re-enlisting because of the incident. It would have been easy to fire a round. Upon coming back from a late night shift in a tower, having worked the towers three previous nights with little or no sleep during the day, your mind in a haze, all you wanted to do was lay down on a cot for a couple of hours before your next shift began, so in a hurry and half asleep, you pull back the chamber without removing the magazine. At that point, if the person in charge does not calmly remind the person not to let go of the chamber bolt, reach down, and push the magazine release button, a bullet would fire.

That first night I pulled tower duty was long. By the time I was relieved from my tower and walked all the way around the tower line back to the Security building, cleared my weapon, stored my gear, found a cot to fall asleep on, it was almost time to go back out for a second shift. But, I had a little over two hours before it was time to start heading back out for a second shift, so I took advantage of it. However, before grabbing a quick nap, I had to use the can. The towers did not have bathrooms. We could not leave our tower, not even for a brief trip down to the base of the tower to take a leak or to dig a hole and take a dump. It was rumored that some people did both in the cover of darkness. Getting caught doing either would be a sure court martial for leaving your duty post. There were times when I was pulling tower duty and I had to go to the bathroom so bad, I thought I would burst. In my early months of pulling tower duty, I always held it, but during the later months, if I had to pee, I stood out on the catwalk and pissed. After doing it the first time, I made a deliberate effort not to ever touch the handrails of the stairs leading to the top of the towers, as I had seen how the wind directed some of the pee on to the stair well. One person, PFC White, had been rumored to take dumps in his tower and then fling it – toiler paper and all – over the tower line fence from the small catwalk right outside the doorway of the tower. He was never caught doing it, but several times after being relieved from his shift, one of my buddies noticed toilet paper on the other side of the fence. He always confronted White with the accusation, not to bust him, but to embarrass him, as he did not like White. About six months after arriving at Miesau, White was promoted to Specialist, E-4. About a month later, he was brought up on charges of sleeping on duty. He was working one of the towers and when his relief showed up they claimed to find him sleeping. He denied it. Nonetheless, he was busted to Private. From that point onward, everybody called him Bolo, which meant screw-up. He isolated himself from everybody, never talking unless required, hanging out by himself in his room, and looking depressed.

After using the restroom, I had dozed off for less than ten minutes when I was awakened by screaming. "BAF. Muster in the Recreation room. BAF. Muster in the recreation room." That was the call for an alert. At the time, four of us were sleeping upstairs.

"Get your gear on and get your asses downstairs," somebody yelled out from down the hall." I slipped all over the waxed, tile floor running down the hall as I put my gear on. The stairwell was dark and narrow and we jumped two or three stairs at a time, single file down the stairs, running into the Recreation room and grabbing our weapons. The BAF consisted of twelve people, and as soon as we were all gathered by the door, Sergeant Sampson blew a whistle.

"That's pathetic," he said. "It took two minutes for everybody to get to the door. From now on, we will be having an alert every night and sleeping will be off limits until we can reduce that time. I cannot believe you guys. Let's get the next shift out to their towers and then we'll try this again." I looked at the clock and could not believe it was almost 2 am and time for my second shift. My next two hours seemed to drag by twice as slow as the first shift. At the same time, my mind was a fog. I had little sleep and could barely keep my eyes open at times. When the shift was over I was looking forward to getting back to the Security building to sit down. No such luck. No sooner had we stored our gear than we had another practice alert. This time we were all gathered together at the door within thirty seconds.

"That's out-fucking standing, gentleman," Sergeant Sampson screamed, overly elated, as if he had won a lottery. "That is an awesome job. We will have an alert every night and as long as you do well on your first response each night, you won't have to do any more the rest of the night." I learned later that morning while I was pulling my tower shift that the SAT Team, which consisted of the three people who had to respond anywhere in the X-Area within a minute, also had practice alerts.

"Okay," Sergeant Ryan spoke, "this place is starting to look like shit, so go and store your gear so we can start the morning clean up." Morning clean up? It was quarter to five. *When do we get to sleep?* I wondered. We had little over an hour before the end of our shift and during the next hour, on both floors, all the trash had to be emptied, the floors swept, mopped, wax applied, and buffed with a buffer, plus everything that was taken out like board games or cards all had to be put away. I was assigned to work upstairs and for the next hour was sweating like a pig.

"Hey, you have to learn to pace yourself," Specialist Moran told me. He had been put in charge of the four of us cleaning the upstairs. "We don't have to clean it all that good either. Just go through the motions man. Are you trying to make everybody else look bad?" I did not heed his advice and continued to do – in my mind -- a good job for what I had been assigned to do. We were done by 5:45. I went downstairs and assisted down there.

"Damn, Turner," Sampson said, "are you crazy? That's outstanding. Keep up the good work." When our relief arrived ten minutes late, Sampson was pissed. The people pulling tower duty from 4 am to 6 am would be in their towers at least until 6:30 am before relief arrived. After the Security building was inspected for cleanliness and the new Sergeant of the Guard signed the paper taking control, releasing Sergeant Sampson and our platoon from duty, we climbed into the back of the trucks that brought us out to the X-Area a little over twelve hours ago and returned to the barracks.

I was one of eight people on the back of one of the two pickup trucks. Two of us on the truck were new to the platoon. I had been there four days; Rogers three weeks, but like me, pulling his first duty in the X-Area. We would end up being good friends and sharing duty together at four different military bases over the next two and a half years. This fat, dirty guy sitting with his back to the cab of the truck on the front bench started giving us a hard time. Everybody called him Bear.

"Hey look at this newbie over here," he said pointing at Rogers. He looks like Beaker from Sesame Street. I think from now on, we'll call him Beaker." Everybody laughed and from that point on he was called Beaker.

"What's your name?" he then asked me.

"Goodwin," I answered.

"You don't look like a Goodwin to me," he said. "You look like a Bob."

"He does, somebody else chimed in."

"I think we'll call you Bob from now on, is that okay with you?"

"Whatever suits you," I said.

"Okay, Bob, why don't you bob up and down on my M-16," he said stroking the barrel of his M-16 like it was his penis. Everybody laughed. From that day forward, everybody called me, Bob.

Once we got back to the barracks, we turned in our weapons and ammo. At that point, it was around 7 am and we could go eat breakfast at the chow hall, which, no matter how tired I was, I loved to eat breakfast. It was always my favorite meal of the day. Drinking a hot cup of coffee with some eggs, pancakes, grits, and sausage could not be beat on a cold morning. There were two things wrong with that. First, it would not be long that I was packing on the weight. Within six months, I gained twenty pounds and weighed in at two-hundred-twenty pounds. Second, going to eat breakfast after a night shift cut into my sleep. It did not take long to learn that during non-working hours, I could not count on having them to myself to eat, sleep, or do personal things like laundry. For example, every Wednesday, the Captain conducted a room inspection of all the rooms and whether we worked all night before, or not, we were expected to have our room ready for inspection, which meant when the Captain came by, we could not be sleeping. We could leave the room if desired, as our squad leader would be present to let the Captain into the room. Or while we were off, if an alert at the X-Area occurred, anybody who was on the base was expected to be on the Alert Force, sign out their weapon, and be transported out to the X-Area to set up a perimeter in the woods surrounding the X-Area. This did not happen every time, but it happened whenever a visiting dignitary wanted to be amused by watching how well all the units responded. Then at least once a month the base commander would have a practice drill, which meant responding to the X-Area and setting up a perimeter. Once that was done, the drill would be called off and we could go back to the barracks. The practice drills were not that bad as they were over and done within an hour. What I hated the most were the times we had to respond due to weather related issues. For instance, whenever it was foggy, if the people in the towers could not see the towers to the left or right, then a fog alert was called. This meant that everybody at the barracks who was not on the Alert Force Alert Team had to suit up, get their weapons and be transported to the X-Area to be positioned between the towers. If the visibility was fifty feet, a guard had to be placed every fifty feet between the inner and outer fences of the tower line. If the fog lasted more than two hours, we were relieved after two hours -- if they had people to do so. Most often than not, they could not scrape together enough people to relieve the fog alert guards, so we would be stuck out there for unlimited hours. The bad news was that it was foggy a lot in Germany. The good news is that the fog occurred during the dawn hours and it cleared out within hours. There was nothing worse than pulling a 12-hour night shift with little or no sleep, then right after turning in our weapon and climbing into bed, our squad leader pounded on the door, screaming for us to get out of bed and to hustle downstairs for a fog alert. This happened after my first night in the towers. *When the hell are we supposed to get some sleep?* I thought to myself. So there I was, thirty minutes later, back out at the X-Area, being posted between Tower Three and Tower Four. About two hundred yards away another guard was posted. At first I walked back and forth trying to stay warm, but before long I was dead tired, so I laid down on the ground in a prone position, facing the woods and rested my head on my M-16 like it was a pillow and fought off the urge to fall asleep. If it were not for the cold, I may have fallen asleep. An hour later, the tower guards were relieved at 8 am. The fog showed no sign of lifting. I did not even bother to get up from my prone position as they passed on the way to the next tower.

"How you doing out here?" the guard commander asked.

"Cold," I answered.

"Stay alert," he said, "we will see if we can get somebody out here to relieve you guys soon." It was not long before "soon" turned into hours and still no relief. I do not think we would have been relieved either. If the fog lasted ten hours, I had the feeling we would have been out there for ten hours. However, when the next shift change for the towers took place the fog was almost gone, and as the tower shift people passed by, they told me to come along with them as the fog alert had been called off. Unfortunately, I could not turn around and walk the shorter distance back to the Security building. I had to walk all the way around the whole tower line. Once back at the Security Building, we had to wait for a ride back to the barracks. Then by the time we turned our weapons in again, it was noon by the time I crawled into bed. That sort of thing happened many times. After a while, I – like everybody else -- resented it because the people who were married and lived off post with their families did not have to put up with that crap. After they pulled their scheduled duty and turned in their weapons, they would hop in their cars and drive home and we would not seem them again until the next shift. It was common for people to do anything to avoid responding to alerts. A siren would blast on the base, signaling an alert, meaning we had to get dressed and muster downstairs. The on-duty Alert Force, who had a maximum of thirty minutes to respond to the X-Area, would determine if more people were needed. Extra people were needed most of the time, as the Alert Force was made up of people from the on-duty platoon who were sick or who did not, yet, have their security clearances. If they did not have a security clearance, they were not allowed near the X-Area, not even to set up a perimeter in the woods. The on-duty platoon was lucky enough to have one or two extra bodies on the Alert Force who could go out to the X-Area, so off-duty people had to be available to be part of the Alert Force, to be dispatched as fog alert guards, or to do whatever was needed.

During an alert, the Sergeant on duty who was in charge of the Alert Force was responsible for mustering as many people as possible to respond. So they would send the on-duty Alert Force people up and down the halls of the barracks, banging on doors, mustering people out of bed, out of their rooms, or from wherever they were to assemble downstairs in order to respond. However, as soon as the siren sounded, people started hiding. By the time somebody knocked on the door, we were either standing on the ledge of a window sill, crouching in a wall locker, or as I did more than once -- after experiencing that first fog alert -- laid in bed, pretending not to hear the siren or the knock, hoping they would go away. Once the Alert Force had enough people, they quit trying to muster people. I laid in bed, refusing to open the door, hoping they would catch people at the chow hall, the small diner across the street from the chow hall, the one-screen movie theater, the four-lane bowling alley, the recreation room on the third floor, the laundry rooms, the recreation center down the street or the gymnasium next door. The chances that they would find enough people at all of these places was slim, so those were the last places that they looked. It was more convenient to stay in the barracks and draft people into service. However, in desperation, they would send people out to all the base facilities to try to round people up. The problem with that, however, was that when people were at one of these places at the time the alarm sounded, they ignored the alarm. They would stay away from the barracks on purpose until they were sure the alert was finished. Some people would hide in the woods behind our barracks. At the movie theater, people slumped down into their seats to avoid being seen. Across from the main gate of the post was a German restaurant and bar that was a real popular drinking spot. If we were there when the alarm sounded, we were supposed to return to the barracks. We could get back on to the base during an alert in order to report for duty, but as soon as the alarm sounded, we could not get off base, as the Polish gate guards, who were contracted to work the gates, would close the gates down and nobody would be allowed to leave. If they did not catch enough people at all those places, then they would get the keys to the rooms and go around unlocking the doors. If they did that and found us inside, we had better play drunk and pretend to be passed out, having not heard the knocking. However, the people on duty knew that was bull, as when they were off duty, they would be pulling the same stunts in order to avoid having to respond to an alert. So, even if we were drunk and not pretending, we were commandeered into duty. Even if we were scheduled to go on to duty within an hour, we had to respond to the alert. During an alert, all shifts became frozen, so changing of shifts where one platoon relieved another were put on hold. Once the alert was over then everything resumed back to normal.

Some people kept what was known as a "Fireball Prevention Device" in their refrigerator in their room. It was four shots of plum schnapps in a highball. As soon as somebody knocked on their door for an alert, they would drink it. Then when they went to sign out their weapon, they would make a point of breathing on the armory guard. Thinking they were blitzed, they would not let them draw a weapon unless they were desperate. In this way, they received brownie points for responding. Others scrambled up the fire escape and hid; some hid in the attic until the alert was over. The attic was also a great place where people on the third floor would hide liquor and other materials during inspections.

One time our platoon was on a three-day break and we were being made to clean for an upcoming GI inspection. My buddy, Sanders, and I were pissed and sneaked off the base and hopped aboard the first train. We did not have a dime on us and pretended not to understand German when the conductor asked for tickets or money. After five minutes, he gave up and allowed us to ride free. We ended up in Cologne, Germany.

By nightfall, I was sorry we had left because I was starving. We each grabbed a wall locker at the train station and slept inside it like bums. I froze my ass off. It would have been better to stay and clean at the barracks, but it was the principle of the situation that drove us to avoid cleaning on our three-day break.

Some people hid in their wall lockers to avoid alerts. For one person that backfired. He climbed into his wall locker to hide. Meanwhile, when they opened the door with the master keys, they drafted his roommate into duty. Jealous that his roommate dodged the bullet, as he left the room, he locked the wall locker his friend was hiding in. Six hours later when the alert was over, the guy in the locker had pissed all over himself and was screaming at the top of his lungs for somebody to let him out, being on the verge of a nervous breakdown.

There was an alert that took place when I first arrived at Miesau. Our platoon was working the night shift in the X-Area.

Sergeant Compton was in charge of the X-Area, and he staged an alert, calling for SAT, BAF and the Alert Force. One of the duties of the person in charge of the Alert Force was to stay in radio contact with the X-Area by making radio contact every thirty minutes and logging the results. Compton had told the people in the X-Area not to answer their radio or phones, and staged people around the outside of the building as if they were dead. When Sergeant Sampson could not get a response from the X-area on either the radios or phones, he called a full scale alert, roused as many people as he could get and went storming out to the X-Area. What they found was a staged scene where people were playing dead. Of course, the Alert Force did not know that. In addition, the people in the towers were lying down on their catwalks playing dead. When Staff Sergeant Sampson arrived at the main building of the X-area, they let him in and he made everyone in the "front room" get on the ground until he cleared the building. Sampson was pissed at Compton and the friction was so bad between the two of them after this that Sampson was transferred to another platoon by Captain Lee; otherwise, Sampson may have hurt Compton if given a chance to do so. Sampson was on the Army boxing team and there were many times he would take off his stripes and take people behind the barracks and settle disputes with fisticuffs. Sampson always walked away without a scratch. The other people did not fare so well. Several people were reprimanded over Compton's X-Area alert. Some lost stripes and their positions as squad leaders, while others were promoted to take their places.

One time they had an alert in which so many people responded to the alert, they had to turn people away. The dog handlers had captured somebody in the woods outside the X-Area. They took him as prisoner to the Security Building in the X-Area. Sanders was working SAT that night and the prisoner was brought into the room where SAT was housed. The prisoner was made to lay face down on a cot. He was shaking like a leaf as Sanders kept yelling at him, "Sprechen Sie Deutsch? Sprechen Sie Deutsch?" Every time he yelled at him, he pretended he was going to hit him in the back of the head with his M-16. The poor guy was trembling and pissed his pants. Nobody knew who he was. Army Intelligence sent interpreters to question him. Meanwhile, back at the barracks, for the first time ever, people were begging to respond with the Alert Force Team. Some people were in their pajamas; some civilian clothes, with all their ammunition belts, flak jackets and steel pots on over the top of whatever they were wearing. I was down stairs observing it all for a while and could not believe that half the people who they let respond to the alert were off duty and drunk. During practice alerts, they would never give a drunk a loaded M-16. I was not about to volunteer to respond. It was not going to happen. *What kind of idiot would volunteer to go set up a perimeter around the X-Area in the dark of the night in the woods where you could barely see five feet in front of you, knowing that you were surrounded by trigger happy drunks who were dying to shoot a terrorist to earn a transfer back to the States?"* I remember watching the first truck load of volunteers drive off towards the X-Area – some of them so drunk they could barely climb into the back of the pick up cab. It was then I decided to get as far away from that scenario as possible and went to the movies.

Before I got back from the movies, the alert was over and everybody was back. It was a simple mistake. On the Miesau Base, besides the X-Area, which was controlled by the United States Army, hundreds of other ammunition bunkers, not a part of the X-Area, were controlled by civilian contractors. Miesau was the largest storage of ammunition in the world. The United States Army guarded and controlled the ones with the nuclear weapons in them. The other ones were guarded and controlled by Polish civilian contractors. In fact on the East Side of the X-Area was a railway yard. From both Tower 4 and Tower 5 we could stand in our tower and watch the Polish Contractors unload railroad cars. Train tracks drove right through the middle of the Ammunition Bunker Area. The railway workers knew that they were not supposed to come anywhere near the perimeter fences of the X-Area as they could be shot. Whenever I pulled duty in Tower 4 or Tower 5 during the day, I would stand in my tower cawing like a crow. I called it the mating howl of a Tower Rat. The workers on the railway would look nervous, probably thinking I would lose it at any moment and fire upon them, as it was no secret that many people went crazy pulling tower duty. One time I was in Tower 5 and a railway worker walked right up to the edge of the outer perimeter fence and started taking a leak. I pointed my weapon at him and started doing the Tower Rat mating call. He could not run away fast enough, dribbling pee all over himself, as he did not even attempt to take the time to put his penis back in his pants. I would do my mating call of the Tower Rat during the night shift, as I learned that the dogs patrolling the woods with the dog handlers would alert on the noise. One time I kept repeating the yell for quite some time, it triggered an alert, and people had to respond out to the X-Area and set up a perimeter. I would make the Tower Rat Mating Call when I was bored and wanted to entertain friends who were pulling duty in the other towers. If they could see a dog handler nearby, they would call me up on the field phone and encourage me to do the mating call. I would do the call and it would echo throughout the X-Area and far beyond into the woods. Then they would watch the reaction of the dog handlers and their dogs, as they heard the eerie noise. The dog handlers were a close-knit bunch who stayed much to themselves. They were the ones who captured the suspected terrorist out in the woods that one night. As it turned out, he was not a terrorist after all. He was one of the Polish contractors working on the railway. It was his first day on the job and as the shift was ending, he went to use the outhouse about five minutes before the end of the shift. When he came out of the outhouse, all the other workers had loaded up into the truck and drove off. He did not know what to do other than to start walking. He thought he could find his way out of the ammunition storage area and back to the main part of the base. Therefore, he started walking. It soon grew dark and he got lost. When he saw the lights of the X-Area, he started walking back towards them thinking those were the lights of the main part of the base, not realizing he was backtracking. When the dogs alerted on him, the dog handlers apprehended him, not knowing who he was or what he was doing out there. To complicate matters, he did not speak English or German, but spoke Polish and we had no translators available. I never heard what became of him other than the Central Intelligence Department took him into custody. I would assume they would have verified his story and released him. However, I pictured them taking him back to their headquarters and torturing him to find out if he would give up information about any connections he might have had to known terrorist groups.

Working in the towers would have been of itself a crappy job, but survivable if that was all we had to do. However, with all of the other duties we had to do between our shifts in the tower, it was miserable and crappy. First, we worked four night shifts of twelve scheduled hours, which meant fourteen hours of work time by the time we first signed out our weapon in preparation for role call and inspection to the time we turned in our weapon. Then we had twenty-four hours of scheduled time off. Following that, we worked four-day shifts of twelve scheduled hours, which, again meant fourteen hours of work by time we first signed out our weapon in preparation for role call and inspection to the time we turned in our weapon. At any time between shifts or during our scheduled time off, when we expected to be eating, resting, and doing personal things, we were on back up for fog alerts, training alerts, real alerts, phoned in bomb threats, cleaning of the barracks for inspections, working at the motor pool to get vehicles ready for inspections, cleaning of our own rooms for inspections, laundry, shining our boots, preparing our uniforms for duty, cleaning our gear, re-qualifying with our weapons at the shooting ranges, and countless other things that would come up that we had to be ready to do at a moments notice. So we had to put up with the boring, tedious duty of standing in a tower four hours per day, eight out of every 9 days, while getting little sleep between shifts. The food at the chow hall was horrible, and the other duty we pulled when not pulling tower duty amounted to nothing more than janitorial labor. It was not a mystery as to why -- during free time -- people boozed it up as much as they could as fast as they could or smoked hash to alleviate the boredom and to forget the circumstances they were in. Most of the people were fresh out of high school; a few were in their early twenties, some with college, and some without. Most people were single. Some people enlisted at a later age and had families. However, for the most part, the majority of the tower rats were single, young, males, who were, for the first time in their lives, outside of the United States and away from the luxuries that the United States offered, like a fast food joint on every street corner, the security of family and friends, strangers who spoke the same language, and a safe environment. Now, take all those things away and put those same people into a high stress, dangerous environment combined with the fact that they are earning paychecks for the first time in their life and have no place to spend them. Most of the money was wasted on booze, drugs, sex, and gambling. It was a depressing environment. People would go home on a thirty-day leave and go AWOL. After six months at Miesau, Riggs, the guy who arrived the same day I did, went home on leave to Los Angeles. He did not return. He was caught and sent back to the military and sent right back to Miesau where he was given shitty assignments and an Article 15. Riggs had the lousiest luck. It took over a year before his Security Clearance came back; so he was given slacker duty. All he ever had to do was work around the barracks. He had to pull night shifts with our platoon, but he was always on the Alert Force. However, since he did not have a Security clearance, he never had to respond to any of the alerts because he was not allowed out to the part of the base where the ammunition depots were, let alone the X-Area. So, most people considered Riggs' duty easy. He hated being away from Los Angeles, and he let everyone know he hated everything about the military. Then after he went AWOL, he was sent back to Miesau where all he had to do was work as a CQ assistant, which meant he worked nights every other day. The Army was going to discharge him for having gone AWOL but it took about two months for them to discharge somebody. All the paperwork was in motion and it was a matter of time before Riggs would be back in Los Angeles, or so he thought. Two weeks before he was due to start processing out of the company to go home, our platoon was assigned a new Sergeant, who was brand new to Miesau. He was a big, tall, fat man. Sergeant Cane was his name. One day after he arrived he called a platoon meeting during our 4-day break and had us all meet in the recreation room on the third floor. He was using the meeting to introduce himself, to meet everybody, and to hear what gripes we might have. Naturally, Riggs spoke up about his dislike for the Army and asked if Sergeant Cane knew the status of his discharge.

"Riggs," Sergeant Cane said with a big grin. "I'm so, happy to meet you face to face, son."

"I ain't your son," Riggs snapped, "and don't you ever forget that." The whole platoon erupted into laughter. Sergeant Cane had a Southern drawl and called everybody son. I think if he tried not to call somebody son, his tongue would have tangled up in his mouth and choked him.

"Calm, down, son, I'm not your enemy," Sergeant Cane said.

"Don't you call me your, son," Riggs said. "I'm not your son, fat ass." The laughter erupted once again.

"You watch your mouth," Cane said as friendly as ever. "That is no way to talk to somebody who has done you a favor like what I have done for you."

"What kind of favor are you talking about?" Riggs asked, looking like he was about to be screwed.

"Well, I've been going through everybody's file since I got here and your file in particular jumped out at me. I saw where you were about ready to receive a General Discharge. Believe me, I had to do a lot of arm twisting and cajoling to get this favor done."

"What favor?" Riggs demanded to know.

"Believe me, son, a General Discharge is not something you want on your resume. So, I talked the Powers That Be into dropping your discharge and letting you stay in the Army." The look on Riggs' face was priceless.

"You did what, Mother Fucker?" Riggs yelled. "I'll kill your fat ass," he screamed, as he started running towards Cane. "I'm going to kill you." We were all busting a gut. Some of the squad leaders near Sergeant Cane grabbed Riggs and hustled him out of the room.

"The man simply does not understand the favor I did for him," Cane said. "Believe me. I would do the same favor for any one of you in this room. From now on, you can think of this platoon as your family. You're like my children and if you work hard for me, I will look out after you." We all thought the guy was an idiot and that he was all hot air.

Sunday, December 9, 1979:

The night was a repeat of the previous night. It dragged by even slower because of the lack of sleep I had during the first preceding day. First, we turned in our weapons. Then we had to sign them out again to go out on the fog alert. Then we signed our weapons back in after the fog alert was lifted. Once I did get to bed, it seemed like a short nap of three hours with periodic wakening every so often from somebody playing their stereo real loud, the slamming of a door, people yelling, or any other numerous noises that could be heard in a dormitory building of three hundred people. So the second night in the tower, I was barely able to keep my eyes open during both shifts. Like the previous night, we had a practice alert in which BAF was called and all the members had to muster in the meeting room. This time Sergeant Ryan had us fire and maneuver out the door leading into the X-Area. The first person ran for cover to an embankment of sandbags while somebody else provided cover. Once at the sand bags, that person provided cover for everybody else as they exited the building in groups of three to various sand bag positions. Once we were all out at the first sand bag positions, the alert was called off. Because we were successful in making it out the door in a fast time, we did not have any more practice alerts that night, so we were allowed to hit the sack in between shifts. However, I never knew when a real alert would be called, so it was always hard to slip into a deep sleep because that was on the back of my mind. If I did get to sleep, I awakened to go pull my next shift long before hitting a deep stage of sleep. Real alerts did not mean we were being attacked by terrorists. A real alert happened whenever an alarm sounded at one of the bunkers. The alarms were set up to sound if the bunkers were breached. A breach could mean that somebody forced their way into the bunker. It could also mean that somebody opened the bunker doors with a key and failed to deactivate the alarm with the proper code. Once the doors were open, if they failed to punch in the code within thirty seconds, an alarm would trigger, which would cause a full-blown alert. The person at the alarm panel would shout, "SAT, Security breach at bunker five," or whatever the bunker number was. SAT then had sixty seconds to be at the location of the bunker where the alarm was sounding. To open a bunker, two people and two Military Police escorts had to be present. The escorts had to accompany the people who were opening the bunker everywhere they went inside of the X-Area and had to stand guard outside the bunker while the doors were open. When SAT arrived at the location of the alarm, they took protective covering from the nearest location like a sand bag bunker, a tree, or by lying prone on the ground. Then they would make everybody lay face down on the ground spread eagle. Then they asked for the password of the day and whether or not anybody was in distress. If the password was given and everybody confirmed they were not in distress, then SAT released everybody and the alarm was silenced. People were authorized to be in the bunkers during daylight hours during the weekday. So if an alarm went off at night, something was wrong. The alarms, however, went off at night all the time during lightning storms. Every time an alarm went off, SAT had to respond. During a lightning storm SAT could be ran ragged within an hour. So, whom ever was the active Security Commander of the X-Area at the time had to make a decision whether or not to call a base alert, which would mean the Alert Force back at the barracks would be mustered. That required getting all off-duty personnel up in order to get their weapons to be driven to the X-Area where two guards would be stationed at each bunker. *Talk about being miserable, having to stand at one of those bunkers during a lightning storm was inhumane.* SAT was required to check the locks on each bunker every two hours. To do that an Army jeep was inside the X-Area for their use. They also did periodic checks of the Alarm system by opening the doors on each bunker to see if the Alarm would sound at the Alarm panel. However, often times the cold weather would freeze the locks on the bunkers and we could not open the door. To un-thaw the ice on the locks, we put rubbing alcohol in a spray bottle, sprayed the key to the lock with the rubbing alcohol, inserted it into the lock, and, presto, it opened.

Monday, December 10, 1979:

    This was the last of the four night shifts that our platoon had to work. I was scheduled once again to work the same shift in Tower Three. That night the first practice alert that took place happened while I was pulling my first shift in the tower. The response time was slow, so later on another practice alert was called. I was pissed that the bozos before did not get a fast enough response time because it meant that our shift was not allowed to go to sleep once we got back into the Security Building. We had to stay awake, waiting for the next practice alert to take place. We never did have another alert that night.

Tuesday, December 11, 1979:

By the time I turned in my weapon after our platoon was relieved from working the night shift, I was dead tired. However, I was excited that we were having twenty-four hours off, walked over to the chow hall, and ate breakfast. At the time, it seemed like a long time, but I found myself sleeping, shining boots, eating, and doing laundry in preparation for the four-day shifts. Laundry was always hard to do because of the lack of laundry facilities. Each of the three floors had a laundry room that consisted of three washers and dryers, but three-hundred people had to share these nine washer and dryers and it seemed every time I needed to use one, they were already in use. I slipped out of the room, took a shower, put on some sweats, went over to the cafeteria across the street from the chow hall, and bought a newspaper in order to catch the football scores from Sunday. Germany was eight hours ahead of Colorado time and during the two years I was in Germany, I was able to hear most of the Denver Bronco games on the Armed Forces Radio Network. I missed seeing or hearing one game during that two-year period. I drove people nuts talking about the Broncos. Whenever people saw me coming, they would yell out, "Hey, Bob, the Broncos suck." I carried a transistor radio with me during Football season in an attempt to catch the Bronco games. We were not allowed to bring radios to our tower, but during the times that I was pulling duty during a Bronco game, I brought one with me. By the time football season started in 1980, I brought a transistor radio with me to my tower all the time, using the battery in the field phone to power the radio. The reception was always poor, so I moved from one side of the tower to the other trying to grab a signal. The radio was a good thing in that it kept me awake.

When I returned to the barracks, I went to see the schedule for the next day. "Turner," Compton yelled out as I walked up to the desk. "I need to talk to you."

"What about?" I asked.

"I'm putting together the schedule for the next four days. Would you have any problems working on the SAT team for a few of those days?"

"Should I?"

"Well, it might not go over too well with some of the other people in the platoon," Compton explained. "Working SAT is reserved for people who have been here for a while and who stand out as good soldiers. You have to be physically fit, too. Do you think you can deal with the people who might be pissed off because you are working SAT, despite having been here only one week? In fact, as far as I know, you would be the first Private to ever work on SAT."

"I can handle it," I said, wondering if somebody else would threaten to kill me as my own roommates did on my first night in the barracks.

"Great. I am going to schedule you for SAT on Wednesday, Thursday, and Saturday. Friday, I'm going to put you out in Tower Four."

That night I went to a movie at the base theater. The movies that they showed were two or three years old, so when I first arrived at the base, I had seen many of the movies already. By the time I left, the movies showing had just been coming out about the time I joined the Army, so I had not seen them, yet. When I arrived back at the barracks, several parties were in full swing in several of the rooms on the second floor where First Platoon was housed. The popular thing to do while stationed in Germany was to buy a Stereo system at the military commissary. Every room had at least one person, if not three people, with super stereo systems, along with speakers that vibrated the plaster off of the walls, playing Led Zeppelin, Pink Floyd, or whatever their favorite music was as loud as possible while drinking until they passed out. Parties like this went on each night for the platoon that was on their twenty-four hour time off or for the platoon that was on their three-day break.

I do not know of a single person on the base who did not purchase a stereo system while stationed in Germany, except for myself. I wanted to buy a stereo system, but I could not afford it. Come January 1, 1980, my paycheck was twenty dollars. When I went to the finance officer to find out why, I was told that for the next twelve months the Army would be deducting the advanced pay of two-thousand dollars I received when I was a recruiter aide.

So, by the time the military took out the deduction for the advanced pay along with the college assistance program I was participating in, I had twenty dollars a month to live on. The college assistance program, called the VEAP, which stood for Veterans Educational Assistance Program, was what President Carter replaced the GI bill with in 1976. Nobody who joined the military between 1976 and 1980 received the GI bill. One of the first things Ronald Reagan did when he went into office was to restart the GI bill again. The VEAP was an optional program we could participate in that allowed us to set aside up to twenty-seven dollars per month of our monthly pay. The government would then put in two dollars for every one dollar we contributed. Once out of the Army, that money could be used to pay college tuition. The problem was that they would only dole the money out in monthly installments once registered in college. The most they would pay was the amount of your college tuition. However, the colleges wanted their money up front. It was inconvenient and made it impossible to use. A few years later when I was in college, I became frustrated with all the red tape involved in getting the money and asked for a full refund. They gave me a lump sum payment of the twenty-seven-hundred dollars I had contributed. I used that money to pay for my college tuition for a year. Although I did not have rent or food to buy, I still had to handle all of my own personal expenses. However, when all of your friends are buying super stereo systems, spending all kinds of money on booze, eating out at German restaurants, hanging out at brothels and you cannot even afford to buy a single cassette tape or a tuna fish sandwich at the cafeteria, it muddles your feathers a bit. It was not that I was mad I had to pay the money back. I was mad that I was not told that I would have to pay it back. If I had known I would have to pay it back, I would not have even taken the money in the first place. It was presented to me as a bonus for being a recruiter aide. Going to the movie cost one dollar. Bowling cost a dollar per game at the four-lane bowling alley. A sandwich at the cafeteria cost at least a buck. With that twenty dollars a month, I was expected to purchase all my own laundry supplies, underwear, shoeshine equipment, and personal hygiene items. So by the end of the month, I was always stretching to make ends meet. Sometimes I had to borrow shoe polish to polish my Army boots or risk being written up. After a while, I quit shining by boots with polish. I kept them clean, but that was it. I fell into the trap of going to room parties. I never could bring my own beer and was always showing up and drinking whatever anybody was offering to share. Like my last year of high school, I found myself drinking every time I had time off, especially towards the end of the month when my twenty dollar monthly budget was spent and I did not have a single dollar to even go to a movie. Like most everybody else, I would drink to the point of unconsciousness. By morning, it was hard to get up at 5 am for duty. Sometimes I had a hangover, sometimes I did not. It is not that I enjoyed drinking. I did not. Drinking made me gain weight and I always hated the morning after, but for lack of nothing else to do, due to lack of money, I drank a lot.

When I did have at least a dollar, however, I preferred to go to the movies instead of drinking. That night of our 24-hour break, after coming back from the movies, I had two beers at the party going on in the room next to mine. By this time, people knew that I was scheduled to work SAT the next day and some of the other people who worked SAT were congratulating me and asking if I was ready for it. Some people were asking whose dick I had sucked. I acted as if it was no big deal and did not care one way or another where I worked. After the free beer was no longer being offered, I went to bed and slept as best I could with the vibrations of loud music from all those expensive stereo systems that everybody owned shaking the plaster off the walls throughout the building.

Wednesday, December 12, 1979:

This was my first day working on SAT. Tedasco, a Specialist Four, was the SAT Commander. He was always nice to everybody. I never once heard him complain to anybody about anything. Tedasco taught me everything I needed to know about working on SAT. The first thing I observed was that working out in the X-Area during the day was a whole lot different than working out there at night. The X-Area, including the Security Building was buzzing with activity. People from the 59th Ordinance Battalion would come in and out of the gate and go to work at the Maintenance Building. If at any time they needed to go open a bunker up, they had to wait for two escort guards.

Besides all the activity taking place with the 59th Ordinance, German, civilian contractors would come into the X-Area to work on the Alarm systems for the bunkers. In addition, the base commander could show up at any time, so we always had to be ready for an alert to be called, so sleeping was not allowed at all during weekdays. SAT stayed busy. Every two hours, we had to get in the jeep and drive to every bunker that was not opened and physically check the locks on the bunker doors to make sure they were secure. A log sheet was on the outside of the door that we had to initial, date, and time stamp when we checked the door. If we were responding to an alarm at the time we were to be starting our rounds, then we had to postpone the checking of the locks, but it had to be done at least once per shift. Sometimes we had to do the lock check when the new SAT team came on duty and took over the responsibility of responding to the Alarms while the old SAT team did their checks. It took on average thirty minutes to drive to every bunker and have a person jump out of the jeep, run up and check the locks, fill out the paperwork, and get back in the jeep to head to the next bunker. If we were in the middle of doing our rounds and an alarm went off, the person at the alarm panel would radio the SAT commander, stating the location. Good SAT and BAF teams would be to the site in less than a minute.

Each member of SAT carried an M-16 and a forty-five automatic. We also had a LAW, Light Anti-Tank Weapon and percussion grenades available to use. In addition we carried a two-foot long pair of bolt cutters in case it was necessary to cut through the inner or outer perimeter fence. Carrying all the weapons, full gear, and the bolt cutters totaled sixty pounds of extra weight.

It so happened that on my first day on SAT, a Congressman was visiting, so everybody was ordered to be alert and at their best. Tedasco told us to keep our gear on so that if we had to respond to a practice alert, we would be ready. At night I noticed the SAT team took their gear off and slept in the SAT room on three cots. When not working tower duty, people on BAF were cleaning in case the Congressman decided to take a tour inside the Security Building. It was a constant job of mopping the floors because it rained steadily. It was fifty degrees, so the rain made the ground sloppy and muddy throughout the entire X-Area. When the Congressman entered through the gate, the base commander and every other officer on the base were escorting him. Along with his own entourage of people, they went straight to the maintenance building where the 59th Ordinance worked on the Nuclear Weapons. At some point the Congressman and his escort of officers went to one of the bunkers. While they, this group of about twenty people, were opening the bunker doors, they failed to deactivate the alarm. Tedasco, Moran, the other person on SAT, and I were all three standing within a few feet of the alarm panel. The guy monitoring the alarms could not see us because we were around the corner, so when the alarm sounded, he shouted, "SAT. Alarm at Bunker Four," at the top of his lungs.

"Do you have all your equipment on?" Tedasco asked for the hundredth time that day, grabbing my arm and looking me up and down, inspecting to make sure I was ready.

"I do," I said trying to sound calm. This was my first response to an alert on SAT and it was not a planned practice alert. For all we knew it could have been a terrorist attack, as nobody had informed us that a bunker was scheduled to be opened.

"Make sure you have the bolt cutters, follow me, and listen for my orders," Tedasco said, as he grabbed his M-16 off his shoulder. "Is your M-16 loaded?" I removed my M-16 from my shoulder and showed him that the magazine was loaded. "Stay close to me." I nodded, heart pounding like crazy. "This is where the alarm is sounding," Tedasco said, pointing to a bunker on a map of the X-Area next to the alarm panel. "Let's go to the first sandbag position."

I followed Moran and Tedasco out a back door that led directly into the X-Area. The route we took when responding to an alarm was up to the SAT commander, and he could determine that going through the main gate, down the tower line in either direction or through one of two back doors into the X-Area would be the best route, depending on the type of alarm it was and where it was in the X-Area. On SAT we had to have every bunker location and Tower location memorized so we knew the fastest and safest way to respond. Other than stepping a few feet out one of the back doors during a practice alert on BAF a few nights ago, I had never been inside the X-Area.

Moran opened a huge, heavy steel door that swung open into the X-Area. "I'll cover you to the sandbags," he said, kneeling down on one knee, using the open door as a shield with his M-16 raised to his shoulder, pointing out into the X-Area.

Tedasco dashed outside, running to an embankment of sandbags about twenty-five yards behind the Security Building. I was right behind him running as fast as I could, carrying my M-16. The bolt cutters, tucked into my web belt, slamming against my thigh, began to slip. Meanwhile, my gas mask popped open, so with both hands on my M-16, running with sixty pounds of equipment, wearing Army boots, trying desperately to keep the bolt cutters and gas mask from falling down into the thick slushy mud, I pressed my M-16 against my chest with my right hand, pressing one end of the M-16 against the bolt cutters, and reached down with my left hand and held my gas mask in place. To top it off, the rain was splattering all over my glasses and they were steaming up, so I was having a hard time seeing.

Tedasco dove into the mud behind the sandbags. I came up behind him and did the same thing, diving to the ground on his right.

"Come on out," Tedasco yelled back at Moran. "I'll cover you." Moran ran to the sandbags and dove for cover to the left of

Tedasco. By this time, we had the attention of everybody at the bunker. They were standing outside the bunker to the left and in front of our sandbag position. Several of the people were wearing suits. Some of the officers were wearing their dress green uniforms. One of the people in the group took a few steps towards the sandbags with his hands on his hips. He was wearing his fatigue uniform, a field jacket, and some gloves. Despite that, he looked sharp, having spent some time starching every crease into his uniform. I assumed he was the base commander, whom I had never met before. However, he was not. It was Lieutenant Hill from the Third Platoon, the head Security Officer in charge for the day.

"Oh for crying out loud," Hill yelled out, acting cocky as he started walking towards the sandbags. "Tedasco, don't you dare do what I think you are about to do."

"Halt," Tedasco yelled out.

"Tedasco, I'm warning you," Hill yelled out, stopping dead in his tracks. "Don't you do this."

"Everybody face down on the ground, now," Tedasco yelled.

"Don't you dare make these men lie down on the ground in this mud and rain in their suits," Hill screamed at the top of his lungs.

"This is your last warning," Tedasco threatened. "Lie face down on the ground."

"Tedasco, I will have you court-martialed for this," Hill threatened. "I swear I will have you court-martialed."

"SAT, lock and load your weapons," Tedasco ordered. I heard Moran chamber rounds into his M-16, so I did the same thing about ready to shit my pants thinking, *oh my, God. I've been here a week and here I am about ready to kill people.* I was so scared. My glasses were fogged up from breathing so heavily, so the people at the bunker were a blur. I took my glasses off and could see that some of them were slowly making movements, as if they were going to lie down on the ground while talking back and forth to each other as if some of them were telling the more hesitant ones that they should comply.

"On my command, and my command only, fire at will," Tedasco yelled out louder than before, making sure that everybody heard him. With that command, people began moving at lightning speed, making themselves flat as possible in the mud, covering their heads with their arms. "Spread your arms and your legs out as wide as you can get them," Tedasco ordered. By this time the people on BAF had taken up positions at various places around the bunker, too. Some of them were behind the bunker; some were at another sandbag position to the left of the bunker, while some were kneeling on the ground using trees as cover. Tedasco called the BAF commander on the walkie-talkie and instructed them to approach the people on the ground and determine if anybody was under duress or if it was a false alarm. We kept them covered. Three people from BAF went to each person and asked if they were under any duress. The BAF commander radioed back that everything was secure and that it was a false alarm. At that point Tedasco declared everything safe and allowed everybody to stand. Hill was still fuming at Tedasco for months after the incident and would have attempted to court-martial him, as he had threatened, if it were not for the fact that after the all clear was given, the Congressman came up and shook Tedasco's hand and commended him for doing an outstanding job. "Son, that was a courageous and outstanding job you did out there today. I'm going to recommend you for a citation," the Congressman told him. Hell, I was impressed, too. It was a day I will never forget. The way Tedasco did what he had to do, despite the rants of a raging Lieutenant threatening to court-martial him if he proceeded to do his job, was an act of courage. If he had backed down to the Lieutenant's threats, he could have been brought up on charges of dereliction of duty.

That was my initiation into SAT. For the next four or five months, I worked about half my time in the towers and the other half my time on SAT.

Within six months, I was promoted twice from Private E-1, the rank with no stripe to Private E-2, a one-stripe ranking to Private First Class (PFC), which is one stripe with a smile connecting the bottom parts of the stripe. Within a week after being promoted to PFC, I was working as the SAT commander. I was told that I was the first PFC to be SAT commander. Prior to that you had to be a rank of E-4 (Specialists) to be the SAT commander. I do not know if that is true, but I took pride in being SAT commander. My first time as SAT commander was a Saturday night. Weekends were easy shifts -- if the weather was good -- because most of the officers did not appear on base during the weekend, so we did not have to worry about having to impress people by having phony alerts. Despite the fact that it was a slow night, I required the other two members of SAT, myself included to keep their gear on the entire 12-hour shift so that we would be ready to respond to any alarms. I did not care if they went to sleep in the SAT room as long as they had their gear on. I required that any time I was the SAT commander. The reason for that dated back to my first day on SAT where Tedasco, as SAT commander, had us in full gear all day long, too, so that we were ready to respond to alerts. During weekdays, it was Standard practice that we kept our gear on during your SAT shift. At night or weekends, however, SAT took their gear off if going to sleep on the cots in the SAT room. That was okay as long as they still responded to alerts within sixty seconds. It was my experience on SAT that we could respond out the door in sixty seconds if our gear was off and we had to put it all back on, but we could not respond to a bunker on the other end of the X-Area even with the jeep within sixty seconds. So, I made it mandatory anytime I was SAT commander that we had to wear gear all the time – including weekends and nights. I found it hard to sleep during a shift anyway because from the moment I laid down, I was waiting for somebody to yell, "SAT."

One of the people I worked with on SAT was Woody. He was an incredible athlete and could run. He was the quarterback on our platoon's flag football team and he was on the Army track team, competing in long distance running and the pole vault. He asked me to train with him for a marathon. On the first day we went jogging we ran for four miles at a fast pace – at least for me. As we rounded a corner a huge hill stood in front of us.

"Try to keep this pace up all the way up the hill," he said. "On the downside we will kick it in high gear." We ran about half way up the hill and I puked my guts out all over the middle of the street. I laid down in the middle of the road and did not move until Woody came back down the hill about thirty minutes later. Needless to say, I did not run the marathon. I did continue jogging on my own on the street behind the chow hall. I was told that wild boars roamed the woods, so every time I heard a noise, I about shit my pants, thinking I was going to be attacked.

Woody trained like a dog before the marathon. Meanwhile, Staff Sergeant Sampson made it known that he was going to run in the marathon, too. Sampson was about as handsome and conceited as any one person can be; he was on the Army boxing team. He was in tremendous shape and could whoop the ass of everybody in the entire company. Woody invited Sampson to train with him. Sampson declined announcing he could not possibly get in any better shape than he already was. During the actual marathon, Sampson was keeping up with him every step of the way. At mile marker thirteen, Sampson grabbed a glass of water from somebody in the crowd and threw it all over his face and chest. The water was ice cold and caused his muscles to contract and spasm all over his body. He cramped up and he fell to the ground in agony, twitching from the cramps. Woody kept on running. About 15 minutes later, an Army ambulance drove by with Sampson sitting on the tailgate of the Ambulance.

"Come on Woody," Sampson yelled at him. "Why don't you quit and climb on board this ambulance with me? Come on, you can't let me drop out of the race by myself." Woody ignored him and finished the marathon. Instead of being proud that he ran thirteen miles in a marathon without any training, he was ashamed that he did not finish the whole 26 miles.

Sanders was another co-worker on SAT. He and I hiked a lot. We often rode a Military Bus over to the Air Force Base on our days off, so we would not be around if alerts were called. We would then eat at the Air Force chow halls, shop at the PX, and then walk back to Miesau. A military bus drove back and forth between Miesau, Landstuhl, where the Army hospital is, and

Ramstein Air Force Base. They completed a circuit once an hour during daylight.

I also worked with Rogers on SAT. He was in real good physical condition, too. He and I wound up being roommates later on at both the Eighth Military Police Company and the 410th Military Police Company.

One of my best friends, Robinson, also worked on SAT with me. He was probably the most popular person in the platoon. He was rock solid muscle from head to toe, an incredible athlete, had friends all over Germany, and having grown up with a household of sisters and no father was very effeminate.

Finally Spriggs, or Springy, as he was called, was another occasional SAT member from Tennessee and would give the shirt off his back to anybody who asked for it. It took an hour for him to walk the one-hundred yard distance to the chow hall because he would stop and shake the hand of everybody he passed and ask them how they were doing. When I was in a hurry, it was quite annoying. But if anybody ever needed anything, he would help.

One of my first times working as SAT Commander we had a practice alert where a few members of the BAF team were playing the part of terrorist and they were instructed to go hide somewhere out in the X-Area. When SAT was called we were told to respond to a break in between towers three and four and secure the site, making sure nobody could come in or out through the pretend break-in of the outer fences. Once the rest of the BAF team responded, the BAF commander, Specialist Meyer left a couple of members of BAF at the pretend break-in site and then took control of the alert. Meyer had been at Miesau for over two years at the time and was gung-ho Army in that he loved weapons, the outdoors, and the thrill of games like this. He lived for the real thing to happen some day. He was different than a lot of the gung-ho Army types in that he never earned the reputation of being a kiss ass like most of the lifer's. Meyer was an Army career man without kissing anybody's ass. He was a natural leader whom we trusted. If we had to go to war, there would not have been a better leader or soldier at our side than Meyer. On the other hand, there were a lot of soldiers who had earned rank in the military by biding their time and re-enlisting, whom we would not want by our side under any circumstances, let alone during war time or any other life threatening situation. Having them in leadership positions because they earned rank by re-enlisting put people's lives in danger. I suspected that with some of the leaders we had, if we had gone to war, the sole hope for survival and victory would have been to shoot them, so that somebody else would have been in charge. Some of the Vietnam vets I met said that was a common occurrence in Vietnam. Somebody like Meyer, however, would have been a perfect leader.

During the alert, which was more like a game of hide and seek, under Meyer's leadership, SAT and BAF fanned out and began a systematic search of the X-Area, looking for the other member's of BAF who were playing the roles of terrorist. A pond was located in the middle of the X-Area and was surrounded by a swamp. It was rumored that Meyer, while one day working on SAT, wearing the full sixty-pound-weight of all his gear and equipment, walked all the way across the pond, holding his breath while walking under water on the bottom of the pond. Meyer would not deny or confirm that rumor, but he was crazy enough to do it. I often times would see him and his roommates play chicken with a razor blade. Meyer would be the first one to start and would cut a short line across his chest with the razor blade, then hand it back to his roommate, daring him to do the same length cut across his chest. Then Meyer would do another line longer than the first one. The game would go on with the lines getting longer each time, until one person could not take it any longer and quit. Meyer never lost. I witnessed him cutting a line with a razor blade from shoulder to shoulder. He liked doing crazy things.

The walkie-talkie that Meyer had was not working and since I had a walkie-talkie as SAT commander, Meyer had me follow him to keep in contact with the main tower. Woody was also with us. Meyer was using Tower Two to communicate to all the other Towers, having them keep their eyes open for the people playing the roles of the terrorists. As we searched, we came to the edge of the pond. I assumed we would walk around the perimeter. "Follow me," Meyer said, as he began wading into the pond.

"They could be hiding under water near the bank. We'll circle the perimeter."

No way in hell they were hiding in the pond, I thought, but was dumb enough to follow him anyway. We risked becoming entangled in underbrush and drowning.

We walked through ten feet of the swamp with Meyer leading the way when we received a transmission from Tower Two that the pretend terrorists had been caught near Tower Six and to head on back to the Security Building. Still following Meyer, I trudged through the swamp. Even though we were walking within two feet of the bank, we were waste deep in water as we made our way back to dry land. Every time we stepped, our feet sank in thick, gooey mud. It was hard to pull our feet free. At times, I wondered if I had pulled a foot clean out of my boot. Once back to the shore, I stepped out of the swamp and wondered if I was covered with leeches, but after a quick check, did not see any.

"Oh, crap," I yelled.

"What?" Meyer asked.

"My Forty-five, it is gone," I said beginning to panic. "I must have lost it in the damned pond."

"Oh, Shit!" Woody said. "We're in trouble. We are going to be busted for going in the pond. It's off limits."

"Screw the pond," I said, "I'm going to be busted for losing my forty-five."

"Are you sure you had it before you went into the pond?"

"I know, I did," I lied. I was not sure that I had it before going into the pond, but I was sure that if it had fallen out of my holster on dry land, I would have heard it hit the ground and would have also felt the lighter weight on my hip. "I'm going to be fucking court-martialed. I'm so busted."

"Where exactly did you step out of the pond at?" Meyer asked.

"Right here," I said pointing behind me. Meyer calmly stepped back into the pond. Without dipping his head in the water, he squatted down so that he could feel around in the mud with his left hand. About ten seconds later, he pulled the forty-five out of the mud. Perhaps the bottom of the pond was littered with forty-fives or Meyer was – or I was – one lucky Son-of-a-Bitch. I could not believe he found it.

"How the hell did you know it would be there?" I asked, feeling like hugging him for saving my butt from a court-martial.

"I didn't," he said, "but I figured the chances were that you lost it when you stepped out of the pond because you would have had your leg at a ninety degree angle or higher as you stepped up onto the embankment." He handed my forty-five back, covered in mud so thick I could not tell what it was. It looked like a giant mud ball. I started wiping the mud off of it by wiping it on to my pant leg.

"I bet this thing is ruined," I said.

"Naw, but I would go back in and clean the hell out of it before you have to turn it in tonight or else it will get ruined."

"Shit," I said, happy as a clown. "I owe you big time for this."

"No biggie," Meyer said.

After wiping the mud all over my pant leg, I re-holstered it and we all went back to the Security Building. As soon as we got back, I went into the bathroom, locked the door, and pulled my forty-five out. I disassembled it in the sink, washed it, and dried it with paper towels. Heck with oiling it and running a wire brush through the barrel. I did not have my own gun cleaning kit like Meyer. I turned it back in that night, hoping it would not rust and that I would not have to fire it someday. I felt guilty about the poor Bastard who was going to come along after me and end up with that forty-five.

Working SAT was great. It sure beat the heck out of standing in a tower for four hours a day. However, it was hard work during the days. There were people from the 59th Ordinance going in and out of bunkers. Some days they would have little or no activity. Other days, they would go in and out all day long, and they were too dumb to open the doors without setting off the alarms. Lightning storms kept us responding to false alarms, too.

December 13, 1979 through December 31, 1981:

Unlike basic training in which I was able to use Army records to reconstruct the exact dates of certain events, I could not do so with the rest of my time in the military. I cannot recall the exact dates when most things took place. For my first seven months at Miesau I worked in the X-Area alternating between working SAT and working in the towers. I hated working towers as much as anybody. At the same time, I felt lucky because some guys spent their whole tour of duty at Miesau, working the towers all the time.

During that first seven months, I did a lot of drinking, gaining twenty pounds of fat as a result, ballooning up to two-hundred-twenty pounds. I was fat, miserable, tired, and drunk a good portion of the time. I hated Miesau and could not wait to get out of the Army. Any time I was on a twenty-four hour break or having three days off, I tried to get off the base, so that I would not be there if alerts were called. If we were not on base, they could not find us to send us out for fog alerts and the like. To get away from base, a common activity was to catch the bus to Landstuhl Army Base where the Army Hospital was located or stay on the bus a little longer and go to Ramstein Air Force base. I often caught a train to Kaiserslautern. I often boarded the trains with little or no money, so I would hide in the bathroom until after the conductor passed. A few times, Sanders, and I would be aboard a train and when the conductor came, recognizing us as Americans, asked in perfect English for our tickets. We played dumb.

"No Sprechen Deutsch," Sanders said, which meant I do not speak German.

"I must see your tickets," the conductor repeated.

"No Sprechen Deutsch," Sanders insisted. So it became a game of who was willing to last the longest. Most conductors would give up after about three or four attempts of asking to see our tickets. It is no wonder why most people hate Americans.

Half the time we got on a train, we had no particular destination in mind. We wanted to stay away from Miesau for as long as we could. We still had to find time to do our laundry, shine our boots, plus tend to our uniforms though. As time at

Miesau went by, I spent less time tending to my uniform and to shining my boots.

A few times during a three-day break we could not get away because the whole platoon would have to go out to the shooting range and re-qualify with our M-16s or forty-five automatics. One time I was selected along with five other people to go and qualify with a bazooka. I learned that when firing a bazooka, there is a kickback blast that is deadly, so it takes two people to fire it. One person held the bazooka on their shoulder to aim and fire the weapon while the other loaded the round and made sure nobody was behind the bazooka within a fifty-foot radius or else the kickback blast can kill them. Once it is verified that the area in the rear is clear, the other person can fire at any time. The blast is deafening and the whole surrounding ground shakes when fired. I imagined that an earthquake would feel quite the same.

Other times during our three-day breaks, part of the platoon would be picked to go on helicopter missions. The missions would involve three helicopters. Two of the helicopters were what I called grasshoppers because to me they looked like grasshoppers. They were long and painted Army green. A big door in the rear of the chopper allowed for passengers or cargo to board the chopper. About twenty Military Policemen could ride in one of those grasshopper helicopters. In the other chopper, a nuclear weapon or parts of a nuclear weapon would be loaded on to the chopper to be transported. The third chopper was your ordinary chopper that most people are used to seeing flying around the city doing traffic reports. This chopper was called the scout chopper. Its mission was to fly ahead of the other two choppers and scout ahead for possible attacks either by air or by ground. The purpose of the helicopter missions was to transport nuclear weapons or parts for them. Sometimes we would go somewhere else to pick them up and bring them back, but most of the time we took them from Miesau to another nuclear storage site. A few storage sites we delivered to made our base seem like heaven. One of the sites we delivered to, the MP barracks was in their security building right inside the X-Area. They had no town within walking distance, nor any base facilities. Talk about nightmarish duty. Miesau had its own helicopter-landing pad where the weapon would be loaded into the chopper. Other times we had to drive out to Ramstein Air Force base to pick up the weapon and board the choppers there. The whole time the weapon was being loaded, we provided a perimeter of security, not allowing anybody within one-hundred yards of the helicopters. The mechanical condition of each chopper was checked. If one of the two grasshopper choppers had anything wrong with them, they would have the MPs ride in that chopper and put the Nuclear Weapon on the chopper that was in better mechanical condition, as they would rather lose twenty MPs than a nuclear weapon. Most of the missions would be delayed or canceled because of mechanical problems with both choppers or because of bad weather. So, the missions consisted of standing around and providing security. In the wintertime we stood outside from dawn to dusk freezing and the mission would be canceled and rescheduled for another day.

Some of our three-day breaks were used up for training. For example we would have mock convoys in which we would get jeeps and trucks from the Motor Pool and practice convoy procedures for transporting Nuclear weapons. The convoy started off by heading out to Ramstein Air Force Base down the autobahn, keeping set distances between the vehicle in front and behind. Rather boring stuff. Then when we arrived back at Miesau, the vehicles had to be washed and serviced. In fact, some three-day breaks were spent servicing vehicles at the motor pool, changing oil and other fluids, and painting the vehicles by hand.

Other three-day breaks were spent cleaning the barracks, getting our individual rooms and common areas ready for some big inspection. An inspection took place once a month that was in addition to our weekly, Wednesday morning room inspections.

To avoid inspections, I took leaves. In the Army we had thirty days leave per year. Throughout the year, I took leave to go skiing in various parts of Europe. Through the military discounts, I was able to purchase discounted lift tickets, discounted ski equipment rentals, and discounted hotel stays. I could purchase or rent lift tickets, ski equipment, and a hotel for fewer than sixty dollars for the entire week. At the time, sixty dollars was a lot of money to me with having to pay back that loan to the Army. I would save money and ski about every other month, skiing for three to seven days at a time, at such places in Germany as Garmisch, Berchtesgarden, and the Black Forest. I also went to Salzburg, Austria a few times. The movie, *The Sound of Music*" was filmed there. In Garmisch, I took a week of private ski lessons from a sixty-five year old woman who was a former member of the Austrian ski team during the decade of the 1930's. Those lessons helped improve my skiing skills. I became interested in ski racing and set a goal to be on the Army ski patrol. In Salzburg, Austria, I was able to ski in July. When I was not skiing, my entertainment was going to the movies or getting drunk. I was drinking either in the barracks, the NCO club, or at the Gasthaus (hotel/restaurant) in Bruchmuhlbach, the little town next to Miesau. I would estimate that one-third of the company, or one-hundred people were drunk at any given time of the night or day. Getting high on hash was done all the time, too, but not so openly. People would smoke hash in their rooms, using coke cans as makeshift pipes. They hung blankets over their doors and placed wet towels at the base of their door in an effort to prevent the smell from escaping their room. I did not get high on my own and never bought the stuff. I drank excessively if given the opportunity – especially if somebody else was buying or providing the booze, as I could not afford to buy my own.

One time Sanders and I were at the NCO club and another member of our platoon, Specialist Henderson, was there drinking. He kept buying us rounds of beer. As alcohol tends to do, it made him depressed and he began telling us all his woes. We wanted to have fun and did not want to listen to his troubles, so we conspired to get him drunk so we could ditch him. We were not drinking the beer as fast as he was buying them and each time he bought another round, we would give him the remaining beer in our mugs left over from the previous round. In short, he was drinking three times as much as us, three times faster. After an hour of solid drinking he went back to the barracks. Several hours later, Sanders and I went back to the barracks. By that time we were plastered.

When we got to the second floor, some medics were rolling somebody down the hall on a stretcher.

"Hey," I said to Sanders loud enough for everybody else on the entire second floor to hear. "I bet that's Henderson. He drank himself to death." Even though it was not funny, Sanders and I laughed, as drunks tend to think that everything they say is funny. Everybody stared at us with a hateful look. About that time the medics were passing us and we got a clear view of Henderson lying unconscious on the stretcher. He drank so much he got alcohol poisoning. They were rushing him to the hospital to save his life. He ended up living, but was in the hospital for a week. When he got back, I apologized to him. He did not even remember being at the NCO club.

Drinking to absurdity was a way of life at Miesau. One time Sergeant East was at a party in the room next to mine. Walker, Rogers, and Bear lived in that room. Walker chewed tobacco all the time. He would use an empty beer can to spit his tobacco juices into. Sergeant East was an alcoholic and would drink anything lying around. After guzzling his umpteenth beer for the night, he saw Walker set a can of beer down. "Hell, if you don't want that beer, I'll take it," Sergeant East said, picking up the can, and guzzled the contents of it down. "Now that's some damn good beer."

"That was not beer, dumb ass," Walker said. "That was my spittoon." Everybody laughed. Some people gagged, but Sergeant East stood up and grabbed another beer. He was drunk all the time. It was hard to tell, but I suspect he was even drunk while on duty. During my last two months at Miesau, I was back to working towers full-time and by that time could care less about the Army, Honor, Duty, and all the other crap brainwashed into our heads during basic training. I was working the 2 am to 4 am shift in Tower Six. By this time I had an attitude of sliding by. When going to my tower, I carried a duffel bag, containing a sleeping bag, a pillow, an alarm clock, and a radio. If anybody asked me what was in the duffel bag, I would not hesitate in telling them. Some people would give me the standard speech about how I would be busted if caught sleeping on duty. The truth of the matter though is that nobody tried to bust us unless we became a troublemaker. Then they would look for ways to bust us. Any person labeled as a troublemaker was not safe from being busted. If we kept a low profile and showed up for duty when assigned and made it appear that we were trying, then that's all that was asked. When drunk, Sergeant East acted as a professional, by-the-book soldier. He was the NCO in charge working in Tower Two that night. I had been up in my tower for ten minutes and had spread my pillow and sleeping bag out across the floor when the field phone rang, requiring me to jump out of my sleeping bag to answer it. "Tower Six," I answered.

"Turner, this is Sergeant East. I'm watching you through my binoculars. I better not catch you sleeping out there tonight."

"What would make you think I would go to sleep, Sarge?"

"I've been watching you and you disappeared. I want you alert and looking out those windows every time I look in your direction. Is that understood?"

"Sure, Sarge. I'm disappointed you think I would not be alert while on duty. I would not want to keep you awake worrying about what I'm doing in my tower."

"This, isn't funny, Turner," Sergeant East said, sounding mad.

"I don't think it is funny, Sarge."

"Tower Two, Out." No sooner had Sergeant East hung up the phone, I was back lying down again, trying to get some rest. I thought he was doing a routine check and that it was pure chance he said he did not see me in my tower while I was lying down. I did not think he had binoculars. If he did, he would not be sober enough to use them. However, five minutes later, the field phone rang again. I rose and answered the phone.

"Tower Six," I said.

"Were you sleeping, Turner?" Sergeant East asked.

"Not, yet, Sarge. Why? What's up?"

"Damn it, Turner. I mean it. If I look over towards your tower again and don't see you on guard, I'm going to have you busted. Is that clear?"

"Sarge, you should know me better than that. I'm not going to fall asleep."

"I'm warning you. I will have you busted."

"Okay," I said to get him to shut up, so I could go back to sleep. I knew he was plastered and would be sleeping soon himself once he was bored playing tough guy. As soon as I hung up the phone, I took my flak vest off and balanced it diagonally in the corner between two of the window ledges. I then placed my steel pot on top of the flak vest and took the broom that was in the tower and stuck it through the armholes of the flak vest. I made a make shift dummy. I laid back down on the floor, stretching the field phone over next to my head, double checked that my alarm clock was set, and started easing into sleep. The field phone rang again. Thinking I was busted, I did not bother standing up. I answered lying on the floor of my tower. "Tower Six, this is PFC Turner."

"Turner. Good job," Sergeant East said, sounding as if he hit a jackpot in Vegas. "That's exactly the way I want to see you standing guard. I've been watching you for a while now and you haven't slacked off once."

"Thanks, Sarge," I said, wondering how drunk did he have to be to think my dummy was me. I could not believe how thrilled he was, too, by the fact that he thought I was obeying his order and staying alert on my post. I must have been the first person to fool him into thinking I was obeying his order. I imagine he had few experiences with people obeying his orders. He was happy and I was able to go to sleep, despite feeling a little guilty for disobeying the order of a drunken superior.

Disobeying orders was not uncommon. I tried to avoid receiving orders by making myself scarce. One time the entire third platoon disobeyed an order from a new Lieutenant that was assigned to their platoon. He was fresh out of College ROTC, boot camp, and the Officer's Academy School. This was his first assignment. He was gung ho on the Army and all of its traditions. He had been at Miesau three days, when on Monday morning at 8 am he showed up at the barracks ready for his first day on the job. The third platoon had finished working a twelve-hour night shift and most of them were settling into bed when he came by knocking on all of their doors, yelling for them to get up for physical training. Big mistake. For one, we did not do physical training. Second, you do not want to piss off a bunch of angry, bitter Military Police who hated the Army, as evidenced by ninety-nine percent of them displaying "FTA" all over their uniforms, which stood for, "*Fuck the Army*." If you wake those people up after working all night long, you are a brand new Lieutenant, a complete idiot, or both. You might as well jump out of an airplane without a parachute.

When the captain arrived to work, he asked why a wall locker was in the parking lot and wanted to know if anybody knew anything about it. "Rumor has it, sir," somebody spoke up, "that it may belong to Lieutenant Rawlins."

"Speaking of Lieutenant Rawlins, where is he this morning?" the captain asked.

"I believe he is in his wall locker, sir," somebody said. The captain turned white as a ghost as he went running outside to open up the wall locker. Sure enough, Lieutenant Rawlins was inside of it. He was a bit shaken, but not physically harmed. When he tried to wake people up for exercise, several people grabbed him from behind and placed a pillowcase over his head so that he could not see anything. They then forced him into a wall locker, took it to the end of the hallway, and heaved it out the third floor window. He never tried to wake anybody up for exercise again. He also got an early transfer out of Miesau because the captain felt sorry for him.

Mental breakdowns happened, too. For example, in July of 1981, I was pulling a night shift in Tower Three when at 2:30 am a call came in from Tower Two.

"Tower Three," I said, answering the phone.

"Who is this?" Sergeant Jarvis asked.

"This is PFC Turner."

"Turner," if you haven't noticed already, SAT and BAF are responding to an alert over by Tower Six. There's an intruder. Be on the lookout. I've got to call the other towers, but if you see anything call a.s.a.p." Jarvis hung up the phone. My jaw dropped. I had not noticed the alert going on. It was so dark, unless you were watching the Security building right at the precise time people were responding out the door, you would not notice. An intruder meant it was the real thing. I was wondering if while up in the tower, I could be shot by a terrorist on the ground. I picked up my M-16 and was watching like my life depended on it. Every once in a while I would see people running for cover from one tree to another tree. Most of the activity was taking place towards Tower Six, and I could not see over in that direction. Within fifteen minutes, the Standby Alert Force arrived from the base area and they began setting up a perimeter in the woods around the entire X-Area. Haines was the guard in Tower Six and had phoned Tower Two saying he saw somebody inside the X-Area. This triggered the start of the alert. The people on BAF and SAT were combing the ground near Tower 6, trying to communicate with Haines as to the location of the individuals he saw. People were on edge, fingers on their triggers, rounds loaded in their chambers, ready to shoot anything that moved. Twenty minutes into the search, Haines came out of his tower on to his catwalk.

"There he is," he shouted. "There he is." He pointed his weapon near where several members of the BAF team were searching. "He's right next to you."

"Where? Where the fuck is he?" they yelled back diving for cover. Haines fired three rounds into the dirt. "He's right there next to you with the glowing red eyes, wearing the Nazi uniform" Haines responded.

It was then they knew that Haines was either seeing one of the many rumored ghosts that haunted the X-Area, or was having a nervous breakdown, or was faking a nervous breakdown. Rumors about Nazi ghosts were wide spread and also a rumor about the ghost of an MP who roamed the X-Area after drowning in the pond – the same pond where I had lost my 45 automatic.

No matter what Haines was seeing or not seeing, they felt compelled to relieve him from duty. It took about thirty minutes for them to talk him into laying his weapon down on his catwalk and to come out of his tower. I was stuck up in Tower Three the whole time. It seems that every time something fun was going on out in the X-Area, I was either in Tower Three or off duty. After relieving Haines, he was required to go to Landstuhl Army hospital for a psychiatric evaluation. Landstuhl was about ten miles from Miesau and a fair number of people who were stationed at Miesau ended up in the psychiatric ward there.

By August of 1980, both my original roommates had left Miesau. Reeder was replaced by Franklin. Reeder had re-enlisted in exchange for duty back at Fort Ord, California. I was a PFC by then. Franklin was a fresh private right out of basic training. Both Seeley and I treated him well and did not allow anybody to put him through any of the "New Guy" rituals. About six weeks later, Seeley re-enlisted for duty working undercover with a narcotics unit. I thought it hilarious that here he was one of the biggest drug pushers at Miesau getting assigned to narcotics. Then it hit me, perhaps he had been working undercover narcotics his whole tour of duty and was pretending to be a drug dealer. Good thing I never bought any drugs from him or anybody else. However, a few times at parties, I took a puff or two of hash. When Seeley left, Franklin and I got a new roommate, Raul Rodriguez. He had the looks of a movie star and was athletic. He was a private fresh out of basic training. As senior ranking member of the room, I was room commander. I do not know if it was my room commanding that caused this or whether it was the insaneness of Miesau or if it would have happened anyway, but within about a month of Rodriguez's arrival, Franklin began acting strange. During all his free time, he would take all of his clothes out of his wall locker and iron them over and over again. If we worked the day shift, he would stay up all night ironing his clothes. If we worked the night shift, he would stay up all day ironing his clothes. It was non-stop ironing. Rodriguez and I were puzzled and annoyed. Then one day Rodriguez and I had come back from working a day shift out in the X-Area. Franklin had been assigned to work that day on the Standby team. After Rodriguez and I turned in our weapons we walked into the room to dump our gear. We found Franklin sitting on his bed crying. He had pissed and defecated on himself. I learned later that this was common for people who have suffered a nervous breakdown. We did not know at the time he had suffered a nervous breakdown. We reported Franklin's condition to our squad leader on the way to the chow hall. By the time we got back from the chow hall, they had transported Franklin to Landstuhl Army Hospital and checked him into the psychiatric ward. A week later, I went up to visit him at the hospital. I ended up seeing both Franklin and Haines along with two other people from Miesau from other platoons, whom I did not know. Haines was the guy who was shooting at Nazi ghosts from his tower. One of the other two guys in the psychiatric ward was there because he had been caught giving oral sex to his drunken, passed out roommate. He was later dishonorably discharged. The fourth person had been carried off kicking and screaming after he suffered a nervous breakdown during an inspection. Many times during an inspection, a Muster Alert would be called where they would see how fast all of the troops could muster all their gear up and meet in a formation. We were inspected to see if we had all our gear and were in proper uniform. One day at the X-Area while third platoon was on duty, a general who was touring the site wanted to have such an inspection so he called for a muster alert where all of the BAF and SAT alert force had to muster right outside of the Security Building inside the X-Area. After everybody was in formation, he yelled, "GAS." Everybody had to yank open their gas mask carrier and put their gas mask on in less than ten seconds. At this point, the guy who had the breakdown, yanked open his gas mask carrier and a coke can, modified to be used to smoke hash, rolled out and bounced around on the ground a few times, stopping at the feet of the general. Many of the MP's smoked hash during their tower duty shift.

"It is not mine," he yelled. "It's not mine. I swear it is not mine. Somebody planted it on me. It's not mine." He kept screaming and carrying on and would not shut up. He was taken into custody and transported to the psychiatric ward of Landstuhl Army Hospital, screaming the whole way, "It's not mine." When I visited the psychiatric ward, I barely recognized him. He looked like a zombie. He was wearing the hospital issued blue pajamas, slippers and a robe. In fact everybody there – about fifty people – were all dressed alike.

Franklin looked like a zombie, too. He had a thick growth of hair on his face as it looked like he had not shaved for a few days. He was doped up on medication – like everybody else – and was drooling on his robe. He could not talk to me – or if he could – he did not. I was in a room full of drooling zombies and was getting claustrophobic, thinking, *What if when I try to leave, they mistake me for a patient and won't let me leave?* I did not stay long. I said a few encouraging words to Franklin and Haines and departed. During my time in Miesau, a dozen people were sent to the psychiatric ward. Most returned within three months and were discharged. Some people who were confined at the ward did not belong there. At the time the Army was on a big kick to curb illegal drug use and alcohol abuse. If they turned themselves in, they said they would give them amnesty and treatment, promising no repercussions. Their treatment for both was to send them to the psychiatric ward and dope them up on medication for a few months while they put your General Discharge papers together and kicked them out of the military.

When Franklin came back from the Hospital, unlike the people who turned themselves in for drug and alcohol treatment, he was not being discharged. He returned to active duty and seemed fine. He no longer stayed up and ironed his clothes all night. Though Rodriguez and I would look at each other and wonder what was going to happen every time he touched his iron. Franklin never brought up the incident and neither did Rodriguez or I. It was like it never happened.

The three of us got along well, and unlike Reeder and Seeley, I trusted the both of them. I was the room commander and felt I did a decent job of making sure the three of us always had our room ready for Wednesday morning inspections. In fact, I always went out of my way to make sure we were able to obtain one of the three floor buffers to shine our floor to a high gloss for the inspections, as a shiny floor always impressed people and as a result they would look at other things less harsh, as they would be too busy admiring the floor. The entire company had to share three buffers. So, not everyone was able to have their floor buffed for every inspection. One of the drawbacks for not having a shiny, fresh, buffed floor was that if it was not shiny, they assumed it was dirty – whether it was or not – and would ding us on it. It did no good to buff out your floor any sooner than Tuesday night or Wednesday morning because it would be all scuffed up within a couple of hours. We tried to buff on a Sunday or Monday and then tiptoe around the edges of the room until after Wednesday morning inspection, but it was not as impressive as buffing it out the night before or the morning of the inspection. Once in a while, we were not able to obtain a buffer, and we were dinged for the floor not being up to par. That all changed when one day, I went down to the supply room to get new gas mask filters in preparation for an upcoming training at the gas chamber. When I got to the supply room, about 4:55 pm, nobody was there. I gently shook the door in case they were inside and I could not see them.

"Anybody here?" I yelled out. No answer. I spied a buffer sitting by the front door of the supply room. It was unusual to see the buffer in the supply room, as they were always signed out. The person who signed it out was supposed to turn it back into the supply room and the next person would have to sign it out. However, it seldom worked that way. One person would sign it out and they would use it. However, instead of turning it back into the supply room where the next person on the waiting list could get it, the other person would then loan it out to their buddy in the next room, who would use it and then loan it out to somebody else over and over again. So none of the three buffers were ever in the supply room. Here I was alone in the basement. The supply room was unlocked and a buffer was sitting within my grasp. How could I not take it? I had to. It was a gift. Quietly, I swung the door of the supply room open, reached in, and grabbed the buffer. I then lifted the damn thing up and hauled ass up to the second floor and went into our room with it. I figured once I got out of the basement without being seen, it was all downhill. If anybody saw me with it, they would assume I had signed it out or borrowed it from somebody else who had signed it out. Since it was a Friday evening, the buffer was not in high demand. I felt like a miracle was taking place. I made it all the way from the basement back to our room on the second floor without a single person seeing me with the buffer. As soon as I closed the bedroom door, Franklin and Rodriguez looked up from their beds. Franklin was writing a letter and Rodriguez was reading.

"Gentleman," I said. "Behold our new buffer."

"They got a new buffer?" Franklin asked.

"No," I said, "but we now have a personal buffer. It is ours to keep."

"What do you mean?" Franklin asked.

"I borrowed it from the supply room," I said, beaming with pride. "This is now our private buffer. Nobody knows we have it and nobody ever will know that we have it. Under no circumstances will you ever tell anybody that we have this buffer and under no circumstances will it ever leave this room, understood?"

"I think that's great," Franklin said, "but how will we keep it a secret? People are bound to see it."

"We can take it apart," Rodriguez said jumping off his bed all excited. "We can hide the pieces inside our community wall locker with all of our other supplies."

"That's a great idea," I said. "You can be in charge of that, Raul." That night Rodriguez took the buffer apart and hid the bottom part of the buffer underneath the community wall locker and hid the top part inside the community wall locker behind brooms and a mop and draped some rags over it. It was impossible to tell we had it. For the next six months, we had passed every inspection with flying colors. Having shiny floors and passing every weekly inspection was why I was promoted from PFC to Specialist ahead of a few other people who had been at Miesau longer than I. My squad leader said that had a lot to do with it, as he said that making sure our room was always ready for inspection demonstrated my ability to lead. What the heck, I was not going to argue with him. I took the promotion and the extra pay. I might not have been able to shoot straight in combat, but if needed, I would be able to buff the hell out of the enemy's floor.

After being promoted to PFC, I decided that I wanted to buy a car. To do so, I would need to get an International Driver's License. A small office building was on post where we could get a booklet to study for the test. However, I decided to bypass that route because a guy in our platoon had the answers to the test, and he was selling them for five dollars. Heck, that sounded like a better deal than studying, so I forked up five dollars for the answers, which consisted of one-hundred, multiple-choice questions and answers. I spent the next two weeks memorizing the answers, A, B, C, or D for each of the questions. Looking back on it all, it would have been easier to read the book and learn the material than trying to remember whether question 33 was A, B, C, or D. I have never claimed to be too bright. After all, I did volunteer for the Army rather than enter college. On one of my three-day breaks I went over to the building to take my test. I sat down at the table and began answering the questions as I had memorized. At question number sixty-eight I became suspicious that Blair had ripped me off because all the answers I had memorized were multiple choices. However, on the actual test from question sixty-nine through one-hundred, the questions were all True or False. At that point I went back to the first question and started reading and answering each question as I thought they should be answered. I figured it was worth a shot, as you could miss as many as 32 questions and still pass the test. Any idiot could do that. But I wasn't just any idiot. After finishing, I took my test up to the front of the room where a tall, fat, German man sat and graded the test at his desk. After five minutes he looked up from my paper.

"You did not pass der test," he said in a heavy German accent that I could barely understand. "In three weeks you come back and you can take it again for the third time, yes?"

"The third time?" I asked. "This was my first time taking the test."

"Dis was your first time?" He asked, looking confused. "Ich thought dis was your second time, so Ich gave you der second test. Oh, vell. You can come back in three weeks und take it again."

"Damn," I mumbled.

"You know," he said, thoughtfully. "Ich hab a 1974 Mercedes Benz for sale for $700. If you buy it, Ich give you license." I was not sure I heard that right. A 1974 Mercedes Benz for $700? How could that be? Back in the States a 6-year old Mercedes would be going for a whole lot of money. Of course Mercedes were manufactured in Germany and they were as common in Germany as Chevy's and Fords were in America. I could not pass up the opportunity. For $700 I would get a Mercedes Benz and my International Driver's License.

"Does it run?" I asked.

"It runs great," he said.

"I do not have $700 right now," I said.

"Perhaps you can get a loan at the Credit Union at Ramstein Air Force Base," he advised me. "They seldom turn Military people down for a loan if you have a checking account with them and set up direct deposit with them."

"Well, I'll catch the bus there today and see if I can do that. If so, I would love to buy your car." Within an hour I was on a bus to Ramstein Air Force Base. I walked a mile over to the credit union and spent an hour filling out paperwork, applying for a loan. My paycheck was still being depleted from having to pay back that $2000 advance I had received as a Recruiter Aide, but I wanted that car that I had never seen. I was thinking I could ship it back to the States when I got out of the Army and sell it for a huge profit. Plus having a car would mean I would not have to rely on catching the bus back and forth from Miesau to Ramstein or having to rely on trains to go skiing. It would give me some freedom from military life. The loan was approved, but it was going to take ten days before the money would be deposited into my account. During the whole time, I was worrying that he may sell his car to another buyer. Unfortunately, that did not happen. I bought the car the same day the money was deposited into my account. He showed me how to start it. It was a diesel engine with a knob on the dashboard that I had to pull out and hold it until it glowed red behind the knob, which indicated the diesel fuel was hot enough to start the car. It took about sixty seconds of pulling on the knob before seeing the glow behind the knob. The problem with having the car was that with repaying the Recruiter Aide advance pay and with a new loan payment added on top of that, I did not have any money left over to buy insurance or gas. Gas, liquor, and cigarettes were rationed and each month we received coupons for each, allowing us to buy as much of each item as our coupons specified. I could not afford to pay for my own liquor. I drank other people's liquor, so I never used those coupons. I did not smoke either. I did want to use my gas coupons, but could not afford it. However, as soon as I bought the car, everybody wanted to be my friend in order to bum a ride or to borrow the car. I never loaned it out, but I did agree to give enough people rides in exchange for gas fare. Within a week, I also had enough money to pay for a month of insurance. That first night, I invited Woody for a ride if he would contribute some money for gas. Some of the money I put towards gas and some of it I put into a pot for insurance. We went driving towards France and went to Saarbrucken. It was not long that I realized, not studying the driver's manual may have been a mistake because I did not have a clue what any of the International Signs meant along the highways. Most of them could be figured out by looking at the pictures – I thought. Remember, I missed more than thirty-two questions on the written test. No problem though. Going the wrong way down a one-way street was good for a laugh once in a while. As we drove back on to the base we saw a pair of glowing red eyes right in the middle of the main road on the base. I stopped the car. As usual, it was raining cats and dogs outside, so it was no surprise to find out that the eyes belonged to a soaking wet kitten. I stopped the car in the middle of the road because I did not want to run it over. Woody and I both got out of the car and approached the kitten. It hissed at us. Germany had a lot of stray cats all over the countryside. They said to stay away from them because the cats could be rabid. Woody reached down to pet the kitten. It hissed again. It was cold, wet, shaking like a leaf, and unable to stand. It could not have been more than four weeks old. Woody picked him up.

"What do you think we should do with him?" he asked.

"If we leave him here, he's going to die," I said. "Let's keep him."

"I'm not keeping him at my apartment," Woody said.

"I'll keep him in the barracks," I said. We ended up taking the cat back to the barracks and made a place for him in my room. I named the kitten Dusseldorf after a city in Germany. I joked that I would one day name my first-born child Dusseldorf. Having pets in the barracks was forbidden and keeping a kitten hid was not an easy chore. The other members of the first platoon helped out. When we had our weekly inspections, we would put the kitten in a box and take it over to the gymnasium next to our barracks. I would hide the cat litter box underneath the community wall locker. However, when the cat was four months old we had two surprise inspections. During the first surprise inspection I happened to be in the barracks and barely had enough time to take the kitten over to the gymnasium. I did not have enough time to hide the cat litter box, nor the cat food that was in the mini-refrigerator. The colonel conducting the inspection entered the room, looked right at the cat litter box, and did not say a word. Perhaps it did not register with him what he was seeing. A minute later, he opened the refrigerator and inspected it for cleanliness and commented how it needed to be wiped down. A half-filled can of cat food was in the refrigerator, yet he did not say a word.

A month later, while I was on a mission with the helicopter platoon, we had a surprise inspection by another colonel visiting the base. This time I was not so lucky. When I returned to the barracks later that night, Sergeant Jarvis, my squad leader, came to my room. He was grinning, but was not happy and wanted to know why I was harboring a cat in the barracks. "You'll be lucky if you don't receive an Article 15 for this," he said. "What the hell are you thinking, bringing a cat into the barracks?"

"Who is it bothering if I keep it?" I asked.

"I'll tell you who it is bothering. It is bothering Captain Lee, that's who. We had an inspection today by a colonel and his aide. When they came into this room a cat ran out from under the bed and climbed up his leg, digging his claws into his thigh. The colonel was furious and so was the captain. Get rid of it."

"I'll see what I can do," hardly able to contain my laughter, picturing the colonel with a cat clawing him in the thigh. I would have loved to seen their faces. I drove over to Woody's apartment and told him about the situation with the cat. He said he had some German friends who might be interested in taking the cat. We ended up giving the cat to a lady who worked as a clerk at our company. She lived off post. Six months later she had to put the cat to sleep because it contracted rabies.

The day after finding the kitten, I was doing my laundry when Staff Sergeant Williams and my squad leader, Sergeant Jarvis, came to see me in my room. They explained that the Captain had decided to start a helicopter platoon. The members of the helicopter platoon would consist of five members of each of the three platoons and Sergeant Williams was to be in charge. Our purpose would be to provide security for transporting the nuclear weapons or parts by helicopter going to or from Miesau. Up to that time whenever the need for such a mission occurred, people who were off duty were volunteered against their wishes to provide the security. However, these missions were becoming more and more frequent and morale was getting low because people had to provide this extra security during their off time. With the new platoon, we would provide the security on a full-time basis and that's all we would do. We would not have to pull any duty in the X-Area at all. Furthermore, full-time meant we worked Monday through Friday with the basic hours of 8 am to 5 pm because the warrant officers who flew the helicopters worked those same hours. During my time at Miesau, night missions never took place. They wanted me to be a member of the helicopter platoon.

"This sounds exciting," I said, "Sign me up."

"Not that you have a choice," Sergeant Williams said, but we were hoping you would be excited about it."

"Hell, yeah," I said grinning from ear to ear. "When do we start?"

"Immediately," Sergeant Williams said. "You'll no longer be assigned to duty in the X-Area. We're having our first meeting at 8 am tomorrow in the Alert Force room to discuss what equipment will be required for missions. Our first mission will be on Monday."

"Monday." I gasped. "I can't make it. I already have plans for that day. That was supposed to be our 24-hour break and I made important plans. Can I be excused from the first mission?"

"Of course not. This is the Army," Sergeant Williams said. "Haven't you learned by now that you can't make personal plans?"

"Aw, come on," I pleaded. "This is important to me. I have a date with a girl in Kaiserslautern."

"I'm sure Kaiserslautern will still be there next weekend," he said. No further discussion."

"This bites," I said. "I'm asking for one day. One day is all. How about a 24-hour pass?"

"Sorry, but the Army comes first," Williams said. "Perhaps if this was not our first mission as a platoon, I might consider it." Williams and Jarvis then both left. I slammed the door shut behind them.

Here Sergeant Williams felt he was rewarding me with the opportunity to be on the helicopter platoon rather than pulling duty in the X-Area. I did not see it that way. I saw it as a missed opportunity because I would not be able to keep my date. By that time I was used to working the four nights, followed by twenty-four hours off, followed by 4 days on, and followed by three days off. My body was adjusting to the schedule and more importantly, during my time off, I was learning to minimize the chances of being called for extra duty, by getting off post as much as possible.

One way I was getting off post was by crashing at Woody's place. Having a car gave me new freedoms that were paying off. Woody arrived at Miesau about the same time I did and met a German girlfriend and the two of them rented an Apartment together. His apartment was about two miles away in the village outside the gates of Miesau. Woody and I had been good friends to begin with, having jogged a few times together, but when I got my car, he invited me to move into his apartment with him to help share costs. I did not have permission to move off post, so I still maintained by bunk and wall locker in the barracks. However, as soon as I was done pulling duty, I would head over to Woody's place. When not at Woody's, I was skiing or going AWOL with Sanders. Sometimes they would lock the base down. For instance, when a big inspection was pending, the Captain ordered that nobody within the Company be allowed to leave. However, if it were during our schedule time off, Sanders and I would go AWOL. One time, we ended up in the City of Cologne, Germany, famous for its huge Cathedral. We had two dollars to our name -- or Sanders had two dollars -- I had none. The first thing we did when we arrived was go to McDonalds. Sanders spent his entire fortune on what little food two dollars could buy. We each ended up with a cheeseburger. There were no empty seats in the building, so we devised a plan to obtain one. Sanders went to the front of the restaurant and faked a seizure. When people rushed to help him, I grabbed a table vacated by one of the good Samaritans. After wetting our appetites, we walked around Cologne all day. By evening we were famished. We had no money for a hotel, so we went back to the train station. Homeless people were sleeping on the stairs leading from the sidewalk down underground into the train depot. We curled up on the cold, cement stairs and tried to get some sleep with the homeless people. About two hours into this nightmare, I was awakened by somebody kicking the bottom of my boots.

"Uhhhhhh?" I moaned, half asleep, half dead from the cold. Opening my eyes, I saw two Polizei, the German Police, going around wakening everybody up by kicking their shoes, "Gehen, Sie," they commanded as they woke each person, "Gehen, Sie." They were making us move from the premises. Sanders and I went into the train station and resumed freezing inside. It was about another four hours of mulling around, cold and bored, before the first train back to Bruchmulbach came into the depot. Sanders and I did stunts like that any time we could to avoid pulling extra duty. We never got in trouble for it, but pulling the extra duty might have been better.

For sure, I was not going to go AWOL my first day in the helicopter platoon when I was assigned duty. It was one thing to go AWOL to avoid extra duty, but going AWOL to avoid regular duty would result in an Article 15.

As scheduled we had our first mission on the following Monday. Missions, except for the helicopter rides, were long, tedious, and boring. I had been on a few missions before, but this was the first mission of the helicopter platoon where all we did was fly missions. At least working in a Tower, we could move around and at night – with risk – we could sleep. Despite being boring, tower duty consisted of fixed shifts and we knew when the shift would end. On missions, we had no relief. It was our job to provide physical security at the helipad while the choppers were loaded with the nuclear weapon or components. In prior missions, I participated as a member of the team that provided physical security for the weapon while it was moved from storage to the helipad or vice versa. To do this meant that a perimeter had to be set up around the storage bunker while the weapon was moved from storage to a long-haul, flatbed truck. Once the weapon was loaded on the truck, a convoy of vehicles escorted it down the road to the helipad. The convoy consisted of a scout jeep that led the convoy, two trucks full of MP's who were to disembark the trucks at a moment's notice and establish a perimeter around the weapon should the convoy come to a halt. The two trucks with the MPs were positioned in front and in back of the truck with the weapon. In the rear of the convoy was another jeep. Each vehicle was equipped with a radio and each operator of the radio had to make sure the radio was set at the proper frequency, so they could communicate during the convoy. Each person had to know the password for the day to use the radio or to challenge someone trying to enter the perimeter. We asked the person for the password to verify whether they had clearance to be near the weapon or to be talking on that radio frequency. Once the convoy reached its destination at the helipad, the MP's would disembark from their vehicles and set up a perimeter around the helicopters while a fork lift would be used to move the weapon off of the flatbed truck on to the helicopter. Two grasshopper helicopters were present, one for the nuclear weapon; and the second one for the MP's.

I was never involved in a mission that went right. Every mission had a flaw. It was a simple process: take a weapon out of storage, load it on to a truck using a forklift, strap it down, transport it a few miles to a helipad, un-strap it, unload it from the truck using a forklift, place it on the helicopter, and fly away. Even things that went right went wrong. For example, the process of loading or unloading the weapon from the truck would – from start to finish – take thirty minutes maximum, which included strapping and un-strapping on or off the truck. However, not once did this process take less than 2 hours. Every officer and warrant officer involved with the mission always had to put their two cents in about the best way to load or unload it or whether it should be loaded or unloaded at all. Nine times out of ten missions were delayed or canceled because of weather. They would load the weapon on the truck and then determine that the convoy could not move forward because the fog made it too high of a security risk because of low visibility. However, rather than letting the weapon sit in storage until it was determined whether fog was a factor, they would load the weapon on the truck, which would require us to set up a secured perimeter. After the weapon was loaded, they would determine it was still too foggy to start the mission, so we would have to wait and wait and wait until somebody made a decision to scrub the mission. The whole time, we stood in a field, providing security. Once a decision was made to scrub the mission, the weapon would be unloaded. Wait. The fog cleared. The mission was un-scrubbed. Re-load the weapon, escort the weapon to the helipad, and establish a perimeter of security around the helipad. Should we unload the weapon? Chances are it would be dark soon and they do not fly night missions. What if the fog comes back? Let's waste some more time deciding on whether or not we should unload the weapon and place it on the helicopter for transport. By the time it was un-strapped from the truck, loaded on to the helicopter, and strapped down inside, the mission was scrubbed due to darkness, more bad weather, or mechanical failure of one of the helicopters. Then the weapon would have to be unloaded from the helicopter, strapped back on to the truck, convoyed back to the storage bunker, unloaded, and put back into storage with the MP's providing physical security every step of the way. Missions were an all day event from sunrise to sunset. When a mechanical problem with a helicopter was encountered and all else was a go, they would work on fixing the mechanical problem. If one of the two helicopters had a mechanical problem, they would load the weapon on to the chopper that did not have a mechanical problem and have the MP's fly in the chopper that had the mechanical problem. The hope was that the problem was fixed well enough to keep from crashing. However, it was the Army's philosophy that they would rather lose a chopper full of replaceable MP's before losing a chopper with a nuclear weapon on it. Who could blame them? If a chopper with a nuclear weapon fell out of the sky and landed in a terrorist's back yard, they could piece it back together and kill millions of people with it.

In those rare cases where at least one helicopter was able to fly, the weather cooperated, and we lifted off, the weapon was flown to another ammunition storage site. Why? At the time we were moving these weapons all over the place, President Ronald Reagan was making speeches about how the United States had dismantled and removed all of the Nuclear Weapons from West Germany and that Russia had better do the same in East Germany. We were playing hide and seek with the weapons, hiding them from the Russians.

When we took to the air with the Nuclear weapon, the scout chopper, which looks like a traffic control helicopter, except it was painted Army Green, flew ahead with two pilots and two to four MP's on board. One time I was in this chopper when twenty minutes into the flight, Sanders, who was sitting next to me pointed out two F16 Fighter Jets in the distance coming towards us. Neither of the helicopter pilots saw them coming. The F16 pilots liked to mess around by roaring past the choppers. A few times, I was on tower duty when the bastards buzzed by the tower. It scared the shit out of me. They moved so fast, I never saw them coming, and I did not expect to see a fighter jet flying so close to the ground. It shocked the crap right out of me. When Sanders pointed out the F16's coming towards us, I held on. Within seconds they blasted one hundred feet in front of the helicopter. The other MP's on board and the helicopter pilots turned white as ghosts and the pilots nearly lost control of the helicopter.

Two other choppers were present on every mission. The big grasshopper choppers, also painted Army green, would be flying a few minutes behind the scout chopper. One of the remaining choppers carried the nuclear weapon and the other carried the rest of the MP's. When mechanical failure took place with any of the helicopters we landed wherever possible. We then rushed out of the helicopters to set up security, keeping in mind which direction to run to avoid decapitation from the blades, depending on the chopper it was different. In the grasshoppers, we ran straight out the back; in the smaller chopper out the side, never to the front. When we exited the chopper, the blades were still going, so we had to hold on tightly to everything or the wind from the blades would blow it away if not secured. We did not have the luxury of waiting for the blades to come to a stop because we had to establish a secured perimeter around the chopper carrying the weapons. We were authorized to use deadly force to prevent unauthorized personnel from getting near the weapon. When an unscheduled landing was made we had to don our gas masks because we had to be ready for an attack. If one occurred, we were told gas would be dispersed to kill unauthorized people from gaining access to the weapon. We did not have a single mission where we lifted off without having to make an unscheduled stop due to mechanical failures of the helicopters. We then landed in some farmer's field, on the main cobblestone street of a small village, anywhere we could. No matter where we landed, the local villagers and farmers came out to see what was going on. Why wouldn't they? If three helicopters landed in your backyard, who wouldn't want to know what was going on? I felt bad for them because once they got near the security perimeter, we had to threaten them with our M-16's. The unscheduled stop was at least an hour while the mechanical issue was addressed. Once duct tape was used to repair some hydraulic hoses on the helicopter that the weapon was being transported on. They felt the repair was marginal, so they unloaded the weapon and put it on the other chopper that the MP's were flying in. Then we had to fly in the chopper repaired by the duct tape.

We never experienced any helicopter crashes. However, we were always prepared. Prior to every mission on the way out to the helipad, we would take all of our dog tags off and put them into a steel pot. One at a time we would reach into the steel pot and pull out somebody else's dog tags to wear on the mission. In the event of a crash, we figured we would get the last laugh and screw with the Army a little and embarrass them by making it harder to identify the corpses. We all agreed that if the person wearing our dog tags died in the crash and the person whose dog tags we were wearing also died, then we could go AWOL under the other person's name and collect the life insurance policy money that the Army carried on us and enjoy our new life for as long as the insurance money lasted.

While on missions, we spent most of our time standing guard without any relief. Our lunches were brought to us on-site either in the form of c-rations or in covered containers. There was never enough food to feed everybody and what food they delivered was scraped together from the bottom of the kettle in the chow hall. Since it rained almost everyday, we spent the whole day on guard duty soaking wet. Also, when the choppers landed at the helipad it stirred debris that stuck to our wet uniform and equipment, so we had to clean our weapon before turning it in and make sure our equipment was clean for inspections. Most of the time the final destination of successful missions was Ramstein Air Force Base. We flew to Ramstein and established a security perimeter at their helipad while either picking up a weapon or dropping one off. We had to deal with the noise from the F-16 fighter jets because the helipad was right next to their runway. When they took off and landed, it was thunderous, eardrum-busting noise. Some days they took off every two minutes.

One of the more memorable locations we flew to for a mission was Flensburg, Germany. The red light district where all the prostitutes hung out was a tourist attraction. It was a beautiful town off the Northern Tip of Germany where many freighters docked. Prior to this mission, several MP's were busted in a mission to Flensburg for disorderly conduct while drunk. Our Lieutenant had his promotion held up because of it. He was the commanding officer on the previous missions in which the trouble occurred. I was not present for that prior mission. All I knew was we had been flying all day and when we arrived at Flensburg, we went to the chow hall to eat when somebody screamed, "Attention," at the top of their lungs. I wondered what was going on because nobody ever showed respect for officers at Miesau by saluting or standing at attention. A major, the post commander, had entered and started bitching us out, telling us he better not see us in town that night because of what had happened on the prior mission. They put us up in an inn way the hell out in the country, thinking that none of us would make it back into town. Sanders and I caught a cab back into town as soon as we checked into the inn. We ended up drunk and strolled down on the docks in Flensburg. We were always discussing possible methods of going AWOL and that night we thought that we had come up with a winner. We saw a ship docked there and decided to climb aboard and hide away in one of the lifeboats. We climbed up the gangplank and walked around on deck until we found a lifeboat. We were trying to peel the cover off the lifeboat when we heard voices. We got scared and hid until whomever we heard talking went inside the boat. The people we heard speaking were not speaking English. Looking around some more, we discovered we were on a Russian freighter. We got the hell off as fast as we could.

After my duty with the helicopter platoon came to an end, I was assigned to the Escort Guard Platoon. Escort guards worked Monday through Friday from 8 am to 5 pm. We worked in the X-Area and lounged around in the Security Building playing cards or sleeping until somebody needed to enter the X-Area. I learned how to play Hearts and Spades, both challenging games that I became quite good at playing.

It was required at all times that any excursion into the Area needed two armed escorts. Most of the time, we escorted members of the 59th Ordinance Battalion who needed to get into the bunkers to work on or inspect a weapon. Other times we escorted Civilian Contractors, like German electricians who needed to work on the bunker alarms; other times we might be escorting a visiting party of VIP's.

Sergeant Spencer was in charge of us. One day he warned us to be on our best behavior because some VIP's were visiting the X-Area and he did not want to catch any of us sleeping or playing cards that day. He wanted us to be busy cleaning the building or cleaning our weapons – anything Army like. It was a cold November morning and the X-Area had snow a foot deep. It was one of those days where you want to stay inside, stay warm, and drink coffee. We did not expect too many people needing Escorts until the VIP's arrived. Then they would need escorts for a few hours. However, first thing that morning, Springy and I were first up, and we had to escort some German Contractors to a bunker for them to do some work on one of the alarms. Springy and I were on the escort for four hours. Under normal circumstances, after being out on an escort after two hours, two other escort guards would come and relieve us. However, while we were out doing our escort, the VIP's arrived. It got crazy busy back at the Security building with everybody playing Army. People forgot about us freezing our asses off outside in the blistering cold wind and 12-inch deep snow, so we were never relieved as we should have been after two hours. When our escort ended, we went back to the Security building, took off our wet boots and socks, barricaded the guard room shut by piling furniture up in front of the door, and then we preceded to go to sleep. All of the other escort guards were on duty in the X-Area. An hour later, Sergeant Spencer came upstairs looking for two people to do another escort. By that time we were fast asleep. Of course Spencer knew we were back from our previous escort and knew he could find us in the escort guard room. The furniture barricading the door did not hold him, as it slid right across the high-polished floor like an ice skater on ice. The noise of the furniture sliding across the floor woke both of us at the same time.

"Get your gear on," Spencer said grinning from ear to ear. "We need you for an escort. When you get back from the escort, do not bother taking off your gear, come straight to see me."

"Sure, Sarge, what's up?" Springy asked.

"Well, it sure as hell was not the two of you," Spencer said. Didn't I give specific orders that nobody was to sleep today? You heard them didn't you, Turner?"

"Sure did, Sarge, but nobody follows orders around here," I argued.

"That's quite alright, go ahead and laugh about it now," Spencer said. "We'll see whose laughing by the time I get done with you." Springy and I went on another escort that lasted an hour. When we returned, Spencer had us put our weapons up and report back to him. He then took us out the main door near the gate into the X-Area. As we stepped out the doors, he grabbed a couple of snow shovels that were leaning against the building. We followed him about twenty yards into the X-Area where he stopped on the road in front of the gate. "Do you see all this snow out here, Spriggs?" he asked.

"Sure, Sarge," Springy said.

"Do you see these roads out here?"

"No, Sarge," I answered, "I can't see any of them. They're covered with snow."

"Well, before you two leave this X-Area, I expect to see every square inch of every road out here."

"But, Sarge," Springy protested, "there's about three miles of road covered in snow."

"Well, you better get started right away," Spencer replied as Springy and I looked at each other grinning from ear to ear, hardly able to believe what we were hearing. "If you work real hard, you might be able to leave before the Spring thaw three months from, now. In the meantime, we will have your meals and mail delivered to you out here. Go ahead laugh it up, now. I bet you won't be laughing in about an hour." He was right. About four hours later after all the other Escort guards and the day shift platoon had left for the day, Spencer came out to check on us. Like a couple of simple-minded Forest Gumps, we busted our butts attempting to clear the roads, but underneath that foot of snow was about three inches of ice. During those four hours of backbreaking work, we managed to clear about 20 feet of roadway. At first we thought we would be smart asses and bust our butts and clear the entire roadway as ordered before the end of the day. We sweated and strained and worked like dogs to clear that 20 feet of roadway. When Spencer came back, he was impressed. "You guys did a good job. I'm surprised. Did you learn a lesson?"

"Hell yeah," I said, "next time we want to sleep, we better find a better way to barricade the door shut."

"Better, yet, next time when I tell you not to sleep during a shift, how about you listen because next time, I won't be so easy on you."

"Yes, Sergeant," I said.

"Yes, Sergeant Spencer," Springy said extending his hand to Sergeant Spencer for a shake. "You're a good man." Spencer shook his head and told us to go get our gear, as the last truck would be leaving with or without us with the last change of tower shifts coming off of their tour of duty. I always had a certain respect for Spencer. He was making a career out of the military. We always knew he would never stab a person in the back. One time during our platoon formation prior to starting a night shift, Spencer announced that the next day after getting off work we were all going to have to go the shooting range to re-qualify with our M-16's.

"Fuck the Army," Cisco yelled out. Everybody laughed, but Spencer.

"Cisco, it seems to me that you are unhappy about something," Spencer said. "Why can't you be more like Turner?

You never hear him complain about anything. He takes everything in stride, does what needs to be done, and goes about his life. He seems much happier than you or most everybody here. He should be an example to all of you." I was surprised he was using me as an example. I guess he never heard me complain much.

I did complain, maybe not as often as others. I would sometimes let it build up inside and then, out of frustration, let it explode. Like the time we were having a Flag Football League Tournament on the base. Every platoon on the base put together a team, including the maggots from the 59th Ordinance Battalion. The base champions earned the right to go to Denmark with all expenses paid by the Army to play in a larger tournament against other bases. For the entire month of September we played two games per week. Our platoon was scheduled to play the Third Platoon in the Semi-finals. The winner of the game would move on the finals to play a team from the 59th Ordinance battalion, which had a guy on their team who used to play for the Kansas City Chiefs. We had beaten them in an earlier game in the month and we had also beaten the Third Platoon in an earlier game, so we thought for sure we had the Championship locked up. We had a good team. Woody was our quarterback and being on the Army track team and a marathon runner, he was fast as a rabbit and was hard to catch. Lieutenant Hill, our Platoon Lieutenant had played at the University of Penn State as a linebacker and was real good too.

I was working as an escort guard and since it was a Saturday I did not have to work that day, but the rest of the First Platoon was working the day shift in the X-Area. The Third Platoon was relieving our platoon for duty that night in the X-Area, working the night shift. The changing of duties was supposed to take place at 6 pm and the game started at 6:30 pm. More than half of our team, including Woody, our star player, was working in the X-Area. If they were relieved on time, it would have been cutting it close to be there for the start of the game at 6:30; however, we did not have a problem during the previous games, so we were not concerned. However, by the time the game started at 6:30 pm, the third platoon, in violation of all kinds of Operating Procedures, had not even arrived at the X-Area to relieve our platoon – not that anybody ever seemed to follow Operating Procedures, but when it came to being out at the X-Area in time for duty, that was important. They were purposely being late, knowing that we may not have enough people to field a team for the game and would have to forfeit the game. However we were able to scrape together some other people who were not on the team to show up and play at the start of the game. They were surprised that we had enough people to play. By 6:30 they could not afford to stall any longer without risking trouble. However, by the time our players were relieved, driven back to the barrack, turned their weapons in, changed out of their uniforms, and made it to the football field, five minutes remained to be played in the game and we were trailing by three touchdowns. But once we had all of our team on the field, the score changed fast, as Woody scored two touchdowns within four minutes. With one minute left in the game, we got the ball back and were moving towards the tying score. It came down to the last play of the game. We were at the fifty-yard line with time for one more play. We needed a touchdown to tie the game. Woody dropped back for a pass and heaved the ball as far as he could. Damned if Sergeant Becker from the Third platoon did not intercept it. He used to be a Specialist in our platoon and was transferred to the Third platoon when he was promoted to Sergeant. He was from Alabama and had a knack of rubbing people the wrong way. It was his decision to delay relieving our platoon on time, so we could not field our team. I was playing center and as soon as I saw him intercept the ball, I knew the game was over. I was pissed. I went running down the field towards him. Meanwhile, he was running up the field towards our goal with the ball. He had a few blockers in front of him leading his way. I went plowing through them, and running as fast as I could towards Becker, I clothes-lined him across the neck as he stepped out of bounds on third platoon's sidelines. He hit the ground like a sack of potatoes. Since it was flag football, I then grabbed his flags off his belt and threw them on to his torso, as he lay there half dazed and confused. The referee blew his whistle and threw his flag at me, hitting me in the back.

"Fifty-six," the referee yelled, pointing at me while calling my number, "you are out of the game."

"That was the last play of the game, you idiot," I said. Then somebody from the Third platoon pushed me in the back. Within seconds the Third platoon had me surrounded and were yelling at me and pushing me. Within a few more seconds, First and Third platoon were having a fight in the middle of the football field. The referee and our Lieutenant Hill were attempting to break it up by grabbing people and yanking them apart. We lost the game, of course, and Third platoon went on the championship game to play the team that we had beaten in a previous game. Third platoon lost the championship game.

For the most part, people in the different platoons got along. Besides things like the football game, there was not a lot of competition between the platoons. Once in a while, we had members of one platoon mad at members of another platoon like when our platoon was working the graveyard shift and we had to deal with the drunken members of the platoon that was on break. People drank a lot at Miesau. I did not drink too much, not because I did not want to, but because I could not afford to do so. When I did drink, it was at a party where I was offered free beer or once in a while going out with friends of mine in the first platoon during our time off and they would buy the beer. I was involved in a lot of drunken escapades, some of which led to being arrested or barely escaping arrest.

For example there was a group of five of us who went into town one night to a local German Gasthaus and played pool while drinking all night. We were drinking quite a bit. There were a few Air Force guys in the bar, too. One of the Air Force guys was there with his pregnant wife. He was barely five feet tall and it seemed he had a real Napoleon complex. He was belittling her all night long, calling her fat ass and stupid every time she missed a pool shot. About 2 am, Rogers confronted the guy, telling him he did not appreciate the way he spoke to his wife. Without saying a word, the guy hit Rogers. He hit him back and a fight started between the two of them. The other Air Force men and the other members of our platoon broke up the fight. However, the owner of the bar did not want us there any longer. He made everybody in our party leave along with the rude Air Force guy and his pregnant wife. We left first and were telling Rogers what a screw up he was for getting us thrown out of the bar. We had a long walk ahead of us – about two miles – to get back to our base. As we were strolling across the parking lot to the road, this car comes cutting across the parking lot real fast almost hitting us. It was the Air Force guy. Now we were all pissed and we began kicking the crap out of his car when he slowed down to give us the finger. We put some large dents in his car doors. He slammed on his brakes, his pregnant girlfriend got out of his car and ran over to Rogers and jumped on his back and was hitting him. Rogers was the one trying to defend her in the bar from her loud-mouthed boyfriend and here she was trying to beat him up. We were all standing there laughing, watching this scene. What I did not know is that while this was going on, Napoleon stepped out of the car. He sneaked up behind me and cold-cocked me from behind in the side of my face. My glasses went flying off my head and the lenses broke on the ground. I was furious. I turned to fight. By then Sanders had grabbed the little prick. This caused his girlfriend to jump off Rogers' back and on to Sander's back. About that same time, two German Polizei pulled up in a car. As soon as they shined their spotlights on us, all the fighting came to a halt.

"Oh crap, we are screwed big time," I said. Rumors were that the Polizei hated Americans and would throw the book at us with all kinds of trumped up charges anytime they could. As it turned out, they were polite, professional, and spoke perfect English. They made Napoleon and his wife get in their car and drive away, despite their angry protesting about the damage we had done to their car. Once the car was out of sight, they told us to leave and not come back, nor to stray from the road. They stood and watched us until we walked down the street about a fourth of a mile. Then they left. Once they did we broke up laughing. When I woke up sober the next morning, I thought it was anything but funny. I did not have any glasses to wear, and I had a hangover. I had to go back to wearing Army issued glasses.

Two other drunken escapades were on Christmas Eve of 1980 and New Year's Eve of 1980 where having drank so much each of those nights, I was unconscious for long periods of time with loss of memory as to what happened. One of the benefits of being an escort guard was that we did not have to work on holidays. At the time, I was not taking advantage of the time off to do anything constructive. I was drinking myself to a stupor. Again, most of the liquor I drank was donated by friends. I did not have the money to buy my own alcohol. As a result I would not use the coupons that I was issued to buy alcohol or cigarettes. Normally, I threw them away. Some people would sell or trade them to German Civilians on the black market. I did not want to take the chance on getting arrested, so I never attempted it. However, one day while working in the X-Area, I was escorting some German Contractors, guarding them while they did some electrical work on one of the bunker's alarm systems. We were standing by their truck before lunchtime, and, in broken English on their part and broken German on my part, we were sharing drinking stories and beer preference stories. At some point in the conversation they asked me if I was interested in selling them my liquor ration coupons.

"How much are you willing to pay for a month's supply," I asked, thinking I could use the money.

"For one month, fifty," one of them said.

"Fifty Deutsch Marks or dollars?" I asked, thinking either way I could buy a few pommes frites (French fries) and bratwurst at the stand outside the main gate of Miesau as a special treat to myself for the month

"Ya, fifty Deutsch Marks."

"You have a deal," I said, not wanting to dicker, as I was not going to use them anyway. We did the transaction right there. Half an hour later, they exited the X-Area for lunch.

Two hours later, I was upstairs playing cards in the escort room when we get a call for two escort guards to come down. Knowing that it was probably the German contractors returning from earlier that day, I volunteered to go. Spriggs was the other escort guard assigned to the job. When we got downstairs to the sally port,

Specialist Jones, who was operating the gates, opened the large gate so their truck could enter into the X-Area. Once they got past the second of the two gates, they were supposed to wait for us to get in front of their vehicle with one MP on each side of the vehicle and then drive slow, as we walked along side of the vehicle all the way to their destination. However, they did not wait. As soon as they cleared the second gate and before Spriggs and I were in position, they gunned it. They went speeding down the road in the X-Area all the way to the bunker.

"You go and get them and bring them back here," Jones yelled out. Meanwhile the SAT team was called out. Spriggs and I went running after them. By the time we got to the bunker where they stopped, they were beginning to climb out of the truck, laughing and having a good old time. They were drunk. I never got a chance to talk to them before the SAT team showed up and told us to escort them back to the gate as they were being made to leave the X-Area.

Oh, crap, I thought. *I'm busted now.* Those idiots went out and bought booze during lunch, using my rations and returned to the X-Area drunk. They were barred from ever working in the X-Area again. Nothing further ever came of the incident.

Another incident involving booze was a summer rafting trip that we took down the Rhein. Our platoon was on a 3-day break. In an effort to boost morale, the Captain allowed those who were interested to go on a rafting trip, using Army rafts from supply. He let us take two dodge pick up trucks from the motor pool, one for transporting our tents, sleeping bags, and rafts, and one for transporting ourselves – all ten of us -- to the Rhein River. We rafted for two days and camped out over night along the banks of the river, drinking lots of beer the whole time. A bike and walking trail paralleled the riverbank and campgrounds were all up and down the river. The river was calm floating with no rapids, so we could lay down in the raft and nap in the sun without bouncing awake. The countryside was beautiful. Every once in a while I dove into the river and swam a bit next to the raft in order to cool off. At times a barge would float by and toss us a rope and tow us along behind them. The two nights we camped out, after setting up our tents, we would go out and do whatever we wanted. I went to a restaurant and had a few beers then went back to the campground and sat around the campfire listening to John Denver tapes. At one point, my flashlight went dead on me. I took the batteries out and threw them in the fire, thinking that was an easy way to dispose of them. Remember, I have never claimed to be too bright, but once I learn something, I do not forget it. I learned not to throw batteries into a fire, as thirty minutes later, a small explosion that sounded like a big firecracker came out of the flames. The batteries had exploded. My roommate, Franklin, was standing next to the fire and battery acid was spewed onto his thigh below his shorts. He yelled out in agony and ran and jumped in the river and washed the acid off. He had mild redness and was okay. That was the downside of the trip. The upside was that I met people from all over the world camping along the river, who were biking through Europe. Sitting around the campfire, drinking beer, listening to John Denver songs, and sharing stories about family and home with the other travelers was a great experience.

Another time I got drunk with some friends and we went to a prostitution house in Kaiserslautern. Well, it was more like an apartment building with a bar in the lobby than a house. In the bar they showed X-Rated movies on the wall and sold over-priced beer. After drinking themselves to a stupor, most guys went through a back door that led to the nine-story apartment building upstairs with twenty apartment rooms on each floor. Each apartment was a one-room apartment with a King Size bed in the middle of it and a small bathroom in the corner. Standing outside each apartment door were the women trying to seduce men into selecting them. Prostitution was legal in Germany and the women all had ID cards showing that they were free of sexually transmitted diseases. I took the trip through the back door. I was so drunk I was falling into walls. I walked down the first floor, feeling guilty each time I passed a woman up. I was looking for the "perfect" woman. By the time I reached the third floor, I was so dizzy I could not stand, so I stopped at the first woman's door. She took me by the hand and led me to the bed where I collapsed. After a few minutes of trying to sleep on her bed, she asked me to leave, so I went downstairs and waited for my friends. I do not remember anything else about the evening.

Another activity Sanders and I did a lot was trying to avoid Parker. He was always trying to find somebody to hang out with, but nobody liked him, as he seemed to have an inferiority complex, always bragging about what a big man he was back in his hometown where his beauty queen fiancé was waiting anxiously for him to bring her over to Germany. He was not a good-looking man himself, so when he bragged about the beauty of his girlfriend everybody teased him about her being a figment of his imagination. That would make him mad and he would brag all the more about what a big man he was back in his hometown, which of course led to more teasing. Sometimes he was so frustrated by the teasing, he looked as though he would break down in tears. One night, Parker saw Sanders and me leaving to go get a few drinks. He asked if he could join us. Not wanting to be mean where we would hurt his feelings, we told him he could join us. We then spent the rest of the evening trying to ditch him. As we raced down to the train station to catch the last train, Sanders and I ran as fast as we could, hoping Parker would run out of steam, but he kept up and made the train, too. We arrived in Kaiserslautern about 6 pm and started trying to lose Parker as soon as we got off the train, but he always managed to follow us to every bar we went to. We tried several bars, most of them being fish bars, where beautiful women would come join us at our table, trying to talk us into buying them a drink. They worked for the bars and if they hooked a customer into buying drinks, they received a watered down version of whatever they ordered. Meanwhile, the girls would order something like rum and a coke and the bartender would serve them a coke with no alcohol in it, so that they could stay sober to reel in more fish throughout the night. Of course, if somebody refused to buy them a drink, they would leave that table and go to another customer's table. The big surprise always came when the bill arrived, as drinks were twenty bucks at minimum. Sanders and I had been victims of it before and knew better. We did not buy the girls a drink and we did not even buy ourselves a drink in the fish bars. Most times we went in to the bars to watch the strip shows. Parker did not know any of this and being the bigwig gentleman he was, he bought drinks for all of us. Later on when they brought him the bill, Sanders and I tried to ditch him again by high tailing it out of the bar while Parker was recovering from the shock of a three-hundred-dollar bill. We thought for sure we had ditched him, as we ducked into a strip club. Darn, if he did not end up walking through the door about a minute later, breathing as hard as he could.

"I thought I lost you guys," he said between breaths, telling us how expensive his bill was. Sanders gave him a lecture about how he should not buy drinks in a fish bar unless it was for himself, and then make it last a while. In trying to ditch Parker, we had not seen a strip act that evening. Parker had never been to a strip club. Since he had spent so much money at the fish bar where two rounds of drinks for six people cost him three-hundred-dollars, Sanders and I were beginning to feel guilty about how we had been trying to ditch him. Within thirty minutes of arriving at the club, a new show started where a woman came out on a stage right in front of our table. The bar was small and the stage was four-foot by four-foot square. The crowd was small. Besides us three, two other people were in the bar. They were German citizens. When the first girl was dancing, Parker turned a beet red and could not even look at her. He kept looking at the floor. This did not escape the attention of the girl, so she gave Parker more attention, causing him to turn even redder. Sanders and I started laughing so hard, tears were rolling down our cheeks. The girl doing her strip dance thought we were laughing at her and became upset. We were asked to leave the club. By midnight we were out of money and had nowhere to go. The next train back to Miesau was not until morning, so we spent the rest of the evening walking around and hanging out at the train station. It was a boring night from that time forward. I learned that that my drinking always resulted in a hangover, getting in trouble, led to a boring evening, or any combination of the three. Parker thought it was a great adventure and bragged about it for some time to come. Sanders and I teased him about the stripper for a long time.

Parker was the roommate of Robinson, my friend, who was the most popular guy on base. He had confided to me that he was gay. Nobody cared because if somebody needed something, everybody knew that Robinson had connections and could obtain anything. Robinson was popular on base because of his connections, having hundreds of friends at Ramstein Air Force Base and hundreds of German friends. Robinson was the single male child in a family of six children and although he grew up to be quite effeminate, he was a great athlete in high school. He chose to join the Army instead of going on to college because he wanted to be around men. Made sense to me. Watching how people interacted with Robinson, I had suspicions that quite a few closet gays were in the military and many of them were jealous that Robinson could be so openly effeminate and not be accused of being gay. Robinson had a great physique and every woman who came in contact with him wanted to turn him straight. Robinson's flaw was that he spent almost all his free time partying and getting high on illegal drugs. Part of his popularity was that he was able to get illegal drugs. It is natural to think that drug usage would be a problem for three-hundred military policemen. However, it seemed most everybody smoked hash. I tried it twice when offered to me at a party and did not like it. I also made sure that when it was offered to me, that the people present were people that I trusted because rumors circulated that some of the military police in the unit might be undercover narcotics officers who were gathering evidence to make busts. I was naive, not realizing a good undercover narc was going to have the trust of everybody. While at Miesau, nobody I knew was busted for drugs unless they were flat out caught in the act of using them on duty, or unless they were discovered in their possession while on duty. Robinson and Parker had become friends while they were roommates and one day Robinson came to me and told me that Parker was going back home to marry his girlfriend. So, indeed, she was real, but nobody believed she was a beauty queen like Parker had claimed. I was one of the first people to find out the truth. About a month after getting married, Parker was able to get permission to bring his wife to Germany. He arranged for off-base housing. Robinson asked me to drive Parker to the airport in Frankfurt to pick her up. I agreed and Robinson tagged along. Robinson and I had a unique relationship in that we argued with each other like husband and wife or like Oscar and Felix from the, "*Odd Couple*." At one point during the drive, I said something that Robinson did not like and he slapped me across the face. I slapped him back. I caught a glimpse of poor Parker's face in the rear view mirror. He was in the back seat with a look of horror on his face, watching us slapping each other while driving eighty miles an hour down the autobahn. By then he wished he had taken the train to pick up his wife. We made it to the airport, and, sure enough, Parker was telling the truth. His wife was drop dead gorgeous. *Talk about the "Odd Couple."* Parker and his wife were like beauty and the beast. I could not believe it. He had the last laugh on all of us. He and his wife moved off post and everybody was jealous. Now people began teasing Parker how they were sleeping with his wife. The poor guy could not win.

About this same time, I was hitting an all time low with my drinking. I was having blackouts. Christmas eve, 1980, I blacked out, but the events leading up to it were memorable. Miesau had a small Recreation Building. It consisted of one foosball table and brochures about vacation packages in Europe that were available to American Serviceman. I visited there once a month and checked on travel packages. I was able to go on a couple of ski trips during my three day breaks and get ski equipment, a hotel room, and ski lift tickets for twenty dollars per day. All I had to pay for was food and transportation. I could never afford a lot of food. On these trips, I bought a loaf of bread and a jar of peanut butter and that is all I had to eat on each three-day trip. The transportation was the most expensive part of the trip. I avoided paying for transportation by hiding from the train conductors in the restroom, which I had done on many other train rides. Two weeks before Christmas, I stopped by the recreation building to see if they had any cheap ski packages available and noticed a flyer on the bulletin board about spending Christmas with a German family. It was a special arrangement they were doing where German families volunteered to let American Service men into their homes for the Christmas holidays. I asked the man running the recreation room about it, and he signed me up for it. In all the years they had been offering this service, not a single person signed up for it. They even got me excused from all duty for two days before and two days after Christmas. It was important to them that a soldier had signed up to participate in the Christmas program off base with a German family. It was good public relations for the Army.

On Christmas Eve about 3 pm, I arrived at the recreation center and waited to be picked up by my German family. They arrived within minutes. It was the Welsher family from Relsberg. Herr Welsher, Frau Welsher, and their 17-year-old son, Robert, picked me and we all climbed in their car for about a thirty-minute ride to their home. It was awkward in that they spoke little English and I spoke less German. Robert spoke enough English to translate most of what was being said. When we arrived back at their home, I met the rest of the family, Robert's younger brother, and their Grandparents. Robert took me to a guest room where I was able to leave my suitcase. I then visited with the family. Conversation was difficult when Robert was not around to translate. The whole family seemed to be overjoyed that I was visiting except for Robert. He came and went several times over the next few hours. We all sat down for dinner around 7 pm. They had an older son who was not home because he did not want to have dinner with an American soldier. I learned that the older people were happy to have American Military bases in Germany as they remembered the brutality of the Nazi's and feared that Russia's brutality would be worse. This was back in the days of the Cold War when nuclear tensions were high between the United States and Russia. East Germany was still occupied by Russia with the Berlin Wall separating East Germany from West Germany. However, the younger generation, who were born after World War II ended, did not like the fact that the United States had bases in Germany. We were briefed everyday about terrorist activities taking place. A lot of the terrorist activities taking place were because some groups wanted the United States to close down their bases in Europe. The family was split down the middle on this issue.

We talked about other things, too. For instance, Herr Welter was the mayor of the village. In addition, we exchanged Christmas presents. I presented the family with a bottle of Cognac. In Germany everybody seemed to drink it, including the children. Minors were not forbidden to drink alcohol in Europe. In turn they gave me a book, "The Klondike." It was written in English and belonged to the Grandfather. He did not speak English, but he had always wanted to learn so he could read that book. He owned it since childhood. A prized possession that he gave to me. After dinner, three friends of Robert's showed up at the house and he invited me to join them. We went up to his room. We were all sitting around the room in various places. Robert had been polite right from the moment I met him. His friends, however, were not so thrilled I was there, though they treated me with respect. Robert told me they were all members of a group that wanted the United States to pull out of Germany and the rest of Europe. Of course he did not say they were members of a terrorist group, as terrorists do not view themselves as terrorists because to themselves, they are in the right and the people they are fighting against are the oppressors who are in the wrong. For example, during the American Revolution, George Washington and his men were considered terrorists from the point of view of England. Likewise, the United States Government viewed the group that Robert and his friends belonged to as terrorists. So, here I was in the home of a nice German family that the United States Army arranged for me to spend Christmas with, and their son is telling me that he and his friends are members of a group that the United States Government considers to be a radical terrorist organization. I did not feel I was in any danger, but I felt I was in an awkward position.

"We do not hold any ill feelings towards you personally," Robert said, "but we do not like the U.S. Government. We feel that they should leave our country."

"I can certainly understand why you would feel that way," I said. "A lot of U.S. soldiers wish we could go home, too. I would feel the same way you do if some other country had military bases in the United States. However, what would happen if we did pull out of Germany? Would Russia march in and conquer Western Europe?"

"They might try," Robert said, "but we want the freedom to be able to fight for and protect our own country from them. I have nothing against the military and think everybody should serve their country. I will probably join the German Army in another year when I turn 18 years old." These people were not radical terrorists; they were no different than me when I was 17. I joined the Army on the spur of the moment decision. These kids were a lot more mature than I was when I was 17. I was twenty at the time, not much older than these kids, so I could relate to them in many ways.

"You do not have to worry," Robert said. "As long as you are a guest in our house, no harm will come to you."

As long as I am a guest in their house, no harm will come to me? What kind of bull crap was that? Of course, I did not take him serious as these were nice people, I did not feel in any danger, and these were high school aged kids. What could they do even if they wanted to? Besides, the Army knew where I was. I was cocky and naive enough to think that I was immune from any possible danger. "A toast to my host," I said, lifting a bottle of beer in the direction of Robert and his friends." We all laughed and took a drink from our beers. We talked for hours. At 11 pm, Mrs. Welsher knocked on Robert's door and said something to him in German.

"My mother says it is time we get ready to go to Midnight Mass to celebrate Christmas," Robert said, translating his mother's words. She wants to know if you will join us."

"I would love to," I answered, wishing instead that I could go to sleep. I was beat. "I haven't been to a midnight mass on Christmas since I was a small child." We walked four cobble-stoned blocks to a large church in the center of the village. It was packed to full capacity. I assumed the whole village was in attendance, wondering if they were all the same faith. It was a catholic church. My family from my mother's side was German and I was forced to attend Catholic Church up through the age of about ten or eleven. After that I attended church on holidays. By the time I left Miesau, I gave up being a Catholic. At this time, however, I still considered myself to be Catholic. The ceremony was beautiful. It was all in German, including the songs. After the mass was over the entire congregation sang Christmas songs in German. The last song was, "Silent Night." It sounded as beautiful in German as it did in English.

After the mass was over, the entire congregation walked down the streets and the sidewalks and headed over to the town hall six blocks away. It was a large stone building. An area the size of a high school gymnasium was all decorated up for Christmas. Tables and tables of food, kegs of beer, a dance floor, a live band, and lots of joyful people filled the room. I was told that it was a party in my honor. I was flabbergasted. I felt like the most important person on the face of the earth. Old men came and shook my hand, insisting on drinking a toast. They acted as if I was personally responsible for winning World War II and freeing them from Hitler and keeping them safe from the Russians. Women would come up and give me hugs. A young German girl gave me a kiss and insisted on keeping my hand clenched tightly in hers while dragging me to the dance floor for every dance. People kept winking at the two of us. After two hours of drinking toast after toast to the United States, the Army, John Wayne, and the forming of new friendships, I was plastered and could barely stand, but was having a great time. The world around me was beginning to spin and I felt foggy. The sound of glass breaking caught my attention as a heavy object flew in through one of the windows from the front of the building. It was a tear gas canister. Soon another window broke as a second tear gas canister flew into the building. The room was crowded with over two-hundred people of all ages. The canisters and the glass did not harm anybody. As soon as the first canister hit the floor and dispersed the tear gas, people began running for the exit doors, shouting and screaming. When the second canister hit, it landed ten feet from me. I got a whiff of the tear gas and it brought back memories of basic training. It is nasty stuff. I looked around the room and noticed all pathways to the exit were blocked. I pushed my way through a few people, breaking through the bottleneck and went over to the nearest window. It was the last window of the three windows that had not been broken by the tear gas canisters. I forced it open and assisted a dozen people in climbing out the window. I followed right behind them. Several people then followed us. People gathered outside the front of the building, ironically still in good cheer. Fifteen minutes later, we all went back inside the building like nothing had happened. I suspected Robert and his friends threw the tear gas as a way of announcing they did not like the people of their hometown honoring an American soldier who was also being hit on by one of the prettiest girls in the town.

When we returned inside, the party resumed right where it left off. I soon found myself drinking toasts again with everybody. The same girl was, again, clutching me tightly and we were dancing to almost every song in between toasts. One German man in his eighties came up to me and said the girl and I made the perfect couple and that one day he could tell we would be married. Thirty minutes later, the same man came up to me and said something that put a stop to my whole evening.

"You are like Elvis Presley," he said. "You come to Germany as a soldier and find yourself the prettiest fourteen-year old wife to be."

"Fourteen?" I asked. The old man grinned and nodded as he walked away. These people here must think I'm a pervert, I thought, fooling around with a fourteen-year old girl. However, they let Elvis leave the country with Priscilla, did they not? I'm not up-to-date on the history of Elvis and Priscilla. But, no matter what, fourteen is fourteen and I knew I had better stay away from her. Throughout the night, several people, including the parents of the fourteen-year old girl, offered their daughters to me in marriage. I assumed they were joking. On the other hand, the older Germans so appreciated the efforts of American soldiers in protecting them from Russia that they were willing to offer their daughters in marriage to a total stranger.

One old man came up to me and handed me a whiskey and insisted on toasting to John Wayne. Drinking that shot of whiskey was the last thing I remembered until I woke up sometime later, dazed and confused as to where I was. It took me a few minutes to realize that I was in the guest bedroom of the Welsher family. I thought it was early the next day, Christmas morning. As it turned out, it was the day after Christmas. I had blacked during the night. I did not know how I made it back to the Welsher house. I could not understand the explanation that the Welsher family had given me, but they had huge grins on their faces as they tried to tell me what happened. At least they were smiling, so it meant I did not do anything to offend anybody. It was a memorable Christmas that I will never forget.

One week after blacking out on Christmas Eve, I found myself at the NCO club on New Year's Eve, 1980, on a date with a woman who had transferred into the unit three days prior. At the club, they were selling bottles of champagne for three dollars a bottle. Neither one of us had ever drank champagne before. We were gulping it down like soda pop in between making out and dancing. After the fifth bottle, I was feeling ill and was thinking that since I had to write a bad check to get the money for the night out, fifteen dollars was getting steep for a night of partying. Payday was the next day and it would cover the check I wrote, but I did not have any extra cash for the rest of the month. Still, I was having a great time, so I splurged on a sixth bottle of champagne. After pouring the first glass of champagne from that bottle, I asked her to take me back to the barracks. She asked Springy if he could help out. He lived in the room next to mine. The two of them half carried, half dragged me back to the barracks. She was drunk, too, but she drank less than half as much of the champagne as I. Once back at the barracks, they helped me into my room. I plopped down on the bed, sicker than a dog. I thought it would not be long before I started to throw up. However, before I knew it, I was waking up eighteen hours later with no recall of anything that happened. My roommate told me that I had vomited several times. I felt like crap for about a week. That was the last time I drank for about seven years.

Of course, I did not spend every holiday getting plastered. On some holiday's I had to work. For the major holidays like Thanksgiving and Christmas, the Army went all out to provide us with the best meals possible. On Thanksgiving the food selection was tremendous. The chow hall was decorated to look like a palace fit for a king and queen to dine. A multiple-course meal with about every type of traditional holiday meat and all the trimmings awaited us. The officers dressed in their dress blue uniforms and helped the cooks serve the food. During the meal, a guy from our platoon, Ramos, started turning beet red. He was choking on a piece of meat. I did not know he was choking, nor did any of the other diners, as he did not seem to be in much distress other than he was turning beet red. As far as I knew, he could have eaten something hot. In fact, he even started to reach for a glass but sat it down, as he turned purple. Then all of a sudden he made a weird noise and a large chunk of partially chewed meat went flying across his table on to the floor. We could not help but burst out laughing at him.

Not long after New Year's, the Mercedes Benz I had bought was non-drivable. It would not start on a regular basis and I was not mechanically inclined to fix it. I ended up selling the car to Haines for four-hundred dollars. He paid fifty dollars down with the balance due the next payday, which came and went without a payment Haines was the guy who a few months before had been sent to the Landstuhl Army psychiatric ward after firing off rounds from his tower at a Nazi ghost. He had been back from the hospital for a few weeks when he offered to buy my car. I knocked on his door and went into his room. His roommates were out, which was good, as I did not want to have any witnesses to my threats.

"Listen Haines," I said, "I need that money for that car, right now, this minute."

"I was going to talk to you about that and ask you if I could pay you next month instead," he said.

"Bull," I said, trying to sound tough and menacing. "You're going to pay the money today or I'm going to beat the crap out of you." I was hoping he was buying my bluff as I had no intention of following through with action.

"I have some of the money, but not all of it," he said.

"Well, then you better crap it out of your ass because if you do not pay me the full amount today, I will put you back in the hospital. You promised me the money and you have put me in a bad situation by not paying. I need the money, now."

"Okay, okay," he said. "I'll give you the money. It is going to leave me a little short for the month," he said.

"That's too bad. You shouldn't have promised something if you could not keep your end of the deal." He ended up paying then. It was a good thing because after we struck up the deal, I turned around and put a down payment on another car from Specialist Moran who had less than thirty days in the Military. If I did not pay him the rest of his money, I was going to lose my down payment and he was going to sell it to somebody else. The car I bought from him was a 1974, light-blue, four-door Chevy of some kind. I paid him four-hundred dollars, leaving myself no money to get it licensed, insured, or registered. I also did not have money for gas. I did not let that stop me though as I drove it anyway, charging my friends money to give them rides to the Air Force Commissary at Ramstein or to Landstuhl. The car came in handy a few times for going to concerts. In Mannheim in September 1980 several of us drove down to see Journey perform. Several months later we saw Nazareth perform in Saarbrucken in a high school gymnasium with less than 100 people in attendance. It was like a private concert. I stood next to the stage wishing the concert was over, as the speakers were so loud, they were giving me a headache, and I thought I was going to have permanent and total hearing loss. At one point, they sang the song, *Love Hurts*. The lead singer looked so mean, nasty and ugly as he sang the song, he would have scared Satan. I was standing right in front of him as he sang the song. It was a great performance, but I did not like the rest of the concert. Four of us went on the trip to Saarbrucken and we stayed the night, renting two cheap hotel rooms. Robinson and I shared a room on the sixth floor of an old hotel. About 3 pm in the afternoon, before the concert, I decided to take a nap. I fell asleep with my legs hanging over the edge of the bed. When I awoke, I was dazed and confused and my legs were asleep. The bed was right next to the window, and as I stood up, still confused as to where I was, my knees buckled and I almost fell through the window, as my legs were asleep.

Another concert that Sanders and I went to was in Frankfurt where we saw several Heavy Metal Bands like 38 Special and other big name bands performing in a soccer stadium. I never have been a fan of heavy metal, so I do not recall whom all the other bands were who played. The attendance was over 20,000 people. Then in September of 1980 I took my first ski trip. I went on multiple ski trips, even taking private skiing lessons several times. I made it known that on three-day breaks, if I was not in my room, I was skiing. Even though the skiing was cheap, I could not afford to go often because I was always short of money. After my alcohol-induced blackout on New Year's Eve, I used skiing as a motivational force to change the course of my life. I decided I needed to start getting back in shape, so I started working out by jogging one to three miles a day in the woods behind our barracks. Despite being afraid that a herd of wild boars would come charging out of the woods at any moment and stuff themselves full on my carcass, I jogged every day. I also weight lifted over at the gymnasium building next to our barracks. My workouts started paying off and I dropped twenty pounds. It was also about that time that our Company Commander decided that he wanted to send people from the 164th MP Company to ski competitions, so he asked me to represent our company. In exchange, I was given a whole week off, was driven to Berchtesgarden, Germany in a military van, and my hotel, meals, and ski equipment were all paid for by the company. *What a deal.* I entered two of the three events at the ski competition, the Giant Slalom and the Slalom. The last event was a 5K Cross Country ski race. I had never Cross Country skied before, so I did not enter that event. The first three days were for practicing in each of the events. On the fourth day both the slalom events were held. I had high hopes of doing well in the competition, but was nervous, as I had never raced before. It was snowing like crazy, so I had to wear my goggles. However, when I put them on, they fogged up my eyeglasses so bad, I could not see. The next best thing was to wear my goggles without my eyeglasses. The trouble with that was that my vision was blurry. When it came time to race in the first slalom race, I started out at a good pace, but then I missed a gate. I never saw it. Instant disqualification. Three hours later when the Giant Slalom started, I thought I had no choice but to wear my glasses and hope they would not fog up so bad that I would be blinded. While waiting in the starting gate, my glasses fogged up. I was skiing blind and missed the first gate. I was disappointed and at that moment hating wearing glasses. I had worn them since the age of ten. I had tried Contacts when I turned 17, but at that time, all I could wear was hard contacts and I never did adjust to them. After several months of agony, I quit wearing the hard lenses and went back to glasses. That night while eating dinner, I decided that I had nothing to lose by entering the Cross Country 5K ski race. So first thing the next morning, I rented Cross Country skis and entered the race at the last minute. I had an hour to learn how to Cross Country ski. I thought, *How hard could it be*? Well, for one, I found you had to be coordinated, working arms and legs together or you fell over. It is harder to stand up wearing skis when you fall on flat ground like the terrain for Cross Country skiing than it is when you fall on a hill like the terrain for downhill skiing. I soon found out that I could not cross country ski. But I was going to try anyway. When it was my time to start, I took off. I managed to go about 100 yards before falling. Getting pissed I stood up and took off jogging. I was jogging at a fast pace with cross-country skis on. It was awkward to do and I was equally clumsy and fell over as many times jogging as I did while attempting to cross county ski, but I covered more ground faster while jogging than I could trying to cross country ski. I jogged the remainder of the race wearing my skis. By the time I crossed the finish line, I fell to the snow, drenched in sweat and laid exhausted on the ground for five minutes. I hung around the race area for the next couple of hours waiting to hear the final results that were announced after everybody had completed the course. I was not expecting that I did that good as I fell down multiple times. However, to my surprise, I finished in third place. That night I returned back to Miesau. A week later I was called into the administration office and was told that a request had come in for me to be reassigned to the Army Ski Team as an alternate on the Cross Country Ski Team.

"However," the desk clerk said, "we can't honor that request because you already have another transfer request pending that should come back any time now. They won't reassign you to the Army Ski Team with your transfer order pending.

"Can I cancel my request to transfer," I asked.

"I'm afraid not," he said. Damn it. I wanted to kick myself for having requested a transfer.

The closer it came for me to transfer out of Miesau, the less I wanted to go. I had spent fourteen months at Miesau. It started out being a horrible nightmare, in a place I could not wait to depart to a place I had come to like. It felt like home. I had a comfortable routine. I was set in my ways, had a good friend who let me crash at his place whenever I wanted, and I had started dating a nice German Girl whose family often invited me to join them for dinner.

It seemed that I could do no wrong at Miesau. I moved up in rank and even when I was in trouble, it turned out positive. For instance, before I quit drinking, I was arrested one night. The circumstances that led to my arrest were that Springy and I were doing our laundry one night while sharing a bottle of Jack Daniels. By the time the first load came out of the dryer, we were wasted and started cutting the sleeves off all of our uniforms. I guess we thought we would look tough - like Rambo. This was back in 1981 and the Army still had not switched to camouflage fatigues. We used the cut off sleeves to make bandannas and green masks and had put them on. About that time, Sanders came into the laundry room. He was sober and dared us to go over to the maggot's barrack dressed like that and raise some hell.

"Hey, why don't we sneak into their building and shut off their electricity," Spriggs said.

"That's a great idea, Springy," I agreed. "First let's cut our pant legs on our uniforms in shreds so we look like the hulk."

"You guys don't have the balls," Sanders said egging us on. So, Springy and I put on our green bandannas, green masks, cutoff army fatigues, and our shredded pants and proceeded to the maggot's barrack across the street. Being as quiet and sneaky as two drunks can be, we ran up to the front door. I grabbed the handles and yanked it open.

"After you, my good, man," I said, holding the door open for him. He ran in, whizzing past me screaming like a psycho as loud as he could. I followed right behind him. I traveled no more than two steps through the front door when Springy ran me over running back outside the building as fast as he could.

"Aw, shit," was all he said as he sped past me, knocking me into the wall, which was not hard to do as drunk as I was. As I regained my footing, I looked up and saw two maggots coming down the stairs as fast as they could. I, too, bolted out the door and ran down the middle of the street towards the main gate. Springy was nowhere in sight. The two maggots followed right behind me chasing me, yelling, "Stop thief."

I was 100 feet away from the main gate, running without a plan, when a military police patrol car darted out of nowhere with their sirens and lights on, stopping dead center in front of me in the middle of the street. About that same time, the maggots grabbed me from behind. Two MP's jumped out of the patrol car, grabbing them, asking what the hell was going on.

"This asshole broke into our barracks, trying to rip us off," one of the maggots lied, though I can see why they would think that.

"We will handle it from here," one of the MP's said. They handcuffed me and put me in the back of their patrol car and the maggots left. As soon as the MP's climbed back into the front seat of the patrol car, they started questioning me. "What is going on?" one of them asked. I told them the story and they laughed. They were a patrol car out of Zweibrucken. I never knew Zweibrucken MP's patrolled at Miesau. When they learned I was in the 164th MP Company, they turned me over to the CQ on duty rather than taking me to jail. Wearing handcuffs, a green mask, a bandanna, and a tattered uniform, I stood there feeling rather stupid as the CQ signed me into custody. Afterward, I went back upstairs to look for Springy. He was nowhere to be found. He arrived an hour later. He said he had run to the motor pool area and hid inside a tank until he felt it was safe to return.

The next morning, I had to go see Captain Tarango. I thought I was going to receive an Article 15 and was standing at parade rest in front of his desk with sweaty palms.

"So, Green Hornet, is it?" Captain Tarango asked.

"Sir?" I asked him.

"The CQ said you were dressed as the Green Hornet, causing trouble last night."

"No, sir," I said. "I was supposed to be the hulk." Tarango broke a smile.

"Well, tell me, what the hell you were doing?" he asked. I told him the whole story.

"Well, Mr. Hornet," he said. "Have you learned your lesson?"

"Yes, sir," I said. "I won't ever drink Jack Daniels while doing laundry."

"I'm not going to recommend any further punishment," Captain Tarango said. "I think you have suffered enough humiliation already. You are dismissed."

"Thank you, sir," I said, saluting and turning to exit.

"Oh, by the way, Turner," Captain Tarango said as I was nearing the door. "If you ever do something like that again, don't embarrass the unit by getting caught."

"No, sir, I won't sir." I had suffered enough humiliation having been caught. Plus I had the added expense of having to replace my uniforms. Dumb De Dumb Dumb Dumb !!!!!

The Green Hornet got revenge on the maggots a month later. I was working a day shift in Tower Three, which was close to the maintenance building where the maggots maintained the weapons. The building was inside the X-Area and they had a volleyball court set up outside the building. While I was in my Tower, they were playing a game and they hit the volleyball over the fence into "no man's land," with the ball landing near the tower against the outer fence. They yelled up to me in my tower and asked if I would grab the ball after my shift and have it returned to them, stating they did not have another ball on hand. "Sure, no problem, I said."

Upon being relieved, I grabbed the ball and dribbled it like a basketball all the way back to the security building. I rather liked it and decided to keep it. I drew a face on the ball and named it Chief Warrant Officer Maggot. For the next few days, I dribbled the ball everywhere I went, so that the maggots could see me with it. They were quite perturbed that I would not give it back to them. Finally after a few days, I got bored with it and decided that Chief Warrant Officer Maggot needed to be promoted. So, I went to the commissary and bought rank for a colonel. A couple of week's later, I was scheduled to work in Tower Three again, working a day shift. So, I let some maggots know the time I would be pulling my shift and told them I would give them their ball back during my shift. At the appointed time, several of them appeared outside on the volleyball court, waiting for me to return the ball. I introduced them to Chief Warrant Officer Maggot and said that prior to his departure, he was being promoted to the status of a real officer. I then poked the colonel rank on the ball on top of the face I had drawn, saluted it, and then threw the ball from my tower to the maggots. The ball, of course, was going flat from having the rank poked through it. They were angry and threw the ball back over the fence. I retrieved it when my shift was over. Upon returning to the barracks, I threw the ball away, but kept the colonel rank. In the next few months, I would put on the rank when visiting Ramstein Air Force base and impersonate an officer while walking around the base.

Friday, February 13, 1981

When it came time to leave Miesau, it took a week to turn in all the equipment I had been issued and to fill out paperwork. One of the last documents I had to sign was a document that said I would not divulge anything to anybody about my assignments with the 164th MP Company. I suppose this book is breaking that promise. However, in looking over the copies of my Army records, I have not come across a copy of that document. Besides, the 164th MP Company no longer exists any longer. What was strange about having to sign the document was that the signing did not take place in any of the offices on the first floor. Instead it took place in the basement in a sub-room of the Armory where the weapons were stored. The person who put the document before me was somebody I had never seen at Miesau prior to that day. The whole experience had a *Men In Black* feel about it.

My next duty assignment was at the 8th Military Police Company Headquarters in Bad Kreuznach, Germany, known as BK for short. Arriving on Friday the Thirteenth should have been my first clue of things to come. Four days prior to transferring to BK, I was promoted to the rank of Specialist Four. I had not even had time to purchase the new rank with all the activity of packing and transferring.

I drove my car from Miesau to BK, which was north of Miesau, with Sanders and Rogers tagging along, as we had put in our transfer requests on the same day for different places. As it turned out, we all received our orders back on the same day and ended up all going to BK, which was not a location on any of our transfer requests. BK is located near the Nahe and Rhine Rivers with a population of about thirty thousand people. Vineyards encompassed the city and the surrounding countryside. The city was famous as a health spa because the natural springs, full of salt and radium, are said to have great healing power.

During both World Wars, BK was a headquarters for the German High Command. In 1981 it was the headquarters for the 8th Infantry Division of the United States Army. The 8th Military Police Company provided security at the base and for some of the smaller military installations nearby, including backup security at some of the ammunition sites near the city.

The barracks for the 8th MP Company was the first building on the left upon entering the front gate. The first building on the right was the office building for the headquarters. I parked my car behind the MP barracks up against a six-foot high stonewall that encircled most of the main base.

Three other people also transferred in from other units at the same time for a total of six new people. Prior to our arrival, six other people transferred in earlier that month. As a result, they had no open beds. We slept on cots in the recreation room on the second, living out of our duffel bags for the next week. Prior to all of us transferring in, the company was six people understaffed, and they could not get the Army to transfer people to them. Now, all at once, they had too many people.

We were all given a short tour of the base, being showed where the main chow hall was located, the commissary, the movie theater, and the other facilities. When we returned to the barracks, the Captain welcomed us to the unit.

Captain Taylor, a young, tall man about thirty, looked like a game show host and acted like he hated his job. He, of course, did not come right out and say it, but that was the vibe he put out. He had us gather in a room in the basement. The basement was where the armory, supply unit, and all the offices were located. Across from Captain Taylor's office was a lounge area with some leather sofas, a few vending machines, a television, and a VCR player. He had the six of us gather there. It was an informal meeting as he allowed us to make ourselves comfortable in the lounge, sprawled out on the leather couches and chairs. He paced back and forth in a calm demeanor in the center of the room.

"Let me start by welcoming you to the 8th Military Police Company," he said. "I apologize for the inconvenience of having to sleep in the recreation room. For a time --that won't last long – we, now, have too many MP's on staff. I guess it is a nice problem to have. But even as we speak, we have several people processing out of the company, so you should all have rooms soon." Once other people transferred out of the company and some people moved off the base, Sanders, Rogers, and myself were assigned the same sleeping quarters with a fourth person, Roger Garner, who had been at the company for over a year.

"Next, let me tell you about the mission of the 8th Infantry Division and our purpose for being here and how the 8th MP Company supports that mission. Should a war with Russia break out, it is the job of the division to be the first to respond to any threat and to prevent the Russians from taking over Western Europe. If Russia launched an attack, the division would be responsible for moving east to meet them and stop them. We have less than twenty-four hours to confront them head on and stop their advancement. It is the job of the 8th Military Police to move out ahead of the whole division within the first two hours of an attack and set up checkpoints on all the roads to direct the movement of the rest of the division. In other words, if Russia attacks, our company will move out first to secure the roadways and to direct traffic so the rest of the division can confront the Russians without getting lost on the way to the war zone.

"That is our mission as it is supposed to be. Now let me tell you the reality of the situation. In the event of a conventional, non-nuclear attack by Russia the Army predicts that within twenty-four hours of engaging the Russians, the division will suffer heavy casualties. Within a week, we estimate we could have eighty to one-hundred percent casualties, and within two weeks, Russia will have conquered Western Europe. It is even worse news for our company. Since we are the first to move out towards the war zone, the Army expects that we will suffer one-hundred percent casualties within the first twenty-four hours. Why is that?" Captain Taylor asked. "Well, for one, the Russians out number us, have better training, and have superior conventional weapons. So I'm sorry to have to tell you this, but basically our mission here is a suicide mission.

"Now for the good news. Russia knows that the U.S. Army knows this information. They aren't stupid. They know that we would never let them take over Western Europe, so if they attack, we would have no choice but to respond with nuclear weapons, turning the conventional war into a nuclear war. Russia knows that they can't beat us in a nuclear war, so we do not ever expect that they will attack. Nonetheless, we have to constantly train and be ready for an attack. We spend about half our time in the field training for this mission. The other half of our time, we provide police protection to the military personnel in this area." The Captain ended his welcoming speech by asking if we had any questions. I thought the whole speech was funny and was surprised that he admitted the Russians would kick our ass in a conventional war. Nobody had any questions.

"No questions," Taylor observed. "Good. Now gentlemen, I hope I did not scare any of you with that speech. Here at the 8th MP Company, our least area of concern is the Russians. Our biggest area of concern and our biggest threat to the 8th MP Company is the Command Sergeant Major. He is the senior ranking NCO in the United States Army and he has it out for us. He hates all MP's. Do not ask me why, but he does. Whatever you do, stay away from him.

"Next order of business," Taylor said, "is tonight's graveyard shift. Although we have more than an ample supply of MP's, according to the Army, we are understaffed for all that we are assigned to do. I hate to do this on your first day here, but I'm going to need you all to work the graveyard shift tonight. I'm told you have been issued gear. I recommend you get some dinner, and a little sleep. Your squad leaders can tell you when and where to report for duty.

"Turner," Captain Taylor said looking at me, "I'll need you to work patrol duty with Sergeant Woodlawn. He'll show you the ropes, so report back down here at 10 pm tonight. The rest of you will be assigned to gate guard duty." *Patrol? Patrol? I have never worked Patrol before. Excuse me. I just came from a nuclear site. I never worked patrol before.* Of course, I did not say what I was thinking but was thinking there must be some mistake. However, I was assigned patrol duty because I was the highest rank of the six of us in the room. The Captain dismissed us.

After eating chow, my excitement prevented me from sleeping. The thought of working patrol duty for the first time had my mind going a million miles a minute. I got out of bed about 8 pm and started getting ready for the graveyard shift, as I had to shine my boots, iron my uniform, shower, put on my uniform and gear, draw a weapon and report downstairs. The shift started at midnight. I was issued a 45 automatic and went with Sergeant Woodlawn to motor pool to get our patrol vehicle. We had a choice of four different vehicles. One was a Ford Pinto; two were VW Vans, and the fourth was a Chevy Caprice. Since it looked the most like a police car and since Woodlawn was the shift commander he signed that one out, leaving the other vehicles for the other MPs. I thought, *How embarrassing it must be for them to patrol in a Ford Pinto. Was this really the U.S. Army?*

Patrol duty was exciting. The adrenaline rush is addictive. Even during dull moments of no activity, we did not know what is going to happen next or when all hell may break lose. For the most part, patrol duty was driving around the city of BK and the surrounding area to do security checks on the various small military installations and ammunition storage facilities in the vicinity. Once in a while, we responded to calls involving a drunken soldier getting into some kind of trouble. Other calls for help were domestic disputes, thefts, and other miscellaneous crimes. Even on the most boring of nights when nothing happened, paperwork had to be completed, like keeping a log of everything we did. So, if we logged a security check of an ammunition storage facility at 2 am, which involved driving around the perimeter of the facility and checking for holes in the fence, then it had better not come out later that a breach in the outer perimeter occurred sometime before we did our security check. However, we seldom did a full security check due to lack of time. In reality we stopped at the main gate of the ammunition site and asked the guard if everything was okay. Not liking Americans, they would nod their head or ignore us. The guards were either German or Polish contractors who the U.S. Army sub-contracted to guard the ammunition sites.

Although we had no jurisdiction over German civilians, an on-duty Military Policeman had authority over all people on a military base and over military personnel outside the base under some circumstances. While on duty, a military policeman even outranks a four-star General. It would have been unwise to exert that authority over a superior except for a serious offense.

My first night on patrol duty was uneventful. The hardest part for both Woodlawn and me was staying awake. We finished work at 8 am. By the time we filled out police reports and turned in our police car, it was about 9 am. We stopped and ate breakfast about 6 am, so I was not hungry, but I was dead tired. I expected to be able to go back to the barracks and sleep. However, to my shock, as well as the shock of Sanders and Rogers, who had pulled gate guard duty all night, we were expected to participate in the morning clean up of the barracks, getting it ready for the Captain's daily inspection. This went on for several nights in a row. At one point we had a day off in that we did not work a graveyard shift. However, we had to participate in work around the barracks during the day. The next day we started working days. I was still on patrol duty and continued to work patrol duty for the next several months, alternating back and forth between graveyard, day, and swing shift. Whenever we were on patrol we were paired up with another MP. Though new at patrol duty, I often times was paired up with somebody of lesser rank than myself, so I was the lead patrolman even though the person I was with had more experience on patrol duty. That is how the Army operated. I was paired up with Sergeant Woodlawn on a swing shift one time, and he decided to go for a ride in the country. As we drove through the city limits of BK, heading for the countryside, some German civilians tried to wave us down. It looked like somebody was giving CPR to somebody.

"Should we stop to help?" I asked Woodlawn, surprised that he was ignoring them.

"No way," he said. "We do not have jurisdiction and if we offer assistance and the person dies, they will sue the U.S. Army and each of us."

"What if the guy is in need of immediate help and dies because we did not stop? Can't they sue us for that, too?"

"It is not our call to make," Woodlawn said. "If we stop, we'll be busted. Besides, it looked as if plenty of people were helping him." *Shit*, I thought. *What use are we if we can't stop to help somebody getting CPR?* An hour later we were in some village ten miles away from BK, cruising the countryside. Woodlawn was driving and was lost.

"I think we are out of radio contact with the dispatcher," Woodlawn said. "We better head back to BK. Get that map out of the glove box." He was doing about twenty miles per hour on the two-way road while we both looked at a map to try to find out where we were and to find the quickest route back to BK. All of a sudden three cars passed us all at once – not one at a time – but all three at once. The first two cars pulled in front of us in the same order they passed us. However, the third car, a brand new 1981 BMW, tried to pass us and the other two cars who were now in front us and used to be in front of him. The BMW flew past us about eighty miles per hour, then flew past the other two cars, and as it pulled back into the lane, barely missed clipping the rear bumper of the lead car. When he did this, he over steered and his back tire went off the shoulder of the road into the dirt. He steered back on the road and looked like he had gained control of the car for a second, but then his back wheels went off the shoulder of the road again. When he tried to correct himself, he swerved across the oncoming lane of traffic and went into the dirt field on the opposite side of the highway. As soon as both wheels hit the dirt the BMW rolled, flipping six times, bouncing like a stray basketball on a basketball court. The BMW came to rest upside down five-hundred yards off the road. Woodlawn pulled off the road, stopping behind the other two cars. We looked at each other. I don't know if my eyes were as big as his, but he looked like he had seen a ghost and was pale. Here we were driving around the countryside outside of our patrol area and our slow driving contributed to a car accident.

"Do you want to go see if he is alright?" Woodlawn asked.

"Hell, no," I responded, "that car could blow up any second." As we debated whether to help, the occupants of the other cars were sprinting towards the rolled BMW. About the time one of the occupants approached the BMW, the driver of the BMW kicked out the back window and climbed out of the car. He was standing there brushing himself off when the occupant of the other car came running up to him as fast as he could. When he got close, he leaped through the air, flying the last ten feet like a football player diving for the end zone and tackled the BMW driver, crushing him to the ground. I do not think he was trying to hurt the guy or fight him. He was helping him because after he tackled him, he climbed up off of him and lifted his feet into the air like he was treating him for shock. By this time, several of the other occupants had reached him, too, and they assisted with holding his feet up in the air and kneeling down next to him. The flying tackle probably did more harm to the guy than the car accident.

"It looks like he is going to be okay," Woodlawn said, "we better get out of here. Besides if we help, we could be sued or court-martialed."

Not all Patrol duty turned out to be bad like that. One time Sergeant Woodlawn and I stopped at a Restaurant in downtown BK to eat dinner. A couple in their nineties served us. As it turns out they were the owners of the restaurant and owned and operated the adjoining hotel.

"You MP's," the old man said, "you shoot Turk's next door?" He made a gun with his thumb and forefinger and pretended to shoot it several times. He then rumbled off something in German that neither Woodlawn nor I understood. His wife translated as best she could. In broken English and part German she explained that the Turks come over from Turkey, entering Germany illegally and take away all the jobs from the Germans. She said they hang out at a bar next door and play loud music keeping them awake all night long.

"No. No." I said. "We can't shoot Turks for you. I tell you what though; I am interested in finding an apartment in BK. Would you be willing to rent me a hotel room? Do you rent by the week or the month?" The old woman translated to the old man. He grinned from ear to ear.

"Yavoh, Yavoh," he said nodding his head up and down.

"How much?"

"Hundred Deutsch Mark," he said.

"Per night? Week? Or month?" Again the old woman said something to him in German. She then suggested to me that I should look at the room first and if I liked it, they would charge me one-hundred Deutsch Mark per month. Reagan was President and had been in office for about eighteen months by then. When President Carter left office, I could trade one American dollar for one German Deutsch Mark, but during Reagan's time in office, the value of the dollar had risen to four Deutsch Mark for an American Dollar, so that made the room twenty-five dollars per month. I knew then that it was going to be a deal I could not pass up. I told them I could not look at the room that night but asked if I could come back the next day. I was not sure when I left if they understood me or not or whether I quite understood them either. Nonetheless, I returned the next day. They gave me a tour of the hotel with the old woman doing all of the translation. The hotel was broken down into two different sections, a front section, and a back section. It was a square shape, four stories high with a little one-story restaurant attached on the North. The front section was the area that they rented to overnight guests. These rooms all had interior entryways. The back section of the hotel was no longer used except for people who wanted to rent a room by the month. It was enclosed on the inner part of the hotel, but each room had outdoor entrances. However, to get to the back section of the hotel you had to enter the building and go through the front section of the hotel. Once on the desired level, you entered the back section of the hotel through a hidden hallway and then found the exterior entry into your room. It was private and quiet. The drawback was that none of the hotel rooms had their own bathroom. The bathroom was a community bathroom that had to be shared amongst the other guests on the same floor. To get to the bathroom for the backside of the rooms, you had to exit your room to the outdoor balcony that was enclosed on the interior of the hotel and walk twenty feet. I rented it on the spot. The room was fourteen feet by ten feet and had a twin sized bed. That was all. Plus, I was the lone tenant in that section of the hotel, so even though I had to walk to use a community bathroom, I had it all to myself. Within days, I brought over my tape deck player, some books, and some of my clothes and had a nice cozy room. When I would come home from work, the old woman would always have a fresh baked pie waiting for me in the kitchen with fruits that she picked daily from their fruit garden. One day I accompanied her and her husband to their fruit garden. The garden was a mile from their hotel and they walked there everyday to pick fruits and vegetables that they served in their restaurant. They were both in their mid nineties and they ran a hotel, a restaurant, and walked two miles each day going to and from their fruit garden. I helped the old woman pick fruit while her husband weeded and watered the garden. Sometimes on my days off, I would explore the hotel. I found a one-lane bowling alley in the basement of the hotel. It was not used and it was covered with boxes, as the basement was used as storage. I talked to them about cleaning it up and getting the bowling alley working again. The old woman was not present to translate for us, so what the old man thought I was saying to him I do not know, but I think he thought I was volunteering to clean the basement.

I kept a wall locker at the barracks with all of my military gear in it and did not tell anybody that I had rented a motel room off post. Prior to going on duty I would walk or ride my bike from downtown BK back to the base, change into my military gear and pull my shift. As soon as duty was over, I changed out of my military uniform into my civilian clothes and headed off base as fast as I could before being assigned to do some menial cleaning of the barracks. I would then go back to my motel room, get some decent sleep, wake up, work out, and start the whole process over again. The drawback was that I could not afford to eat meals off the base, so unlike living on the base, I could not walk a few hundred yards to a chow hall and grab a meal. I did not want to ride back to the base to eat my meals, so I skipped one or two meals per day, eating a meal at the chow hall on base either right before my shift started or right after my shift ended depending on whether or not I was working day, swing, or graveyard shift. The benefit of this was that I was losing weight. Plus with my workouts, I was getting back into tremendous shape. Right from the start of arriving at BK, we had to do monthly Physical Fitness

Tests. Our squad leader, Sergeant Thomas, who looked like the identical twin brother of the father on the television show *Eight is Enough,* would march us over to do the tests at the track on the base. He would then apology to us for making us do the physical fitness tests, saying it was required by the base commander. I was glad to be doing it. In high school I always excelled in sports and physical activity, and for the first time in the Army, I was being given a chance to challenge myself. I had been training on my own for several months by this point, trying to get in shape for ski season. Also, having less than a year-and-a-half in the Army, I wanted to get back into shape before going home. After leaving the military, I discovered that the drill sergeants falsified records in basic training, showing we had taken physical fitness tests that we never took. In each one, they rated me average in the three categories. I was insulted when I found out. At Miesau, we did not do any physical fitness either. It was too dangerous for an officer to attempt to order us to do physical fitness tests. Sergeant Thomas did not seem scared to be having us do physical fitness tests, but he seemed like he was self-conscious about us not liking him by him being the one who had to supervise us and score the tests. He teamed our squad up in pairs. Then one person would hold our feet and counted how many sit-ups we did within two minutes. Then we switched. Afterward we did pushups where one person counted how many pushups we did in two-minutes. The last test was the two-mile run. Two miles is hard to do wearing combat boots.

Starting with the sit-ups, I blew everybody out of the water, doing 120 in two minutes -- One sit-up per second. I hardly broke a sweat. Before the full two minutes was up, everybody else had run out of steam and quit, so they were watching me. Sergeant Thomas broke a smile and for the first time seemed happy to be doing his job.

"That's incredible," he said. "Did you see that? Did you see that? That's a perfect score on the sit-ups." Next we had to do pushups. Again, I blew everybody out of the water. I mustered 97 pushups in two minutes. After I reached about 40, everybody was cheering me on. When time was up, I collapsed on the ground and rolled over to my back. Sergeant Thomas was dancing. "I do not believe this. Our squad is going to have the best scores in the company. Nobody is going to believe this." Next we had to run the two miles. "If you finish in less than 12 minutes, you'll have a perfect score," Sergeant Thomas said before signaling us to go. He had us all run at the same time. Two other people finished faster than me, but I did run the two miles in eleven minutes and thirty-five seconds. The next day, I was somewhat of a celebrity at the company. Several people were congratulating me on my scores. My next three months at BK I ended up with perfect scores on all of the physical fitness tests.

At the time I transferred to BK, I had started to date a German girl, Monica, back at Miesau. I tried to keep the relationship with her going. In fact within about three weeks of arriving at BK, I asked the captain for a four-day pass to go skiing. He gave me the pass and I made reservations for Monica and me at a hotel in Garmisch. She had never been skiing before and I was going to teach her. I drove to her house on a Friday. We had lunch with her family and then headed out for our ski trip. We got about two miles from her home and my car broke down. It died and never ran again – at least not while I owned it. Her father arranged for a tow truck to pick it up. I had it towed to the one place I knew that was close – the Miesau garage. It was an auto shop that rented a garage bay for two dollars per day for people who wanted to do their own repairs. Even though I was not stationed at the base any longer, they let me bring my car there. I had the tow truck driver park the car on the side of the garage. I never returned there to fix it. I knew as much about cars as I do about brain surgery – nada. That night, I spent the night at Monica's home. She still lived with her parents. They had a young kid from France staying there, too, as a foreign exchange student. The next day we all went out to a fair and rode on carnival rides. I noticed Monica had her eyes on the French Kid. I suspected something was up. The next day, I caught a train back to BK. A few days later when I called her, she broke up with me, saying she was dating the French kid.

Perhaps if the Eighth MP Company was more like Miesau, I would have liked it. For instance, once our duty was over, if missions, alerts, or other pressing issues, were not taking place, they expected you to clean. Even if we worked a graveyard shift and did not get off until 8 am, they expected us to report downstairs to be assigned regular day tasks, such as cleaning, mowing lawns, painting vehicles at the motor pool or any other mundane tasks. At Miesau, unless it was required training or an emergency situation, once we pulled our shift we were free to go do whatever we wanted, which most times meant sleeping.

In addition, after doing mundane chores, they made us sign an attendance chart for having attended training for knowledge that we would be tested on annually in order to advance in rank; however, the classes were never conducted.

Third, we went out to the field on a regular basis and played Army. I could have put up with the first two things; however, camping was something that, all my life, I disliked. I do not like spiders, snakes, worms, bugs, getting dirty, and sleeping on the ground. I hated camping. Going out to the field and playing Army was a camping trip in which we played war games like little kids. During my first 20 months in the Army, I had to go out to the field once and that was for four days during basic training. When I joined the Army, I joined the Military Police, figuring I would be assigned to a military base and would perform police duties. In basic training, I learned that MP's, during times of war, also handle the care, custody, and control of Prisoner's of War and are involved in convoys. At Miesau, I was nothing more than a glorified security guard, but at least our company never had to go out and play Army and camp in tents.

Within a week of arriving at BK, I resigned myself to the fact that I disliked the Army and was going to do my time, slacking off, having fun, and then return back to the States to start college. I had taken three college classes at Miesau through an extension of the University of Maryland. If enough people signed up, a professor would teach on the base; otherwise, it was canceled. The Army offered to pay for each class, and if we signed up, our Captain gave orders to each platoon to do whatever they could to make sure we had time off to attend. I signed up for every class that was offered. Three of the classes had enough enrollees where they did not cancel the class. All three were classes on Law Enforcement. The professor for the first class I took was a Medical Examiner for the Army. He worked for the Central Intelligence Department (CID) and performed autopsies when required. That alone made him interesting as a professor; however, his most interesting resume filler was that he was one of the negotiators in Paris, France in 1972 when President Nixon had Henry Kissinger attempting to make peace with the North Vietnamese and the Cambodians. I had always assumed that Henry Kissinger met with a big wig from North Vietnam, sat down at a table, and tried to hammer out peace. Not so. Our professor was one of 200 negotiators for the United States, not to mention the translators who were present all working on a peace deal. During the peace talks, Nixon was bombing North Vietnam and Cambodia twenty-four hours per day, seven days per week. The bombing had been going on for thirty days straight. He said the North Vietnamese were on the verge of surrendering unconditionally after about two weeks of negotiations because the bombings were taking a heavy toll in both North Vietnam and Cambodia. However, after thirty days of consecutive bombing, Nixon halted the bombing raids due to political pressure from people who wanted the war to end. If the bombing had continued for another two days, the war would have ended with North Vietnam surrendering unconditionally, the professor said. As it was when the bombing stopped, the peace talks failed and the war lasted two more years. Later in 1974, the United States hightailed it out of Vietnam with our tail between our legs. This tale fascinated me. The professor fascinated me, and I could not wait to get out of the Army so that I could take all the money I was saving and start college.

I had resigned myself to finishing up my tour of duty because I was disappointed in all the lies the Army recruiter told me about Military Police Duty and was fed up with the false records being kept on training and was getting burned out on working too many hours with too few breaks. However, I was enjoying some activities in BK.

For instance a friend of mine on base talked me into signing up for a 10K race that BK held every June. I started jogging with him. He could run fast and I would throw up daily for the first two weeks trying to keep up with him. We jogged at least five miles per day. Meanwhile I was doing about 2000 pushups and 2000 sit-ups per day. I trained for four months for the race. I did not expect I was going to do as well as my friend as he always out ran me. However, on the day of the race he said he could not run because of an injured knee, so he dropped out of the race. I finished third in the race.

In addition, once a month, the division practiced how we would respond if the Russians launched a conventional war attack against Western Europe. We never knew when the practice attack was going to be called and when it happened, we had an hour to respond in full gear, heading out to station MP's at various check points. The alerts lasted anywhere from one to three days. From the time I arrived in BK, I managed to escape these alerts by going AWOL every time one was called. Sanders and I reported for the company formations, but would not load our duffel bags with our overnight gear on to the trucks. After role call was taken at formation and we were dismissed to go get our weapons and ammunition, we would sneak off upstairs to our room, change into civilian clothes, head to the train station, and board the first train out of town. We would go wherever the train was going and spend a few days in that place and then return. It was always the same upon our return. "Where have you two been the past three days?" We always played dumb, claiming we did not know anything about the alert and that when we discovered everybody was gone we took a short trip. We were reprimanded each time, told not to ever pull a stunt like that again or we would be charged as being AWOL. But each month we did the same thing and the outcome was always the same. Heck, I would have done anything to get out of going to the field and going without a shower for three days. Of course on our AWOL trips we could not afford a hotel so we wandered around doing nothing for three days. Looking back on it, we may have had a better time in the field, as while we were AWOL, we could not eat or shower due to lack of money. At least in the field we would have had meals.

I was used to the way things were at Miesau where we had free time unless an emergency surfaced. That free time was not encroached upon. The 8th MP Company took the approach that we did not have free time and that we were expected to work twenty-fours per day. One morning after working the graveyard shift, Sanders, Rogers, Garner, and myself had climbed into our bunks to get some sleep when our squad leader, Corporal Dugan came banging on our door to wake us up for barracks duty. He wanted us to spend a couple of hours cleaning the barracks getting it ready for the daily inspection. Sanders, Rogers and I had been there a month. Garner had been at the company for over a year. It was his first duty assignment, so he did not know any better. We were tired of being woke up after pulling midnight duty, so Sanders, Rogers, and I lined each side of the door way with wall lockers – two on each side of the door, facing back to back. On top of the lockers, we stored our duffel bags full of gear. At first when Corporal Dugan knocked we ignored him, pretending to be asleep.

"I know you guys are in there and that you can hear me," Dugan shouted.

"Man, you guys," Garner said, sounding like he was going to cry, as he was probably seeing his military career flash before his eyes. "We better open the door and let him in. He sounds mad."

"Shhhhh," the three of us said at the same time.

"You better keep your mouth shut, Garner," Sanders said.

"Unless you open this door this minute, I am going to go get the master key to the room and let myself in and you will all be in trouble," Dugan said.

We had been through this same scenario several times and every time he would go get the key and come let himself in and we would pretend to be asleep. We never did get in trouble. However, in the past, we did not have the wall lockers on each side of the door.

When the knocking subsided, we knew he had left to get the key. Garner was all upset. Meanwhile, Sanders, Rogers and I all positioned ourselves on the front side of the wall lockers waiting for Dugan to come back and let himself in the door. After a few minutes he did.

"I'm coming in the room, now," Dugan shouted from outside, the keys jingling in his hands. We could not see the door from where we were on the other side of the lockers, but we could hear the doorknob turn. Then the door opened. "What the hell is this?" Dugan asked as he entered the room, seeing the wall lockers on each side of the door. Of course, he could not see us because we were on the other side of the lockers. We then knocked the duffel bags off, so they came crashing down on top of him. "What the hell?" Dugan thrashed and cussed and we scrambled back into bed. He managed to crawl out from under the duffel bags and left the room. He never did come back to wake us.

"We are in so much trouble," Garner kept saying. "We are going to be court-martialed."

"Shut your fat-ass up," Sanders said "or else, I'll go over there and beat your ass."

"Why are we going to be in trouble, Garner?" I asked. "We were in bed asleep. Can we help it if he was clumsy and bumped our lockers when he came in here?"

"I'm going to go downstairs and explain everything," Garner said.

"You better not move from that bed," Rogers said. Garner quieted down and we got some sleep. Later that afternoon when we got up on our own, Sanders and I were downstairs in the lounge playing some foosball and were told that Top wanted to see us. Top was the senior ranking sergeant in the company. Every company has one. Our Top was a thirty-year veteran who trembled. He reminded me of Barney Fife – a nervous fellow.

"Sanders, Turner," Top said as we stood at parade rest in front of him, "what's this I hear about you and your roommates giving Corporal Dugan a hard time? Dugan is a good man."

"Top," Sanders said shaking his head, "apparently you do not know Corporal Dugan the way we do. He wakes us up every morning including the mornings after our grave yard shifts and expects us to participate in the barracks clean up. He does this to everybody. We've heard rumors that the platoon is taking up a collection of money to hire some Turks to break his legs." Top turned white as a ghost and looked like he had aged two years in ten seconds.

"Is this true, Turner?" Top asked, his voice shaky.

"I do not know if it is true or not, Top," I said, "but I have heard those rumors, too." Of course I had heard them, as Sanders – every morning - jokingly suggested the idea of hiring Turks to break Dugan's legs.

"You two are dismissed," Top said, looking gravely ill as we left. Before the day was out, Top transferred Dugan to another platoon and we had a new squad leader the next day. That would not be the last time that I saw Top look so aged and ill. While stationed there I caused him to have near a break down over one incident and contributed grief to him on a regular basis.

One such incident involved the Captain's secretary, Private Robinson. He was already at the Eighth MP Company when I arrived. He had been there for several months, having come there straight from basic training. He was a year younger than I and seemed naive, having little knowledge of life outside the barracks. When he arrived at the company, he was assigned to be the Captain's secretary for no other reason than he knew how to type. This was back in 1981 before the personal computer was in use and everybody, including the Army, typed all forms in triplicate, and the Army had a lot of forms to type, so people who knew how to type were more valuable than the Special Forces. I did not dislike him. I did not like him either. To me he was Robinson. Nothing more, nothing less. However, I did notice that whatever Robinson wanted, the captain always tried to bend over backwards to accommodate him. Robinson wanted nothing more than to fit in with the rest of the guys in the platoon. So, he wanted to work patrol duty. The problem was that many people who outranked him, had been at the company longer, and they seldom were allowed to work patrol duty, if ever. They worked gate guard duty all the time. I do not know how it was that on my first day in the unit I was sent out to work patrol duty. In my mind I was still a 16-year old, irresponsible kid and wondered how I was being given adult responsibilities. The same thing happened when I arrived at Miesau. Within two weeks, they had me working on SAT, and by the time I was a PFC, I was the first non-Specialist in charge of SAT. Meanwhile people spent years at Miesau and never worked SAT. I also had the chance to work on the helicopter platoon, and the escort guards. I pulled little tower duty at Miesau. Others did nothing but tower duty. I seemed to be a golden child in the Army. So in a way, I was able to relate to Robinson. One day as I arrived at the barracks from my off-post hotel room, I was told the Captain wanted to see me. I went to his office.

"Turner," he said, I understand you've been doing an outstanding job since you arrived here."

"Thank you, sir," I said surprised. I had been there two months at that point and other than sleeping in the patrol car on midnight shifts and blowing by people in need of help so that the Army would not get sued, I did not feel like I had done much of anything. In fact, BK did not have much crime, and I had yet to even make an arrest or respond to a crime. Patrol duty meant doing a lot of security checks and sleeping in the car.

"You know my secretary, Robinson?" The Captain asked.

"Sure," I said. "Everybody knows Robinson."

"Well, I'm going to assign him to do some patrol duty on swing shifts a few times per week," the Captain said "and I want you to be his partner."

"Me, sir?"

"Yes, do you think you can handle the job?" The Captain asked. "Show him the ropes and keep him safe?"

"Yes, sir," I said, feeling I had been awarded care and custody of his sole child. "No problem, sir."

The next day, Robinson and I were partners and we had been privileged with having the Ford Pinto as our patrol car. The shame of it all. I was doing everything by the book showing Robinson every security check that had to be made, how to log it into the books, how to handle radio calls, and how to fill out a patrol log, figuring everything we did would get back to the

Captain and I would be busted if anything was not done to regulation. Nothing exciting was happening. Then about the time we decided to go by the chow hall to eat, we had a call that an alarm was going off at the ammunition storage site about five miles north of BK. These alarms were triggered by deer, rabbit, or sometimes by the weather. Whenever an alarm went off, the first unit on the scene was supposed to drive around the outer perimeter to where the alarm was sounding and secure any breaks in the chain link fence, making sure nobody exited or entered. If there was not a break at the site of the alarm, we were supposed to circle the exterior. We were the first unit on the scene, so I radioed to another unit who was responding that we would do the perimeter check and told them to check with the Polish gate guards to make sure everything was okay and that they were not being held hostage. If Robinson was not working, I would not have made a perimeter check, as some of the ammunition sites were so large it took thirty minutes to drive around them, so we could not finish all of our assigned security checks during the course of our shift. We were assigned so many security checks to do during a shift that even if working non-stop, without a break, we could not physically check each building. As an example we had to check the post library by getting out of our car and checking to make sure every door and window was locked by trying to open each one. If we found one unsecured, we had to call for back up, enter the building, and make sure it was secure. There was not enough time to do that with every building, so we drove by and looked for anything out of the ordinary like a bunch of people with ski masks loading library equipment into a stolen vehicle. If nothing was out of the ordinary, we falsified our log, stating we physically checked the building, and then moved on to the next building. Likewise with these alarms, we checked with the gate guards that everything was okay. If they did not have people pointing guns at their heads, and they treated us with their usual contempt, then we logged it as a false alarm. Since Robinson was with me, and I was not sure if he was spying for the Captain or what, I did everything by the book. So, I'm driving this Ford Pinto patrol car – *how embarrassing* – around the perimeter of this ammunition site.

Never having been around the perimeter of this site before, I found that the further we got off the road, the harder and harder it was for the Pinto to navigate the rough terrain. Sure enough, about a mile off the road, I bottomed the Pinto out on top of a mound of dirt in between two large ruts in the dirt road. We were stuck. I knew the other patrol car, which was the Volkswagen van, was en route to the front gate of the ammunition site, which was at least five miles away from us.

Robinson exited the car and assessed the damage. We were high-centered, stuck on top of a rut. I had him push while I tried to get the vehicle going. It would not budge. I tried radioing the other patrol car to inform them we were stuck on the east side, but they could not hear our radio signal.

"Robinson," I yelled. "Start hoofing it over to the west side of the ammunition site and flag down the other patrol car before they head back to BK."

"All the way to the other side?" he asked.

"If you hurry you can make it back to the main road before they do, but you better start hoofing it now. That's an order. Go. I'll keep working on getting us unstuck." He started jogging towards the main road.

"Run Robinson," I yelled. "If I miss chow, I'm going to beat your ass. Faster, Robinson. Faster." He was running at a good pace, so I went back to the car and repeatedly tried to reach the other patrol car by radio. They had been to the front gate and were heading back to BK when they heard me calling them. I explained our situation and told them to come down to see if they could tow us. "On the way here, you're going to see Robinson running towards the main highway," I said. Stop and pick the poor bastard up." About that same time, Robinson was about five-hundred yards or more away, and I could see that he stopped running, but was walking as fast as he could. "Run Robinson, you asshole. Run." I was yelling at him at the top of my lungs, having some fun with him. "You have four more miles to go. You better catch up to that other patrol car." He looked back over his shoulder towards me and almost tripped as he did so. "I'm going to count to three, Robinson. If you aren't running by the time I get to three, I'm going to shoot you in the ass." He started running again. About thirty seconds later the other patrol car turned off the main highway on to the dirt road. Robinson started waving frantically for them. I can imagine what was going through his mind. I had a feeling I was going to be in big trouble the next day, but I did not want to miss chow at the mess hall. I was starving, and if we were not back before they closed, I would have to go without dinner because I did not have any money to stop and buy dinner. Once the other patrol car arrived, we used it to push the Pinto off of the mound and hightailed it out of there. Robinson did not seem the slightest bit offended that I threatened to shoot him or made him run like a dog to catch the other patrol car. He seemed to be having a good time. We did not make it back to the chow hall before it closed, so I went hungry for the rest of the shift. That night when I got off of work I was famished, so I did not bother going back to my hotel. I slept in my bunk at the barracks, so I could eat breakfast as soon as the chow hall opened. I hated that little hotel room. But it was my own private space. It was the first true independence I experienced in my life in regards to living by myself. It was boring when I was at the hotel, but anything was better than living in the barracks. My hotel room gave me a place to go to be alone when I wanted to be able to sleep and not get stuck doing barracks duty in the morning.

That night when I started my swing shift, I checked next week's duty roster that had been posted that day. To my surprise, Top had put me on graveyard gate guard duty for seven days in a row. I had patrol duty twice. Robinson must have blabbed about how I threatened to shoot him in the ass and that was the payback. I had been in BK for almost three months and had not pulled any gate guard duty, yet. It was boring duty where we stood at the front gate and pretended to check ID's of people entering the base. If they were wearing a uniform, we waved them through. If they had any officer insignia on, we were supposed to salute as they passed. Gate guard duty was twelve hours long with three people assigned to the shift. We worked two hours at the gate, had four hours off, during which we had to be doing chores during the day; otherwise we were allowed to sleep at night. After our four hours off, we pulled another two-hour shift. The bad part about working the graveyard shift was that sometimes the relief person never showed up because they were sleeping. The three people who worked the gate were also responsible for raising and lowering the flag each day. The people working the graveyard shift had to raise the flag each morning at 7 am. The day shift had to lower the flag at 5 pm. When the flag was raised or lowered, the senior ranking member of the gate guards would go to the Eighth Infantry Division headquarter building right behind the gate guard shack and start a tape that played revelry. Then they went to the gate guard shack where the main gate would be temporarily closed for the ceremony. Meanwhile, one of the guards would march over to the cannon while the senior ranking MP would march the other guard and one other off-duty MP over to the flag pole where the two of them would raise or lower the flag. Once the flag was either folded or flying on the pole, the MP at the cannon would fire it. Then the two MP's who raised or lowered the flag would march back to the headquarters' building and stop the revelry tape while the MP who fired the cannon marched back to the gate to re-open it. While revelry was playing, everybody who was outside had to stop and salute the flag. If they were in a car, they were required to stop their car and get out and salute the flag, too.

Every time I worked gate guard duty, I was the senior ranking MP and would either fire the cannon or would march the other MP's out to the flag pole to lower or raise the flag. One day when it was time to lower the flag, it was raining quite furious, so when we went to lower the flag, we were wearing our rain gear. After starting revelry, I marched the other MPs out to the flagpole, and gave the order to lower it. One MP held the flag to keep it from hitting the ground while the other one unscrewed the clasps that secured it to the rope on the flagpole. However, the one MP could not loosen the clasp. I tried it by hand, but it was to wet to grip.

"Wait here," I ordered. Other than running the flag back up the pole, I had one other option to consider. "I'm going to find some pliers." I marched back to headquarters to find the place deserted. I went to the basement and started opening closet doors, looking for a pair of pliers. Other than finding the biggest cockroach I had ever seen in my life, I had no luck with finding anything that would be useful. I pictured that the Command Sergeant Major – if he was witnessing this event – was having a cow. He hated MP's. During my search for the pliers, the revelry was playing over and over again and people were standing outside, saluting the flag in the rain and getting soaked to the bone. Next, I went across the street the MP barrack. I first checked with the CQ to see if he had any pliers. No luck. The supply room was closed in the basement, so I began knocking on doors. I knocked on ten doors before I found somebody who had a pair of needle nose pliers. I took those and ran back outside, marching back over to the flagpole. Using the needle nose pliers, I loosened the clasps, assisted with folding, then signaled for the cannon to be fired, which was the signal that the ceremony was complete. I then marched the other MPs back to headquarters where we stored the flag and laughed about the whole event. From that day forward, whenever I was on gate guard duty, I always made sure, I had a pair of pliers with me in case something like that happened again. The Command Sergeant Major had not witnessed the event, as he had left post. To my surprise, nobody questioned me about what happened. I thought that somebody would have been mad, having to stand out in the rain for ten minutes while saluting a flag. A normal ceremony took two minutes. But nothing was ever said, and nothing ever got back to the Command Sergeant Major; otherwise, he would have used it as an excuse to chew out Captain Taylor about how incompetent the MPs were.

Meanwhile, besides working gate guard duty, I was still working patrol duty once in a while. One night I was assigned to work with Sistrunk. He had been in the Army for almost a year longer than I had been. He had been stationed at Miesau, too, prior to transferring to BK. He used to be Woody's roommate at Miesau when Woody still lived on post. Sistrunk often came back to visit and would come stay at Woody's apartment, where I usually hung out, too. One night Woody and I had arrived at his apartment after finishing a 12-hour shift when Sistrunk showed up. He told us he had this great money making deal that was going to make us all a fortune. He then took a package out of his coat pocket. The package was about twice the size of a deck of cards and was wrapped in tin foil. He unwrapped the tin foil and showed us what it was. Woody's eyes got huge.

"What is it?" I asked out of ignorance. Woody and Sistrunk laughed like I had made a joke, but I did not know what it was.

"It is hash," Sistrunk said, "and this is just the beginning. This is a sample of it."

"Where did you get it?" Woody asked.

"You know the owners of the Mystical Disco?" Sistrunk asked. Woody nodded like he knew them. Mystical Disco was a favorite Disco hang out outside of Miesau. I did not care much for Disco and had been there three previous times in a drunken stupor with nothing better to do. Woody hung out there all the time. "Well, they gave it to me to sample. They want us to sell it for them. We can make a fortune."

"Are you crazy?" I asked. "I'm not going to deal drugs."

"He's right," Woody agreed. "We can get busted big time for dealing."

"Let's try it," Sistrunk begged, packing it into a pipe.

"We'll try it," Woody said, "but no way are we selling drugs." Sistrunk lit the pipe, took a puff off of it, and passed it to Woody. Woody took a puff and passed it to me. This was my first and last time that I smoked hash. We were sitting at the kitchen table when I took a puff. The next thing I knew, I was sitting on the couch hallucinating. A poster of the rock band Scorpion hung on the living room wall and the members of the band were talking to me. Meanwhile a stack of empty beer cans sat against the far wall of the living room, and one at a time a can would dart across the living room and back to its spot in the stack of cans.

"Woody," I said, "If I try to fly out the window, grab hold of my legs. As a child, my mother told me that the original TV superman died, having smoked some dope and while hallucinating thought he could fly and jumped off the roof of a building." Woody and Sistrunk laughed their heads off at that, thinking it was hilarious. "Seriously," I told them, "I'm seeing some weird things, so don't let me fly out the window."

"Hey let's go get something to eat in Kaiserslautern," Woody suggested. The next thing I knew, we were driving down the autobahn at eighty miles per hour. I let Woody drive because he did not seem to be hallucinating quite as bad as I was. I was in the back seat looking at the occupants of other vehicles as they passed by, convinced that they were out to get us. I was paranoid.

"Why are those people laughing at us?" I asked as every car passed. People were beginning to look like Mister Potato Heads. It was the grace of God that we were not in an accident where we were all killed ourselves or innocent people. At the restaurant, I was convinced that everybody in the entire restaurant was laughing at us. The truth is we were high and making asses of ourselves, ruining their dining experience. I was afraid to order any food as the paranoia got worse. About this same time I felt a ringing tone in the top of my head that was driving me crazy. I was convinced that this whole experience was going to leave me permanently brain damaged and that if the ringing that seemed to originate at the back of my skull on top of my head did not stop, that it would not be long before I killed people out of frustration. I do not remember leaving the restaurant. The next thing I remember was waking up the next day on the couch back at our apartment. I had a major headache. From that day forward, I never did drugs again. The whole hallucination thing was an awful experience. When Woody and Sistrunk woke up, I questioned them both about it, asking if that hash made them hallucinate, too.

"I don't think it was the hash that made us hallucinate," Sistrunk said. I think it was the Angel dust that was laced in the hash."

"You put Angel Dust in the hash?" Woody asked. "You asshole. Why didn't you tell us?"

"I didn't put it in there," Sistrunk said. The owners of the club did. They said it is high in demand and that we will be given a percentage of the profits if we sell the hash for them."

"Were not selling any drugs," I said.

"I told them we would sell it for them," Sistrunk said.

"You did what?" Woody asked. "We are so dead. They will kill us if we don't sell them."

"You mean they will kill Sistrunk," I said. "We aren't involved in this."

"You guys have to help me," he said. "Go with me back to the club tonight and I'll tell them we can't sell it for them." We agreed to accompany him, arriving at the club at 10 pm, expecting the place to be packed, as was the case every night of the week. However, the place was closed and looked deserted with the exterior lights off and the interior lights dimmed.

"You did tell them we were coming tonight, didn't you Sistrunk?" I asked.

"Yes, they're expecting us," Sistrunk said.

"Oh, crap," Woody said, laughing. "We are so dead." We got out of my car and attempted to go in through the front door, but the doors were locked. We knocked on the door. "Man this is odd. It looks like nobody is here. What the hell is going on?" A man opened the front door and gestured for us to come in. The three of us were escorted to a table in the center of the club. It was dark and hard to see. I had never been in the club except when it was packed shoulder to shoulder with people. We sat down at the table with three other Germans who were the owners of the club. They recognized Woody and seemed happy to seem him. Woody seemed to be the most popular person everywhere he went. Sistrunk and these three people bantered back and forth in German. I was quite impressed with how well Sistrunk spoke German. The three men looked angry. At one point, Woody and I made eye contact while watching the conversation between Sistrunk and these men. When the conversation became heated, as Sistrunk handed the three men the remainder of the hash by sliding it across the table to them, Woody mouthed to me, so I alone could see it, "we are going to die." They picked up the package, gesturing towards the door, indicating for us to leave, cussing at Sistrunk in German. We jumped in my car and sped back to the apartment. Woody and I were quite pissed at Sistrunk.

Now here it was five months later, I ended up being transferred to the same place as Sistrunk and we were on patrol duty as partners. Even though Sistrunk had been in the Army for almost a year longer than I, he outranked me by two days as a Specialist, so that made him the senior partner. As such, when we had been assigned to drive the VW Van as a patrol car, he insisted on driving. That evening, we were exiting the main part of the base after having eaten dinner. It was windy outside with a cold rain falling. We were a block from the main gate of the base when Sistrunk saw a black soldier walking down the street with his hands in his pockets, trying to keep them warm. He was walking back to his barracks, which were about two blocks outside the main part of the base. Sistrunk veered the van towards him.

"Watch me fuck with this, Nigger," he said and stopped the van right behind him. I was puzzled as to what Sistrunk was doing, as the guy was walking down the street, causing no trouble. In fact, I had seen him eating in the chow hall when we were eating. Sistrunk rolled down his window and yelled, "Hey soldier, come here," motioning the guy over to the van. As he stepped up to the door, Sistrunk explained to him that it was against the Uniform Code of Military Justice for a soldier to walk down the street with his hands in his pockets, so he was under arrest. I sat in the passenger side of the van unable to believe what I was hearing. I had no idea Sistrunk was so bigoted that he was hassling this black soldier for having his hands in his trouser pockets on a cold, wet day.

"You've got to be kidding," the guy said as he turned to walk away. At that Sistrunk opened up the driver's side of the van and jumped out in front him. *Oh crap*, I thought. *Trouble.* I jumped out of the van, too, having been left with no choice, but to back up Sistrunk. I stood behind the soldier off to his side and noticed dozens of people watching from the windows inside of this guy's barrack. I knew things were going to get ugly.

"I'm ordering you to take your hands out of your pockets," Sistrunk said. "Or else, I am placing you under arrest for a Uniform Code violation."

"Just try to arrest me, then," the guy said, attempting to sidestep Sistrunk. Grabbing his handcuffs with one hand and the guy's forearm with another hand, Sistrunk pushed the guy up against the side of the van.

"Spread your legs," Sistrunk said. I then noticed that nobody was looking out the windows any longer, instead people were running out of the front of the barrack towards us yelling and screaming. I was wearing a walkie-talkie and grabbed the microphone and called for assistance. That action probably saved lives for as soon as Sistrunk pushed the guy up against the van, he took his hands out of his pockets and started swinging wildly. I jumped in and grabbed him from behind. Meanwhile dozens of people surrounded us, grabbing at us as we tried to subdue the soldier. Within seconds, back up patrol cars were arriving one after the other. Some people took off running while others stood and fought as the other MPs helped to break up the mob so that Sistrunk and I were able to get the handcuffs on the guy. People from the crowd were yelling that we had arrested him for no reason at all. I agreed with them, but I could not join them in beating up Sistrunk. As an MP we had to rely on each other for protection under all circumstances. We ended up taking the guy back to the station where he was charged with disobeying a lawful order and disorderly conduct. I was disgusted and wanted more than ever to beat Sistrunk's ass. This was twice now that he had endangered my life. The next morning I went downstairs into the office where all the squad leaders had their desks. I asked Sistrunk' squad leader and my squad leader if I could speak to them in private about the incident that took place the night before.

"Hey, we heard about that," my squad leader said. "I heard you and Sistrunk did great, handling that riot last night. We were talking about that this morning." My squad leader and Sistrunk's squad leader were black. I did not quite know how to tell them that the whole incident was racially motivated. Technically in the right, the reason Sistrunk did what he did was not because he was trying to enforce the law. According to his words, he wanted to "harass the Nigger." It all happened at lightning speed, and I reacted with how I was trained and that was to back up my partner. However, I felt ashamed of the whole thing and felt embarrassed to be telling these two men what had happened. I found the best way to tell them was to tell them the whole story as I witnessed it. At first, they looked at me in disbelief. As I told them the events of what happened, the disbelief seemed to turn to anger. I could not tell if the anger was due to Sistrunk's bigotry causing a riot or whether they were angry because I was ratting out a fellow MP. After I finished telling them the whole chain of events, they both looked a little hurt by it all and did not seem to know what to do.

"I don't know what can be done, if anything at all," Sistrunk' squad leader said.

"Nobody enforces that code," I said. "That was an excuse to harass that guy."

"You know it is going to be your word against his word, don't you?" My squad leader asked.

"Of course," I said, "but I can tell you, now, if you ever put me back on patrol duty while Sistrunk is working patrol, I will refuse to be his partner, and I will not back him up on any calls. The guy should be barred from ever again working any patrol duty. We could have been killed along with any of the other MP's who responded to our call for back up help. Not to mention, people in the riot could have been killed if back up had not arrived. Sistrunk is a danger to be on patrol."

"Will you fill out a sworn affidavit to everything you told us?" my squad leader asked.

"No problem," I said. I spent the next hour writing down what happened. When I was done, they told me they would turn the papers over to the captain for further investigation. The investigation did not take long. Before the end of the day, the duty roster was changed. To no surprise, Sistrunk had been removed from patrol duty. However, to my shock, I, too, was removed from patrol duty. From that day forward, Sistrunk and I were two of the people who were continuously assigned to gate guard duty. My squad leader said Sistrunk was pissed off about being removed from patrol duty and that the Captain never gave him an explanation as to why, so that there would be no retaliation against me for ratting him out. The Captain must have been tired of my stunts and pulled me from patrol duty, too, or that was my punishment for being a rat.

About the same time that I was pulled from patrol duty, Sanders, was tired of working the gate and wanted more action. So, in exchange for extending his three-year active duty enlistment by six months, they transferred him to Baumholder, Germany, where he was assigned to the Central Intelligence Department and began working and training as a detective. Baumholder had a reputation for being a hellhole. It had over twenty thousand infantry people stationed there and three hundred MP's. It offered a lot more excitement than BK, which had mainly officers and their families stationed there. Also about this time, Rogers began having an affair with an Army officer's wife. He had met her while on gate guard duty. She saw him as she came on post and had the hots for him. This affair would later be the cause of him requesting a transfer to Baumholder, too.

Meanwhile, I was getting in more trouble every day, which, also, led to me being transferred to Baumholder at the same time as Rogers. My additional troubles were due to my rebellious attitude. For instance, one day, while working gate guard duty, the Command Sergeant Major entered the base. He glared at me. Then he came walking over to me where I was standing right outside the door of the gate guard shack. "Soldier," he yelled, reminding me of some of the drill sergeants in basic training. "When was the last time you had a haircut?"

"I cannot remember the exact date, Command Sergeant Major," I said. My last hair cut was about one year earlier while I was still stationed at Miesau. I never liked the way I looked in an Army hair cut. One day I told my squad leader that until the Army started paying me extra money to get a haircut on a monthly basis that I was no longer going to get a haircut. He looked at me like I was nuts.

"Why," he asked, "would the Army pay you extra money to get a haircut?" I explained to him my reasoning, which was quite simple. The Army paid women soldiers extra money every month to purchase personal hygiene items, such as tampons and other personal items because those were things that women soldiers needed, but men soldiers did not. It was my argument that men were required to get haircuts, monthly and to shave daily, things women were not required to do, so men should get extra money to pay for a haircut and to pay for shaving cream and razor blades. I informed my squad leader that until the Army started paying men extra money for monthly haircuts that I would no longer be getting a haircut. I told him that as soon as I get out of the military, I planned on filing a discrimination suit against the Army. My squad leader, knowing how stubborn I could be, shook his head and told me to do whatever I wanted, but do not expect help from him if I got busted. So, here it was a year later and nobody had, yet, called me out on the carpet about the length of my hair until now. One reason nobody harassed me about it before now was because whenever I went on duty, I would slick it back and hold it in place behind my ears with hair gel. But now it was also hanging down below my collar. In addition, the Command Sergeant Major was always looking for any reason to harass an MP.

"Well, soldier, you are going to get a haircut, today," he said storming off, not giving me a chance to tell him that I was not going to get a haircut. Less than five minutes later, Captain Taylor came strolling out to the gate guard shack. He did not look happy. The Command Sergeant Major did not call him to report that I needed a haircut; nor did he direct him to send somebody to relieve me from duty, so that I could go get a haircut. Instead he chewed him out for allowing me to work with a non-regulation haircut. But it did not end there. The Command Sergeant Major ordered Captain Taylor to personally relieve me from duty and to work my shift while I got a haircut.

"If I get a haircut, it may affect a future lawsuit for discrimination against the Army," I explained to him, messing with his mind. He looked like he wanted to cry. He begged if I would at least go get a trim. I agreed to that because I felt sorry for him. He said he would send somebody out to relieve me from the gate in a few minutes and for me to proceed directly over to the barbershop, as he had no intention of pulling gate guard duty despite what the Command Sergeant Major ordered. I went to the barbershop, got a short trim, and went back and finished my shift. I thought for sure that the Command Sergeant Major would come and check my haircut, blowing a gasket when he saw how long it still was. But he did not. I could not believe that my rebellious attitude was not getting me in trouble. When I told my superiors that I was going to sue the government for discrimination and not get a haircut, that was all a bunch of bull, as I knew I would not win, never mind the fact that I would never be able to afford a lawyer for such a lawsuit either. My real reason was that I did not want to get a haircut. I thought for sure they could see that. Either way, no matter what my reason was, I expected to get in trouble for refusing to conform. However, it seemed everybody was bending over backgrounds not to displease me. It later became known to me that a secret investigation was going on for the first four months that I was at BK. When the investigation was complete and charges were filed, I understood why I was getting away with so much rebellion. About a week before I arrived at BK, one of the MP's picked up a girl at a disco bar and brought her back to the barracks. He handcuffed her to his bed and raped her. Of course he was arguing that it was consensual sex and that he had no idea that she was fourteen. He may have gotten away with it if the story ended there. But it did not. After he had "consensual sex" with the girl, one at a time, over the course of several days, sixty other MP's had "consensual sex" with the girl. She was handcuffed to the bed the whole time. When she was released and the authorities were notified, nobody was arrested and the whole investigation was kept secret. The Central Intelligence Division interviewed people over the next few months, gathered evidence, and eventually arrested and charged sixty MP's with the girl's rape a few weeks after I was relieved from gate guard duty and told to go get a haircut. The Captain and his staff, of course, knew all about the investigation from the start and knew it looked bad for those involved and knew once charges were filed it would get worse. Once the charges were filed all sixty MP's were confined to the barracks while awaiting trial and were not allowed to leave except to go to the chow hall. None of them were allowed to pull duty of any kind except for work around the barracks. The Captain was in a huge bind. So everybody who had not been involved in the rape was essential and that much more important. So, a little rebellion was overlooked. Though I still had not been given any more patrol duty, I was put in charge of all the gate guard shifts that I worked, long hair and all.

I was also assigned to work another special mission. The duty was being on standby for the Space Shuttle. Every time it blasted off for space, MP crews at bases around the world were put on standby alert. During the launching and the landing of the space shuttle, a crew of twelve in BK was assigned to Stand By Alert. That required us to report downstairs in the lounge with our weapons, ammunition and all our gear and be ready to be deployed if for some reason the shuttle had to do an emergency landing or in case it crashed somewhere during the launching or re-entry. From our location in BK, if the space shuttle landed anywhere in Europe, we were to be on a helicopter within minutes, flying to the crash to set up a secure perimeter around the shuttle, and at all cost, prevent it from falling into enemy hands. We were told that even if the shuttle crashed in the middle of Red Square in the Soviet Union, we would be going in after it. We had to report for duty an hour before launch time, with our weapons, ammunition, and gear, while wearing our nuclear, biological, chemical (NBC) suits with our gas masks strapped to our sides in the gas mask case. We had to wear our NBC suits in case we were deployed, as it was equipped with deadly gases that would be disbursed to kill anybody within a close radius so that it would not fall into enemy hands. A year after I got out of the Army was when the first space shuttle blew up during take off and all of the Shuttle parts landed in the ocean. The most recent incident in which the shuttle blew apart during re-entry was over land and the government put out a warning that if anybody was caught trying to keep pieces of the shuttle, they would be prosecuted. The punishment was quite severe. That was one way for the government to scare people from trying to scavenger for pieces of the shuttle that poised a threat of dispersing poisonous gases. When on the Stand By Alert team, if deployed, our job would have been to set up a perimeter around the shuttle, using any means of deadly force necessary to keep unauthorized people away until other teams could remove or destroy the shuttle before the enemy obtained it. While waiting for the shuttle to launch or to land, we had to remain in the lounge area where food was brought to us, as sometimes the launch was delayed for hours and the twelve of us would be sitting around this tiny room wearing our nuclear suits, sweating like dogs. Once the launch took place and the shuttle was in orbit, we were free to remove our nuclear suits. We had to sign in and out of the barracks, being allowed to leave to go to the chow hall or to do a supervised chore. The shuttle never crashed or blew up while I was in the military.

Two days after having been relieved of duty at the gate in order to get a hair cut, we were scheduled to take a test given by the Army that is used to determine whether or not we could be promoted in the future to the ranks of Sergeant or higher. The Army was trying to improve the training of the soldiers and wanted every soldier to take the test. It was called the SQT, which stood for Standard Quality Testing and measured our overall knowledge as a soldier. If we did not get a passing score on the test, we would be ineligible for future promotions. The higher our rank, the more detailed knowledge we had to know, and the higher our score had to be. Our commanders at BK were making us work during off time and then ordered us to sign papers stating we participated in training that day. When it came time to take the test, I refused. My platoon sergeant ordered me to take the test. I refused. I was then sent to see our Lieutenant who threatened that I would be given an Article 15. I told him I would not sign an Article 15 and that I would prefer a court-martial. He then backed down telling me that if I did not take the test, the Army would have no choice but to bar me from re-enlisting.

"I'm not stupid enough to want to re-enlist in the Army," I told him. He was pissed and walked out of the room to confer with Captain Taylor. After a few minutes he came back into the room and handed me a blank affidavit to sign. He said I could fill out the affidavit stating why I did not want to take the test and it would go on my permanent record and I was blocked from re-enlisting in the military. "Thank you, sir," I said, "that's the best news I have heard in a long time." He gave me a look like he wanted to kill me, but knew better than to risk his career. I completed the affidavit, stating that since the Army was relying heavily on the test to determine who was available for promotion, and since the commanders at the 8th MP Company felt it was more important to have us do chores rather than training (though ordering us to sign attendance documents, stating we had attended a class), I was refusing to take the test. I stated that by taking the test I would show how much knowledge I was lacking – not because I was stupid, but because I was never trained. By not taking the test, people would never know whether I knew the knowledge or not.

All they would know is that I refused to take the test. Since I thrashed the 8th MP commanders, I thought they would throw the affidavit away, thinking they would not be dumb enough to put it in my permanent record where it could incriminate them of wrongdoing. But before I left the military, I found otherwise. The rationale for them putting it into my record is that they either did not read what I wrote or did not care, thinking it was too unimportant to ever come back and haunt them.

When they threatened me with charges of disobeying an order to take the test, I called their bluff, asking for a court martial, so that the false records about us being given training would come out in the open. They dropped the matter. In fact, I do not know if it was punishment or reward for standing up to them, but I was promoted to Acting Sergeant. Acting Sergeant meant that I was given the stripes of a Sergeant, but was not paid for it. In their mind it was punishment because they also pulled from all duty, including barracks duty. I was reassigned to being one of three CQ's. In BK a CQ was on duty at all times. It is an official sounding title. The CQ keeps a log of all events that take place, takes messages, signs people in and out for passes, and a whole bunch of other miscellaneous duties like answering incoming calls. Most people were assigned CQ on a temporary basis, for example, one guy was CQ for about six months while recovering from a broken leg, and he could not do any other duty. I was being assigned CQ duty on a permanent basis. They told me I could be CQ for the rest of my time in Germany. While still stationed at Miesau, when I had put in for my transfer for White hat duty, I requested stateside assignment. Instead I was transferred to BK. Little did I know I would soon receive orders to transfer to the States to Fort Hood, Texas. But at the time I was assigned to CQ duty, I did not know a transfer was coming and although I was being given CQ duty as punishment for my rebellion in going AWOL once a month, terrorizing the Captain's secretary by threatening to shoot him, turning in a fellow MP for being racist, refusing to get a haircut, and refusing to take the SQT test, I liked the idea of spending the rest of my time in the military working as a CQ in BK. Each CQ worked a 24-hour shift followed by 48 hours off with no extra duty. While on duty, I wore the rank of sergeant, thus the title of Acting Sergeant. But when not on duty, I wore my assigned rank, which for me was Specialist, one rank and one pay grade below a Sergeant. Even though the CQ duty was for a 24-hour shift, on weekdays, we did not have to report for duty until 5 pm and we worked until 8 am the next morning. On weekends we had to pull a full 24-hour shift, unless of course, our 48 hours off happened to fall on that weekend. Then we had the entire weekend off. I loved it. I was adjusting to my off-post apartment and liked having the 48 hours off to work out. I was also doing a lot of reading. When I was back at Miesau, another MP attempted to get me to attend a weekly Wednesday night Bible study with him. He was always trying to recruit people to join him at the Bible study. One Wednesday night when I was off, he cornered me as I came back from dinner. I could not think of an excuse and wound up going to Bible study with him. Miesau had five-hundred people stationed there and the Bible study consisted of three other people besides me. They held the study in a room at the gymnasium. I did not have a Bible, so one of the men gave me a Catholic Bible. As soon as the Bible study was over, I could not get out of there fast enough. As most people do with their Bibles, I put it away and did not read it. My family was Catholic, and up to the age of ten years old, we attended church every Sunday. After that my mother decided to give my brothers and me the choice to choose for ourselves whether we wanted to go to church or not. Of course, we chose to stay home and watch football games or play. In other words, we were not a religious family. Now that I was the owner of a Bible, it struck me funny that during all the years that we did attend church, I never once heard a priest or nun mention the Bible. Going to church, I had the impression that the priest was the most holy man to walk the face of the earth and was equivalent to God. I remember the church performed a lot of rituals, which I did not understand. One time when I was about five or six, I was at church with my aunt and while we were kneeling a bell rang. It was barely audible. Next thing I knew, my aunt slapped me across my face so hard, my cheek burned and tears welled up in my eyes. "Whenever you hear that bell ring, you're supposed to put your hand over your heart," she told me. Believe me; I did not want to be slapped like that again, so I made sure to put my hand over my heart whenever the bell rang. To this day, I have no idea what that stupid gesture symbolizes. The rituals of the Catholic Church made little sense to me. They reminded me of some of the rituals that the Army did, too. For instance, saluting a flag during revelry or every time you passed one made little sense to me either. *If you don't salute the flag, will it know?* With all my free time on CQ duty, I started reading the Bible for the first time in my life. I read it from front to back and it left me with many concerns regarding the lack of spirituality in organized religions. As a result of reading the Bible and coming to the conclusion that religion and all their rituals are different than spirituality, I refused to salute a flag (citing religious preferences) for the remainder of my time in the military, thus becoming even more rebellious. My sergeant tried to convince me that not saluting the flag could lead to serious trouble, but I refused to do so the rest of my time in the military.

Another incident that stirred up trouble was during one of my shifts on CQ duty. With the rape of the 14-year old girl having taken a lot of people off the duty roster, and with all the people leaving the unit when their enlistment was up, we were short-handed. Then a murder of a 20-year old German woman who lived in BK had people hopping. Captain Taylor volunteered our unit to help the German Polizei do searches in fields and forests to look for her body. All available personnel who were not working patrol duty or gate guard duty or who were not restricted to base due to a pending rape trial were sent out during the days to search all day long. This went on all week long and her body was never located. That Friday night as I came on to CQ duty, Captain Taylor instructed me not to bother waking anybody up on Saturday or Sunday morning at the usual 8 am to do barracks clean up. He said he would allow them the weekend off from barracks duty since everybody had been working so hard. For a Friday night, the CQ shift was quiet. I did not have to reprimand anybody for being disorderly due to drunkenness, loud parties, and property destruction. My CQ runner and I were able to take our usual naps.

Each CQ was assigned a CQ runner – somebody in the unit who could not do normal duty due to an injury. The CQ runner assisted the CQ to do physical checks of the premises or check on problems in the barracks as they arose. Thus they were called a CQ runner. Whenever I was working CQ, I would let my CQ Runner go to the lounge and go to sleep for the first part of the evening. If I needed them, I could wake them, as the lounge was to the left of the CQ desk, which was in the basement right at the bottom of the stairs and was the first thing seen upon entering the barracks. As the CQ, I would sit at the desk and read books, do pushups, and sometimes go on rounds while the CQ runner manned the CQ desk so I could check out the condition of the barracks and make sure the fires were extinguished and that damage was minimal. When we first came on duty as the CQ, we were supposed to do an inspection of the barracks and choose whether or not to relieve the other CQ. If the barracks was dirty or damaged, we could choose to decline the responsibility of CQ duty until the issue was addressed. Then we notated the condition of the barracks in the CQ logbook and let the other CQ leave. On weekdays, the other CQ left nine hours before at 8 am, so by the time the evening shift started at 5 pm, we did a quick visual inspection, logged in as CQ and started our shift. By 2 am, when the Armed Forces TV would go off the air, I would wake my runner from his sleep in the lounge and have him stay at the front desk, while I slept. I told him to wake me if any problems arose. I did not want to lay down in the lounge, so I would drag out a lazy boy chair from the lounge to sleep in, moving it to the front desk. Well, the night the Captain told me not to wake the Company up for morning cleaning, he also told me not to call him at home under any circumstances, so I was glad things were quiet that night. With all of the extra duty people had to do during the MP shortage and with half the MP's waiting to stand trial for rape, morale was at an all time low, and nobody felt like partying. About 2 am, I unzipped my boots, un-tucked and unbuttoned my shirt, turned the TV down to low, turned the radio on, and conked out in the lazy boy chair. I was snoozing and so apparently so was my runner. The next thing I knew, somebody woke me up by kicking the bottom of my boots.

"What the fu—" I started to say but stopped short when I opened my eyes to see the Command Sergeant Major standing in front of me with a snarl on his face and both hands on his hips?

"Who is in charge here?" he demanded to know.

"I'm the CQ in charge," I said answering back.

"Sergeant, this barracks is a mess," he said. "What the hell has been going here? I want you to wake every swinging dick in this building and get them to clean this mess." I glanced at the time on the clock while standing up. It was 7 am.

"Command Sergeant Major," I said addressing him while tucking my shirt back in and buttoning it up. "Captain Taylor gave me strict orders to let everybody sleep in this weekend."

"I don't give a damn what your Captain told you, soldier," he said. "I inspected these barracks inside and outside and there is trash everywhere. You get your Captain on the phone right now and tell him to get his ass down here right now. You let the troops sleep in as he said. I'm going to come back here in an hour and if Captain Taylor isn't personally cleaning this barrack, I'm going to bring the wrath of God down on this place. Do you understand?"

"Yes, Command Sergeant Major," I said, turning the radio and TV off. He then turned and marched out the building. I could not believe he did not say anything about my hair this time. By now my hair was longer than it had been on the day he had me relieved from gate guard duty. But he did not remember me and was finding more enjoyment in humiliating a Captain than in badgering some peon enlisted man.

"Crap," I said, pushing my runner who was standing next to me. "What the hell are you doing falling asleep? You were supposed to be covering for me. Damn, Taylor's going to be pissed. Go start waking everybody up and get them on cleaning details."

"But the Command Sergeant Major said Captain Taylor should clean," my runner reminded me.

"Do you want to wake Taylor and tell him that?" I asked. "I sure as hell do not. Hold on. I'm going to call him." I picked up the phone and dialed Captain Taylor's house.

"What the hell does that son-of-a-bitch asshole want now?" Captain Taylor yelled on the other end of the phone. It was obvious he had been awakened by the call.

"Sir, the Command Sergeant Major came and inspected the barracks and is insisting that the barracks be cleaned up within the hour."

"That son-of-a-bitch," he said. "Okay, wake everybody up and have them clean, then let them have the rest of the weekend off."

"Sir," I said, "the Command Sergeant Major said he wants you to personally clean the building. He said when he comes back in an hour that if you aren't cleaning, he will bring the wrath of God down upon us." Taylor went into a tirade, ranting and raving about the Command Sergeant Major being sick in the head and that no way in hell he was going to clean anything. In between the cuss words, he told me to wake everybody up and have them clean and that he would deal with the Command Sergeant Major on Monday morning. I sent the CQ runner up to wake everybody up. Meanwhile, knowing my relief would arrive within an hour, I sat back down in my lazy boy chair and took it easy. When my relief came, I briefed him on the situation and told him what Taylor had ordered and I left. I did not give a damn, as I had forty-eight hours off coming, so I headed over to the chow hall, ate some breakfast, and then rode my bike back to my little hotel room, where I went to sleep. *What a life. I had it made.*

Why I kept doing things to get in trouble, I don't know for sure. Maybe I was fed up with all the false promises made by the Army recruiter, the false records made in basic training, the low morale at the nuclear site created from boredom in security duty, the false records created at BK, the politics, and the games played by people like the Command Sergeant Major, who found pleasure in making other people miserable. Not to mention, we were told that the majority of American Soldier deaths in Vietnam were not due to combat injuries suffered during battles with the enemy, but due to inadequate training and misuse of the weaponry. These were classified as "friendly fire" deaths. With the way the military falsified training records, I could see why people did not know how to use the weaponry and accidental deaths occurred. In addition, I met people who served in Vietnam who claimed that American Soldiers purposefully shot and killed other American Soldiers because they did not like the other person. These, too, were classified as "friendly fire," but never as murder. So, why I did what I did next, I guess I was bored and had low morale and liked to mess with the minds of my ranking superiors as a way of protesting all the crap.

The incident occurred during a big inspection. Prior to the inspection, I took the single souvenir I had from Miesau -- a red table cloth that I stole from the NCO club one night when I was drunk -- and hung it from my wall above my bunk with signs attached to the wall that said "Better Red Than Dead," and "Go Big Red." I was not there during the inspection, but eyewitnesses who were said Top nearly almost had a heart attack when he and the colonel entered the room and saw the signs with the red table cloth on the wall. They said Top began shaking uncontrollably and veins popped out of his neck and forehead. The inspection came to a halt, Top called for a company formation in front of our building. I was walking back from lunch when I heard the call to assemble. In all my time at BK we had never had a Company formation before. Top stood in front of the Company still shaken and beat red – probably from his blood pressure at an all time high. He said he was humiliated when the colonel inspected that room. "I do not know who is responsible for this, but whoever bunks in that room, I want to see them in my office immediately. In my opinion that was an act of treason. Somebody is going to be doing some hard time in Leavenworth for this. I think you know who you are and what I'm talking about. If you do not know what I'm talking about, then this does not apply to you, so leave it at that. Whoever is responsible, I want to see you in my office within five minutes." I was in big trouble. I knew he was talking about my red flag, so I followed Top from the formation straight back to his office.

"Top," I said, ready to confess. "Somebody told me it was the red table cloth in my room that you were referring to in the company formation."

"Does that commie flag bullshit propaganda belong to you?" he asked. "I tell you, I have never seen a man so upset in my life as the colonel was when he saw that commie flag on your wall with those signs. Nothing I can do will save your butt over this. You're going to be court martialed. There won't be any offer of an Article 15. This is as close to treason as you can get. Do you want to explain to me why you did it?" *Great*, I thought. *My second threat of a court martial in two months. First the threat of a court martial over refusing to take the SQT test and now a court martial for hanging a red table cloth on the wall. How stupid was I for getting into these dilemmas?*

"Top," I said, looking puzzled at him. "I do not understand why the colonel would be so upset about me being a Nebraska Cornhusker football fan. Why would I be court-martialed for that? Is it illegal to be a fan of the Cornhuskers?"

"The Cornhuskers? Are you from Nebraska?"

"I'm from Colorado, but I like the Cornhuskers," I lied, as anybody who is a fan of Colorado Buffalo football, as I was, despises everything about the Nebraska Cornhuskers. "They're my favorite team. Red is their color. Would you like me to go explain things to the colonel?"

"No, do not dare speak to that man, right now. I had a hard enough time calming him down when he saw what we both assumed to be communist propaganda." I had a hard time keeping the smirk off my face. Top was still shaking when he dismissed me. I did not hear another word about the incident. However, before the week was out, Rogers, Randall, and I were all called down to Top's office and we were asked to transfer to another platoon located in Baumholder, Germany. By this time, Sanders had been stationed in Baumholder for a few months, working as a detective for the Central Intelligence Division. He loved it there, saying the duty was non-stop excitement. I loved the duty I was pulling as CQ; it was too good to be true. Plus, I, now, loved my off-post apartment, so I did not want to transfer. Rogers wanted to transfer to Baumholder because the affair he was having with the married woman was turning ugly and rumor was that officers around the base had heard about it, which was an embarrassment to the company. Randall was open to the idea of transferring, too, because he was not the most popular guy in BK. He had a bad reputation for not taking showers. People claimed he stunk. I was born without the ability to smell, a condition called Anosmia, so I could not smell him, so his body odor did not bother me. Other than that, I knew nothing about the guy, other than to me he looked like Sergeant Carter on the TV show, Gomer *Pyle*. When asked if we wanted to transfer to Baumholder, it was presented in such a way that we did not have any choice. We all three transferred to Baumholder on July 21, 1981.

I learned a few years ago that at the time I was stationed in Baumholder, so, too, was the late, infamous, serial-killer, Jeffrey Dahmer. Sanders was one of two detectives dispatched to two separate suicides at the barracks of a medical unit in Baumholder. The deaths were classified as self-inflicted drug overdoses, but at the time Sanders told me he was suspicious about both of them, but had no evidence to prove that they were anything other than suicide. Sanders had questioned other people in the unit and was suspicious about one of them. He said that person was Jeffrey Dahmer. Of course, this was years before Dahmer had been convicted of murder. But it is of no surprise that before torturing and killing his victims, he drugged them and then tried to perform partial lobotomies on them in an attempt to keep them in a zombie like state of mind. Perhaps those two deaths in Baumholder were Dahmer's early attempts at experimenting with drugging people and in the process he overdosed them by accident or on purpose.

Baumholder was huge compared to BK. At BK we could walk from one end of the base to the other in about five minutes. Baumholder was spread out so far, it took a while to walk from one end to the other. It was hard to tell where the base ended and the town began as physical boundaries such as a wall or fence did not surround the base. It was a bunch of buildings like barracks and office buildings intermingled within the town itself. Baumholder seemed to have it all. It had all the traditional chow halls, one right across the street from my new barracks, a bowling alley, a gymnasium, a library, several strip clubs, several churches, schools, base housing and the majority of the Eighth Infantry

Division was stationed there. One thing about infantrymen (or grunts) is that they hated MPs. The Command Sergeant Major back in BK was a perfect example of that. He used his power as the senior Command Sergeant Major to make the lives of MP's miserable. It was well known that if we were out and about while off duty and encountered by grunts, we would have our ass kicked. In fact, a former MP I knew at Miesau had been busted for drugs and was reclassified to an infantry unit at Baumholder. I ran into him a few times at a chow hall. Every time I saw him, his face was swollen and black and blue from bruises, as he was beat daily in his new unit because he was a former MP. Approximately 330 MP's were stationed in Baumholder. Twenty of them were in the new platoon I was assigned to. The other MP's were assigned to another MP company. We rotated patrol duty with them on a monthly basis. For one month they would be responsible for providing patrol duty on base while our platoon of twenty would be involved in field exercises and training. Unlike at BK, when we were supposed to do training, we trained. We did not, however, do physical training. When we rotated, our platoon would be responsible for patrolling all of Baumholder for an entire month. This was nice – in my opinion – because I hated field exercises and patrol duty was the most exciting part about being an MP. It was why I joined the MP's. However, we had no time off, working 12-hour shifts either days or nights. Once in a while we worked a 12-hour shift, and then trained for field exercises after getting off with no time to change clothes, shower, or eat. By the end of the month, I was exhausted. When not working patrol, we, also, painted vehicles at the motor pool and re- qualified with our weapons. I even qualified with a bazooka, the LAW (a weapon that fires small rockets capable of taking out tanks), the M-60 machine gun, and the 50-caliber machine gun that shakes a person like a milkshake in a blender as it is firing.

The first four weeks I was at Baumholder, I worked the night shifts on patrol duty. Right from the start, the weekends were filled with action from having to arrest drunken soldiers fighting in bars or driving while impaired. The weeknights were quiet most of the time, except for a domestic dispute from time to time. The patrol area was huge and part of the patrol duties included making trips to outlying bases once per shift. When we trained during the day and then pulled a 12-hour night shift, it was hard to stay awake on some of the slow nights. But we had to turn in paperwork showing that we physically checked certain buildings on the base for locked doors and windows. Just like in BK, it was impossible to check every door and window, so we did a drive-by inspection and forged our paperwork. The problem with fudging our paperwork like that was Sergeant Howard. He was a strange man. I thought he was crazy. The rumor was that while in Vietnam, he was on a helicopter that was shot down. When the helicopter crashed, his skull was crushed and they had to put several metal plates into his head to hold it together, so it was said he did not have all of his mental faculties firing on all cylinders. I do not know if any of this was true or if he really was crazy, but I like to think he was crazy because if he was not, he was the meanest, most obnoxious asshole in the world. Sergeant Howard was the highest-ranking Sergeant on night patrol, so he was in charge. At the end of the night he would question every document I turned in, asking, if I checked the doors and windows. "Am I going to find them locked like you said on your report?"

"How am I supposed to know?" I answered. "They were locked at the time I checked. But the possibility exists that somebody could have entered the building since then and exited through a door or a window that is now unlocked. In fact, somebody could be breaking in as we speak." *What else could I tell the guy, the truth?*

"Wrong answer," Howard would say. "If I go to the high school right now and find an unsecured door or window, I'm going to bring you up on charges of forgery. So, it is your choice, before you get off work, do you want to go and do a perimeter check of the high school and re-do your form or do you want to risk me going out and checking the perimeter myself."

"You can do whatever you want to do," I answered back, "but I can tell you one thing for sure, I'm not doing another perimeter check for two reasons; one, we already did a check of the building, and if it has become unsecured since that time that is out of our control; and, two I did not forge anything. I was ordered by a superior to complete the form as you now see it. So bring me up on charges if you want because I doubt they would stick."

"I was not born yesterday," Howard said. "You better hope I don't double check all your work." So, I knew right from the start that Sergeant Howard did not like me and he seemed to have it in for me. I had transferred to Baumholder labeled as a troublemaker.

On my fourth night working patrol, Howard accused me of a heinous crime. I was assigned to patrol with Sergeant Brown, and after we turned in our paperwork after our shift, it showed that we patrolled the officer housing area of the base and found that all the houses were secure. We had patrolled it a couple of times, driving through looking for suspicious activity. We did not see any. It was a quiet night. Howard did not see it that way. He called Sergeant Brown and me into a small meeting room. Howard was sitting on top of a table in the room and motioned for us to sit down. He had our reports in his hands.

"I've looked over your reports," Howard said. "I saw a glaring lie on the page where you mentioned that the Officer Housing Area was secure. I don't think you patrolled that area at all. If you did, you were negligent. I know because I drove through that area myself right before the end of our shift and at House number 42, I discovered an unsecured tricycle on the side of the house."

"A tricycle?" I asked, looking at Sergeant Brown and then to Sergeant Howard. "How can a tricycle lying next to a house, make an area unsecure?"

"It is the tricycle itself that is unsecured," Howard said. "Once you leave something like that out in the open, you are going to tempt thieves, and before you know it, crime will be running rampant."

"You don't live on earth, do you?" I asked. Howard looked at me and shuddered like he had been blasted with cold air.

"It is you who does not live in reality," Howard responded. I guess you don't realize how much hot water you are in for forging this report, claiming the area was secure when it obviously was not."

"Can you prove that tricycle was there when we patrolled the area?" I asked. "Or perhaps it was there, but we did not see it. Either way, you are full of shit." Howard was getting pissed and Sergeant Brown was looking distressed.

"If you didn't see it, then I could charge you with negligence in duty instead of forging reports."

"We did patrol the area," Brown said. "We must have missed the tricycle."

"Go ahead and make yourself look like a fool and charge us," I said.

By this time Howard was realizing that he was not intimidating us like he had hoped, so he changed his tactics.

"I'll tell you what the two of you are going to do," Howard said. "I want you to go back out to that house, wake the occupants, and ticket them for leaving their property unsecured."

"That's bullshit," I said. "You can't be serious. You want us to give somebody a ticket for leaving a tricycle outside? Where the hell are they supposed to put it? Do you want us to ticket them for not putting their car in the house, too?"

"I do not know what type of game you're playing, Turner," Howard said, standing up shaking, "but this is the Army and you are a Military Policeman, so act like a professional and perform your duty."

"You're the one playing games, trying to screw with us," I said as I got up to walk out of the room. "If giving people tickets for tricycles is your idea of being a Military Policeman, then shove it."

"Brown, you make sure that he is the one who issues the ticket," Howard said to Brown as I walked out of the room. Brown caught up with me in the hallway.

"Turner," he said, "you have to mellow out. Let Howard play his stupid games. It makes him feel important. Don't go getting yourself an Article 15 by disrespecting him."

"How can anybody respect that dumb ass? This is bull. "Are they going to court-martial us if we don't do it? Howard would be laughed out of the Army if he brought us up on charges for something like this."

"You don't know Howard and how this company works. He could charge you for disrespecting a Non-Commissioned Officer and Failure to Obey an Order. It does not matter how stupid he is or how stupid the order is."

"This is stupid. Let's go get it over with." We went back out to our patrol car and drove back out to the house. A tricycle was leaning up against the side of the house. We knocked on the door, but nobody answered.

"What are we supposed to do, now?" I asked. "Should we set up a perimeter around the house, call for backup, shoot tear gas into the house, storm inside, and arrest the kid who left the tricycle outside?"

"I don't think we have to take it to that extreme," Sergeant Brown said. "We will write up a report that says, as ordered, we came out to the house to ticket the occupants for unsecured property, but nobody was home. We will turn that in with our paper work." We drove back to the police station. I expected Howard would still be there to mess with us, but he had left and went home and was probably in bed asleep before we started to write the last report. I could not help but think about my first day at basic training, I got yelled at by a drill sergeant for leaving my wall locker open while I was less than ten feet away from the locker. He told me I could be court-martialed for failure to protect government property and made me do twenty-five pushups. At that time, I was still gung ho about the Army and could see why a drill sergeant might play mind games like that as an opportunity to make you do pushups. But to wake up a family and give them a ticket for a tricycle was mean-spirited and an abuse of power.

From that day onward, I did not make any pretense at all to like Howard. Meanwhile, he always pretended to be everybody's friend, while always looking for a way to bust them. Under Howard's command was Corporal Gibson, my squad leader. I could never figure him out. When he was talking to me face to face, he would act like my best friend and act like he was on my side, including bad-mouthing Howard. At the same time, whenever he was around Howard, he acted like his best friend. So, I did not trust him. My suspicions were that he was a kiss ass, so I never bit into his comments about Howard by responding, as I knew anything I said would get back to Howard. This seemed to frustrate him that whenever he would make a remark about Howard, I would not respond. I remained silent as if I did not hear him. I thought he was Howard's pawn and that he was harassing me because I was not bending over and kissing Howard's ass. It felt Gibson was trying to do anything he could to provoke me to fail in order that he could get on Howard's good side. During my first week there we had a face-to-face chat in which Gibson told me I made a huge mistake by refusing to take the Army's SQT test a few month's earlier. "Tell me what you are going to do with the rest of your life after you get out of the military," Gibson said with his hands folded on his desk and a look of concern on his face.

"I plan on going to college when I leave the Army," I answered. "My plans are not definite, yet."

"I bet you're going to regret that you did not take that SQT test because I guarantee that within two years of leaving the Army, you'll find that you can't make it in the real world and you will want to re-enlist but won't be able to do so."

"I seriously doubt that I will ever want to re-enlist," I said. "Once I finish with my enlistment, I'll never come back."

"I thought the same thing," Gibson said, "but I found out that it is a lot tougher out there than what I thought. The Army offered me a career that I did not have in the real world. I don't think you're going to be able to cut it out there in the real world."

"That may be," I said. "But I don't want to make a career out of the Army, so I will never re-enlist. When people get promoted for the single reason that they re-enlisted, then something is wrong, so I like the concept of the SQT testing where promotions are based on knowledge, but they should also take into consideration performance as a soldier, too. But if they are going to rely solely on the test results of the SQT, then they should give valid training, instead of falsifying the training records. The SQT is a bogus way of determining promotions because the training for the SQT tests is lacking and or falsified."

"Are you accusing somebody of falsifying records?"

"I am," I said. Not knowing that my sworn affidavit was in my personnel file and that Gibson had already read it, I explained to him what happened with the SQT and my reasoning for not taking the test. "I refused to take the SQT because our training records were falsified."

"I really did not know that," Gibson lied. "All I'm trying to do is to get you to reconsider your position," Gibson said. Three years ago, I was you. I speak from experience when I say I know you'll regret your decisions." At that point I could not tell if Gibson was sincere or whether he was not. Although within the next four months, I would be brought up on charges 4 more times. He was never directly involved in bringing charges against me. It was not until after I left the Army and was given a copy of my records that I realized to what extent that falsifying took place during basic training and at the 8ᵗʰ MP Company.

Other than being harassed by Sergeant Howard and harboring resentment towards Corporal Gibson for insinuating that I was a screw up and would be a failure in life, those first few weeks working patrol duty went quick and were exciting. I was involved in making several arrests, including several fights while making those arrests.

Then things became less exciting. During September in 1981, the U.S. Military participated in the NATO Exercises in Germany. We played war games. It was a two-week exercise in which we lived in tents and played Army. Other than having to camp outside in a tent for three days and two nights during basic training, this was my first real time that I went out to the field. Since arriving in Baumholder, I had not had a single day off, having worked 12-hour patrol shifts at night for the thirty-days prior to our scheduled departure for the field. In fact, I was pulling patrol duty the night before we left. Upon getting off of work, I was supposed to head straight back to the barracks, load my gear, and head out to the field with the rest of the platoon. The whole platoon was working their butts off with double duty like this. But most days, we at least had a few hours of sleep before having to go back to work that night. On our departure day, that would not be the case. We were scheduled to get off at 8 am then move out to the field with no sleep. We were required to have our gear packed the day before, so as soon as we returned back to the barracks, we could sign our vehicles out of the motor pool, load our gear, and head out. But Howard had other ideas. Once again I had been teamed up with Sergeant Brown on patrol. He had me drive so that he could fill out the reports as we worked our shift. When we turned in our reports, Sergeant Howard said he would not accept them as they were because they were not neat enough. He wanted us to copy them over again. Sergeant Brown told him that would be no problem and told him he would have me get right on it.

"Turner, you copy the reports over," he said. "Meanwhile I will go turn our vehicle in."

"Excuse, me," I said as he started walking out the door, "I am not copying anything. If you want to kiss Sergeant Howard's ass, then you copy the reports."

"Don't make me pull rank on you," Sergeant Brown said.

"You don't have the balls to pull rank," I shouted at him while taking my nightstick from off my belt and threw it as hard as I could against the wall. Assuming it was going to bounce off the wall and hit him, Sergeant Brown ducked and covered his head while Howard fled out of the room like a dog with his tail between his legs. "If you had the balls to pull rank, you would also have the balls to tell Howard to kiss your ass. I'm not re-doing any of this damned paperwork and neither should you." At that moment, the on duty desk Sergeant and dispatcher came running into the room.

"What the hell is going on in here, Turner?" the Desk Sergeant asked.

"Howard wants these reports to be rewritten before we get off work. I don't think we should have to do that. If they need to be rewritten, then Brown should do it as he was the one who wrote them in the first place."

"Hey, we all know that Howard is an asshole," the Desk Sergeant said, but don't go getting yourself court-martialed over something so trivial. Think about it. How long can it take to re-copy the forms?"

"You're right," I said. "Since Howard cannot get off work until he turns in all the forms from all of the patrol units, I will re-copy them. I hope he knows that I am a slow writer and that this could take hours, maybe even days."

"Have at it," the desk sergeant said and left, shaking his head.

"I'm going to go turn the patrol car in," Sergeant Brown said and left also. I grabbed some blank forms and sat down at the table and began copying the forms over. I deliberately wrote slow, attempting to make every letter the same standard dimension. I was making little progress when thirty minutes later Sergeant Brown returned from turning in our patrol car. "Howard said forget about re-copying the forms. He said we should turn them into the desk sergeant and head back to the barracks and load our gear up so we can move out." I could not believe it; Howard caved in and was too cowardly to come back into the room to deliver the news himself. He probably sensed that I was ready to rip his head off. We hitched a ride back to the barracks from the patrol unit that relieved us. We were back barely in time to load our gear. The vehicles we needed had already been drawn from the motor pool. I was too tired to care about what happened back at the police station. I assumed I would have to be answering for my outburst. But to my surprise, we went out to the field and did our war games for the next two weeks and nothing was said. Nobody asked me anything about it at all. But I would find out before the end of the month that the matter was not dropped. As it turned out, the paperwork for a court-martial takes a while to move through all the red tape.

In the meantime, for the next two weeks, while we were playing war games, I created more trouble for myself. Being out in the field was not as bad as I had anticipated. The first day, our platoon was positioned at various check points along the route that the 8th Infantry Division was to travel to get to the site of the NATO War Games. I was stationed at an intersection in a forested area. If it were not for the Infantry Division traveling through the area at the time, it was a peaceful, quiet place. My job at the intersection was to make sure that somebody did not make a wrong turn. The vehicles were supposed to be spaced far enough apart in the convoy that if ambushed, one vehicle would be lost at most. I was stationed there for four hours. I had my duffel bag leaning up against a tree near the intersection. Inside the duffel bag was a waterproof bag that contained a boom box radio that I planned to use to catch the Denver Bronco game on the Armed Forces Network that upcoming weekend. At some point during the convoy, some grunt or grunts stole the water proof bag that contained the radio, but they left the duffel bag. Thank God for that because, otherwise, I would have lost my equipment, plus all my extra clothing. I had to laugh about it, thinking the reason somebody stole the waterproof bag was because God had wanted them to do so because inside the bag with my radio was a large and expensive King James Bible that I had purchased in BK through the Bible Study group that I was attending. I was able to purchase a transistor radio and hear the Bronco game, anyway, so it all worked out for the best.

When we arrived at the main site that would be the headquarters for the Eighth Infantry Division we set up tents. To my surprise, we were not sleeping in our pup tents. Instead we set up big 10-person tents that enabled us to sleep on Army cots. The entire two weeks, it rained non-stop. So, we were wearing ponchos the whole time we were outside. But at least we had clothes back in our tent that were dry in our duffel bag. In the meantime, we had another set of fatigues drying out in the tent while we were wearing a wet pair of fatigues. Some people made their own alcohol by placing wheat bread on top of their canteen cup and pouring rubbing alcohol over it, letting it drip into their cup, using the bread as a filter. The Army cooks served hot meals out in the field from portable kitchens. So, at the main camp, it was a first class set up. We were not allowed to have fires, so at night it got dark in the woods and was easy to get lost. For the first couple of days, I was enjoying the War Games, except for the fact we had to dig holes in the ground to do personal business and then bury it with a shovel. Shitting in the rain with a poncho draped over you while slinging an M-16 Rifle on your shoulder was inconvenient, too. We also had to take a turn providing sentry duty inside the camp and outside the camp. As it turned out; however, we did not spend too much time at the main camp. Each day, our platoon was sent on various missions in two-man teams and positioned at bridges and intersections to make sure that tanks and heavy Army vehicles did not turn the wrong way where they might exceed the weight capacity of a road or bridge and damage it. Rogers and I were stationed at a bridge for several days. It was our job to prevent tanks from trying to cross the bridge (should any happen along) as the weight of the tank would cause the bridge to collapse. We were given a three-day supply of c-rations and told to stay put and prevent tanks from crossing the bridge. We set up our tents and decided to work in shifts, working two hours and taking two hours off during the day. At night we did four-hour shifts. I took the first shift and Rogers went to bed. Soon afterward local German kids started gathering at the bridge and were treating me like a superhero and were offering to trade anything they had of value for c-ration items. This one kid, Hans, hung around all day. Earlier I had traded him a candy bar from my c-ration lunch for a pocketknife. He acted as if it was the greatest thing he had received his entire life. When I started my 6 pm shift he was still there. It was pouring down rain, my socks were drenched, and I was cold. The kid's mother called out from a house about a hundred yards away for him to come home, so he scampered off. Ten minutes later, he returned and said his family wanted me to join them for dinner. Rogers was asleep. We had been out there a whole day and not a single tank came by and even if they did, they were too wide to fit on the bridge. Hans was inviting me over to his family's house for a hot meal in a warm house. *Screw the bridge*, I thought. *I'm going to his house for dinner*.

I deserted my post, ate a nice dinner, made new friends, and let my feet dry out a bit. During the course of dinner, Hans gave me a pocket-sized new testament Bible written in German. Of course I did not know enough German to be able to read it, but in my heart it replaced the King James Bible that had been stolen from my duffel bag earlier that week. When I returned to the bridge about two hours later, Rogers was up wondering where in the heck I had been. He was pissed that I did not wake him to go to dinner, too. For years after leaving Germany, I wrote to Hans and his family. Hans was 14 at the time I met him and his family. When he turned 18 he sent me a post card, telling me he had joined the German Air Force. For years we wrote to one another about once a year, but that tradition faded with time.

After spending another night guarding the bridge, Rogers and I were picked up the next morning. Our squad was being sent on another mission. During the war games, we had been issued blanks. So, I was surprised when they picked us up, we were told we were being sent on a real mission. At the time, the Red Brigade, an Italian terrorist group, had been active in Europe and earlier that week had attempted to kidnap an American General, but failed. A few months later on December 17, 1981, they succeeded in kidnapping General Dozier, an American General in Italy. A report was sent out that the people responsible for the failed kidnapping had been seen hiding in a wooded area not far from where our eight-man squad was positioned on bridges and roads. Our lieutenant had heard this and volunteered our squad to search the woods to find the terrorist. The lieutenant came to every traffic control point, picking us up. As he stopped we climbed into a back of a deuce-and-a-half truck whereupon we were given a brief account of what was happening. Within thirty minutes, everybody had been picked up from our traffic control points and we pulled off the one-lane, paved road onto a dirt road. The deuce-and-a-half truck was too big to go down the dirt road, which was more like a swamp because of all the rain. We were ordered to dismount and to take cover behind some bales of hay one-hundred yards further down the dirt road. Everybody, except for Weller sprinted for cover behind the hay. The lieutenant ordered Weller to stay with the truck, keeping it secure.

"Everybody listen up," the lieutenant said. "We've received a report that there are some heavily armed men in these woods who are believed to be the terrorists recently responsible for trying to kidnap an American General. I volunteered you men to search the woods and find them." Of course he volunteered us.

Like General Custer, our lieutenant wanted to make a name for himself. We all thought he was nuts. Everybody stared at him.

Not believing what I heard, I spoke up for everybody. "Excuse me, lieutenant," I said. "I assume when you volunteered us, that you also acquired real ammunition? You realize we have nothing but blanks in our M-16's, don't you sir?"

"They would not have authorized the use of real ammunition, so I did not ask" he responded.

"Who are they?" I asked. "That is crap. They authorize the use of real ammunition all the time for missions. I would dare to say that searching for armed and dangerous terrorists is a real mission."

"I'm warning you, Turner," the lieutenant said. "If you do not quit stirring up trouble, you're going to be in a heap of trouble yourself."

"I don't think asking for real ammunition is stirring up trouble, but fine we'll do it your way. So, if we find these terrorists, do you want us to yell, 'bang bang,' or throw rocks at them?"

"This is going to be our base of operation," he said, ignoring my last question. "Half of us are going to stay here, providing a perimeter around the woods while you four search the woods." He pointed to the four people on his left."

"So you're going to send those four on a suicide mission while we hide behind these bales of hay that aren't going to protect us from gunfire? Good plan."

"Turner, I will deal with you back at camp; otherwise, I would be sending you in there, too. If these four have a problem with my order, then I will deal with them, too."

"I hope you do deal with this later," I said, "telling people all about it, as you'll be lucky not to lose your commission. It's an illegal order and possibly suicidal." Suddenly Weller started shouting for the lieutenant regarding a radio transmission coming in from the radio mounted in the truck.

"Weller," the lieutenant shouted, "keep your mouth shut, you're breaking protocol, possibly giving our position away to the terrorist." *As if they could not see our truck.*

"Sir," Weller shouted from the truck, "HQ radioed us to scrub the mission. The people in the woods have been identified as some local hunters."

"Thank you, Weller," the lieutenant shouted back. "You heard the man, the mission has been scrubbed." About that same time, the rain stopped and the cloud cover broke and a ray of sunshine shone down on Weller, encasing him in a rainbow.

"Look at that rainbow on top of Weller," Thomas said. Thomas was an obnoxious, hard-drinking man who liked to party and get into bar fights. Meanwhile, Weller was a zealous Christian who was trying to convert the whole platoon into Christianity by inviting us, all at various times, to join him at church for Sunday Services or bible studies. He attended a Holy Roller gospel church of the Assembly of God Faith. I tagged along a few times to both church and bible study. I was the single member of the platoon to ever accompany him to either one. I liked the church. I found the preacher to be entertaining, and his wife always provided great snacks at the bible studies. Everybody in the platoon made fun of Weller except for me. I admired his faith. No matter what happened to him, good or bad, he was always praising God and thanking Jesus.

"I swear to God," Thomas said, "if Weller starts floating up to heaven, I'm going to run and grab his ankle and go with him."

"Weller, next time I order you to keep silent, you better follow my orders," the lieutenant shouted as we all approached the truck. As we neared the truck, the cloud cover once again blocked out the sun and it soon started raining again.

"Praise, God, huh, LT?" Weller said. "They were hunters and not terrorists."

"Yes, praise God," the lieutenant said, glaring at Weller. I had a feeling the lieutenant was pissed that his chance for glory had been ruined and that he somehow was blaming Weller for that.

When we returned to the main camp, the lieutenant went into the tent looking for Sergeant Howard. Within an hour, Howard had tracked me down.

"Turner," Howard said as we stood near a tree away from the activity of other people. "I'm greatly disappointed in you. The lieutenant informed me that you deliberately disobeyed orders from him today. When we return from the field, you're going to be given an Article 15. I would not be surprised if you are busted down to a private." Having been through the threat of an Article 15 before, I was not falling for his bluff. I knew that when threatened with an Article 15, most people blindly accepted it and signed the necessary papers agreeing with the terms, which resulted in fines, loss of rank, barracks restrictions, and extra duty. However, a person did not have to accept. They could opt to be tried through a court martial process.

"I am greatly disappointed, too," I said. "I thought the lieutenant had more sense than what he displayed today. However, I don't recall disobeying any orders. I simply questioned the legality of them, and just so you know, I would rather decline the Article 15 and take my chances with a court martial."

"You better keep your nose clean or I'm going to personally see to it that you are busted to Private." He then turned and walked away.

"If it will make you feel good about yourself, go for it," I said as he was walking away. "Good luck to you with that project."

The next day was a Sunday with no missions. Several of us decided to commandeer some jeeps and go to a high school in a nearby town, as we heard we could get inside and take showers. We were forbidden to go into the town because of concern that if a bunch of military people descended upon the town, it would wreak havoc with the local citizens, so the town was off limits. Eight of us decided that it was worth the risk, so we all loaded into two jeeps, with four people in each jeep and went into town and found the high school. Sure enough, it was unlocked and we were able to shower in the locker room. It was refreshing. On the drive back to main camp, we were driving down the autobahn. Driving an Army jeep fast was out of the question, as they were infamous for flipping over even at low speeds. So, we were cruising at fifty miles per hour, being passed by cars doing twice that speed. A loud, metal on metal, crunching sound caught all of our attention. A car traveling in the opposite direction on the other side of the autobahn lost control and hit several other cars, causing a multiple-car pile up on the autobahn. The original car flipped over several times and came to rest upside down about half the size it used to be.

"We should pull over and help," I suggested.

"No, keep driving," Sergeant Brown said. "We are not supposed to be out here, remember?"

"Then we should radio this in, so they can dispatch ambulances," I suggested, reaching for the microphone on the radio.

"Hell, no!" Brown said, yanking the microphone out of my hand. "What part don't you get? We're not supposed to be out here. Do you want to get us all busted?"

"It would be better we were busted than to let somebody die," I said

"Do you know for certain somebody is dying in that car wreck?" Brown asked.

"No, but the car was smashed."

"I did not see anything that should have been a concern to us, and I'm positive nobody else saw anything either," Brown said.

"You're a chicken shit," I said and did not say another word. Sergeant Brown was fuming. Once again within an hour of getting back to camp, I was being lectured. This time Sergeant Gibson took his shot.

"I agree with Sergeant Brown," Gibson said. "You had no evidence that anybody was hurt, so there was no need to get involved. But I commend you for wanting to help." Gibson was trying to act like my friend in this matter, but I knew he was itching to go tell Howard how we had all gone to town when it was off limits. So, I agreed with him to end the conversation.

"I'm sure somebody called for help,"

"That's the spirit," Gibson said, putting his arm over my shoulder. I wanted to throw up on his boots. "There are a lot of things you can't control. You will have to learn to accept that; otherwise, you are going to be in more trouble than you are right now."

"I can't argue with you about that," I said, wanting to end the conversation and forget the whole day. Sure enough as soon as Gibson left, he headed straight over to Sergeant Howard's tent and ratted on all of us for going into town. I couldn't believe Sergeant Brown told Gibson about the event because he was so concerned if we radioed for help, we would get busted, yet we got busted anyway because he told Howard's brown-nosing sidekick. We all ended up getting assigned extra field duty when we returned to Baumholder for going into town.

Upon returning back to Baumholder after the war games, we were not scheduled to be on patrol duty for another two weeks, but we had a big inspection coming up at the end of the month by the Inspecting General. So we had to get all of our equipment, uniforms, vehicles, and the barracks cleaned. Living in a tent for two weeks made me appreciate the barracks. The barracks were not so bad. Living in separate rooms with one or two other people was more like college dorm life. When we first arrived at Baumholder, Rogers, Randall, and I were all three assigned to the same room. Rogers and I had heard about Randall's reputation of not showering, but we also found out he was messy. He would not clean anything. We constantly had to rag him to clean his stuff, so that our room would be ready for inspections. Rogers was always complaining about how awful Randall smelled from not taking showers. Like I said, I was born without the ability to smell, so his odor did not bother me. Prior to playing war games, Rogers had put in a request to be moved to a different room because by that time, he could not stand living with Randall any longer. When we returned from the field, a bunk opened up in another room, as another member of the platoon finished his three-year enlistment and was discharged as a free man. Rogers moved to his room. Meanwhile, Carlson, another MP, told me that several people were thinking about giving Randall a blanket party where they would burst into the room while he was sleeping, throw a blanket over his head, and beat the hell out of him. I told Carlson to tell anybody who was thinking about bursting into my room to think twice about it because I would hurt them.

"If they want to give Randall a blanket party," I said, "they better be willing to give me one, too, and I will hurt people in the process. Anybody who bursts into this room to give a beating better be willing to take a beating. Just because he does not take a shower is no reason to beat him. The guy needs to have his head examined, not beat." Carlson warned everybody of what I said.

Being the senior ranking member of the room, I was the room commander, not that it held much authority, but I was constantly ragging Randall about keeping his area clean, as he would throw his stuff all over the floor, so his half of the room was always a mess. I ordered him to have his area spotless for the upcoming inspection. During the days the whole platoon was doing various chores around the company getting the area ready for inspection. For example, we painted the hallways, scrubbed the bathroom, painted the vehicles at the motor pool, and landscaped around the barracks. The old Army motto applied: If it moves, salute it, if it does not, paint it. We worked like dogs for an entire week. Then with one week before the inspection, once again, our lieutenant – still trying to make a name for him self -- volunteered eight of us to go out into the field for a training exercise as a favor to some ranking officers. The eight people he volunteered were the eight people, myself included, who went to town that was off limits in order to shower during the war games. This was our extra duty punishment for ignoring the order to avoid the town. The training exercise involved the eight of us playing a game of hide and seek. The 8th Infantry Division was testing some new radar on some tanks and they needed us to hide while they used the radar to track us down. In teams of two, we signed four jeeps out of the motor pool, loaded up a weeks worth of supplies and equipment, and were told, as a group, to head anywhere we wanted within Germany. We were given a 24-hour head start.

When we left Baumholder, we zigzagged for eight hours all over the place, coming to camp in a remote area. We thought no way in hell would they locate us. They were not scheduled to start looking until the next morning. We were so sure they would not find us, we did not even bother to leave the next morning. Having spent the night sleeping in our jeeps because it was dark, cold, and rainy by the time we arrived, we all gathered around the jeeps, eating our c-rations for breakfasts. About 11 am, we heard a loud rumbling that kept getting louder. Tanks were driving up the road to our exact location. Their radar pinpointed our exact location before they even left Baumholder, and they drove straight to us. The new radar system in the tanks was so sophisticated, they could detect the shoeshine on our boots. They were upon us before we knew what was happening and had us surrounded. We thought we were going to have our asses kicked, being out number two-hundred grunts to eight MP's. However, they were happy to see us and proud of how fast they located us. They invited us to join them for lunch, as they brought hot meals with them. The rest of the day we made plans on what we were going to do the rest of the week. They wanted us to stay within that vicinity and to take our jeeps off road into as much rough terrain as we could and attempt to escape from them. They would try to keep up with us in their tanks, as they wanted to test them. Meanwhile, we had blanks and would act as enemy soldiers, trying to take out their tanks by getting them stuck. For the entire week, we slept in our jeeps. It was freezing and raining cats and dogs. The grunts had their tents with wood stoves and inside the tanks, they had heaters to keep them warm, too. They shared dinner with us that night. The next morning right before we headed out to play, Sergeant Brown said he had received a radio transmission, and that he and I were to return back to Baumholder, as Top wanted to see me. Not knowing what it was about, I was nervous the whole two-hour drive back. I had a feeling that Sergeant Brown knew what it was about, but he would not say anything. The anticipation was killing me as I entered Top's office and stood at parade rest in front of his desk, looking like hell from the past two days of sleeping in a jeep. I had not shaved during the past forty-eight hours.

"Specialist Turner," Top said, "this is never an easy situation, but you have nobody but yourself to blame for this, and I find no pleasure in having to do this. I'm sorry I had to call you in from out in the field, but as soon as we are done, I'll see to it that you get right back out there."

"No problem, Top" I said. By the tone of his voice, I could tell I was in hot water.

"I would have done this before you left for the field, but it took longer than I thought to get the paperwork back from headquarters. I have taken the liberty to draw up Article 15 papers for you to sign."

"Article 15 papers, Top?" I asked as if it was news to me. "May I ask why?" I had a gut feeling it was for when the Lieutenant had volunteered our squad to look for armed terrorists without ammunition. Gibson had said that was going to happen.

"Certainly," he said. "You have been charged with being disrespectful to a Non-Commissioned Officer." *A non-commissioned officer? The lieutenant was a Commissioned Officer.* This caught me a little bit by surprise.

"Being disrespectful to a Non-Commissioned Officer?" I asked. "Who was I disrespectful to, Top?"

"You don't recall being disrespectful to Sergeant Brown?" Top asked.

"I do not. "

"Do you recall throwing your baton at Sergeant Brown?"

"I recall throwing my baton at a wall," I said. "I would have hit him with the baton when I threw it, as he was standing a few feet away from me at the time. Also, I'm sure I would have called him a few disrespectful names, too."

"So, you don't think what you did was disrespectful?"

"To Sergeant Brown?" I asked. "No," I said, answering my own question. "I was angry that night, as I felt he should have been the one re-copying his own paperwork. For that matter, I don't think we should have been told we had to copy it in the first place. I was angry at Sergeant Brown for allowing Sergeant Howard to piss all over us. I have the utmost respect for Sergeant Brown as a man, but that night I was angry at Sergeant Howard and intended to fully disrespect him. Sergeant Brown happened to be standing a little bit too close to Sergeant Howard."

"That's not the way Sergeant Howard saw things," Top said. "He brought it to my attention and we reviewed the situation and determined that you were disrespectful. So, I've drawn up these Article 15 papers."

"So, you're telling me Sergeant Howard is accusing me of being disrespectful to Sergeant Brown?

"Didn't I just say that?"

"So, Sergeant Brown, himself, did not accuse me of being disrespectful?"

"He doesn't have to," Top said.

"If I sign the Article 15, what all does that involve, Top?"

"You'll be busted down two ranks from Specialist to Private, be fined $500, and be restricted to barracks for two months and will be assigned extra duty." This did not sound like a good deal to me. I knew I had an option not to sign the papers. I do not think Top knew I was aware of that. If he was, he did not think I would refuse to sign because what I said next floored him. I could tell by the way his jaw dropped.

"Top, no disrespect intended," I said, being sarcastic, "but I won't be accepting your offer. Like I said, I was not disrespectful to Sergeant Brown. I was angry at Sergeant Howard and I overreacted. If you were bringing me up on charges of being disrespectful to Sergeant Howard, I might agree with that. But to tell you the truth, I do not think Sergeant Howard has the balls to bring me up on charges for fear that I would opt for the court martial and it would become known how incompetent he is. With all due respect, I do not think Sergeant Brown is that great of a leader, as he and I have had our differences. But I confront him with those differences face to face. If I wanted to be disrespectful to him, I might be tempted to accept the invitations I have received to join the Ku Klux Klan from other members of this platoon. Since arriving in Baumholder, I have been asked to join the KKK three separate times. My answer has always been, 'No.' I think the KKK is nothing but a bunch of cowards. If you have to hide behind a mask and then form a mob to attack a single man, then I want nothing to do with them. These are the people you should be busting for being disrespectful. I have respect for Sergeant Brown, but not those animals in the KKK. I may have been angry that night, but I was not disrespectful to anybody but Sergeant Howard, and this is his chicken shit way of getting even. I did not act in a professional manner by throwing my baton, but if you bust everybody who loses their temper, who will Sergeant Howard be able to harass? I will make you a deal."

"What's that," Top said after a few seconds of staring at me with his mouth open, looking shocked that I was refusing to cave into him.

"I will sign these Article 15 papers, on the condition that you relieve Sergeant Howard from duty for being incompetent. He is not playing with a full deck. Otherwise, instead of signing the papers, I will opt for a court martial. You will have a hard time convincing people I was anything but angry that night. If I was disrespectful that night to Sergeant Brown, I am sorry, and I owe him an apology and I'll accept whatever punishment that involves after being convicted through a court martial."

"I doubt we will have a problem convicting you," Top said. "I know you will end up spending time in jail and will be dishonorably discharged."

"I'll take my chances," I said.

"Fine," Top said. "I will tell Captain Taylor to proceed with a court martial. Until then, you are dismissed."

"Do you want me to go back to duty in the field?" I asked "Or am I restricted to barracks or something?"

"As it stands right, now, you are free to go about your regular duties, so I expect you to head back out to the field."

"One last question, Top," I said. "I suspect I will soon be brought up on charges of being disrespectful to the lieutenant, too. Do you know what the status is regarding that? I'm hoping to be able to have a court martial for that, too, so that it can be brought to somebody's attention as to how the lieutenant endangered our lives."

"I am not at liberty to say at the moment," Top said, "but you are in a heap of trouble over that, too. You will be lucky if you are offered an Article 15. You will probably go straight to a court-martial for that."

"Thank you," I said, turned and exited Top's office where I met Sergeant Brown out in the hallway. We returned to the field.

On the ride back, he apologized and said he had nothing to do with the Article 15. I told him he had nothing to apologize for because I refused to sign it, and that I was sorry for having thrown my baton. He said he understood and knew that I meant no disrespect towards him.

The court martial, now hanging over my head, ruined the rest of my week. From that point on, I was wondering what prison was going to be like. I also wondered if Top was a secret member of the KKK. I had been asked by people at Miesau, Bad Kreuznach, and Baumholder to join the KKK. I always refused and never went to any secret meetings when invited. If I were smart, I would have attended, so I would have known who was in the KKK. Ever since I had been at Baumholder, I had heard people refer to Sergeant Brown as a *Dumb Nigger* behind his back, laughing at him. It was said that the reason he was promoted to Sergeant was because he re-enlisted. I pulled patrol duty with him in Baumholder. I thought he was an excellent Policeman. I wondered if one of the reasons everybody was trying so hard to bust me was not because I was a "screw up," as Gibson kept telling me, but because I had refused to join the KKK. Now, I had also made it known that I thought people in the KKK were cowards. But never having attended a meeting, I had no idea for sure who was in the KKK and who was not. As far as I knew, maybe not many people at all were in it. I always suspected that the people who invited me to attend meetings were not even in it, but trying to run a rouge chapter of the KKK, appointing themselves as leaders. I wish I knew. When I mentioned the KKK to Top during our meeting, he did not even bat an eye, making me believe he was aware of it and maybe even a member. The one person for sure I knew was not in the KKK was Weller. He was the platoon religious fanatic. I was the single person who ever accepted his invitations for Bible study and church. I was glad I did. I did not go with him all the time, but was glad every time I did. He attended an Assembly of God church that was in downtown Baumholder. The church was held in the apartment of the preacher, which was on the second floor of a two-story building. On the first floor was the most popular strip club in Baumholder.

It was quite a large apartment and the pastor and his wife conduct church services in the apartment several days per week as well as several Bible Studies. He was an entertaining preacher. He was five feet, four inches tall and pudgy. He always dressed in a three-piece suit and his hair was blow dried like a game show host. His wife was a shorter version of him, except she wore business suits. He entertained while he preached, bellowing out a sermon that could be heard out on the street, drowning out the loud music and barroom noise from the strip club on the first floor, which is something because the strip club often had live heavy metal bands. After church or Bible study, they provided a meal and snacks for anybody who desired it. They were great people. I loved going to be entertained by his preaching. He would act out all the parts of the people in whatever Bible verses were applicable to his sermon.

Another time, I joined Weller for a sermon at the local high school by a traveling preacher, Dave Roever, a phenomenal man who was severely burned in Vietnam. I do not know how anybody could hear his story and not believe in a Higher Power. Another traveling preacher, Gene O'Neill, who is the author of the book, *I'm Going to Bury You*, told a remarkable story about his conversion to Christianity. I was not as zealous as Weller. Often, I did not feel like going to church or Bible study, so I chose not to. Also, if something went wrong, I'd be the first to be cussing up a storm or arguing with those whom I thought caused the wrong. Weller, on the other hand, was not affected by anything. A grand piano could be dropped on his head and he would praise God for it.

Perhaps Top was not in the KKK. Perhaps I was a big "screw up" as they were saying. After all, I had gone straight from basic training, to being assigned to Recruiter Aide duty, where I got high with the recruiters. Then I went to Miesau a place of lunatics. Perhaps the people at Baumholder were professional soldiers who demanded a fellow soldier be of the utmost professionalism at all times and obey all rules, too. One thing I learned at Miesau was that I would not take crap and often times would dish out the crap.

The rest of that week out in the field, we spent the majority of the time four-wheel driving our jeeps in some rough terrain with tanks following close behind us. Those Army jeeps were tough. At one point, I was speeding across a field, steering with one hand and shooting blanks from my M-16 at a tank with my other hand. I went flying across a ditch, landing so hard on the other side I dropped my M-16 and thought my arm was broken. It was not, but the jeep was dented. The other three jeeps were not any better. By the end of the week, they were dirty, dented, and had broken headlights and taillights. At the beginning of the week, they looked brand new, as we had spent a lot of time at the motor pool the previous week, scrubbing and painting them for the big inspection coming up on Monday by the Inspecting General. It ended up being a fun week and even though Baumholder was the last place I wanted to go to, it was sweet returning there. Before turning in our jeeps at the motor pool, we all went back to the barracks to unload our gear and turn our weapons back in. It was an early Sunday evening. The cobblestone streets in Baumholder, as in most German towns, were quite narrow. On this particular day, for some reason the street in front of our barracks was quite packed with cars. When cars parked on the streets, they had to park partially on the sidewalks to leave room for cars to drive down the street. There were cars on both sides of the sidewalks, making the passageway quite narrow, leaving no room for cars to park. So, instead of parking the jeeps, we unloaded our gear and turned in our weapons four people at a time while the other four people each stayed in their respective jeeps, idling in the middle of the road. Weller was in the lead jeep, idling in the middle of the street, unable to go any further because the car parked on the sidewalk in front of him was sticking out a little too far, making passage impossible. The other three jeeps were behind Weller. Meanwhile, another car turned down the street. Seeing the jeeps blocking his way, he honked his horn for them to move. Nobody could move anywhere, but the guy in the car did not know that and kept honking his horn. The lieutenant, who was working in his office that day, preparing for the big inspection the next day, was getting irritated at the honking and stuck his head out the window, and in the same brilliant manner in which he handled the terrorist in the woods, he issued a command.

"Weller, move that fucking jeep out of the way," The lieutenant shouted.

"But, Sir," Weller said, "I can't because –"

"I don't want to hear your excuses, Weller," The lieutenant said, "I'm ordering you to move that jeep right, now, or face disciplinary action. I'm tired of your constant excuses."

"You really want me to move this Jeep, sir?"

"Let me put it to you this way, Weller," the lieutenant screamed. "If you don't move that fucking jeep right, now, I'm going to bust your ass down to Private."

"Yes, sir," Weller said. He then put the jeep into gear and drove straight ahead into the car that was sticking too far out from the sidewalk into the street. The car was a BMW that belonged to the lieutenant and Weller hit it hard, crumpling the entire rear end of the car. The lieutenant was furious and brought Weller up on charges. After a few months, it was found that Weller did nothing wrong and the charges were dropped. But for a while, Weller had charges hanging over his head, too. He praised God the whole time and constantly prayed about the charges being dropped. His prayers worked. I was not having the same luck. But then again, I was not praying for them to be dropped. My problems kept compounding. I was waiting for a court martial hearing to be scheduled for being disrespectful to Sergeant Brown, plus I would soon be brought up on charges three more times within the next few months, being offered an Article 15 on each one.

But before the other charges came about we had our big inspection on Monday as scheduled. All the work we did around the barrack was for naught, as the Inspecting General never came to our barracks as having stopped off at the motor pool, he was flabbergasted to see the condition of the four jeeps that we had taken out to the field the week before. When we turned them in, they were dirty. Not to mention the dents could not be fixed and repainted, nor could the lights be replaced. Even if somehow we could have done all that within a 24-hour period, nobody ordered us to do so, and the first thing you learn in the Army is to lay low and to never volunteer for anything. The Inspecting General canceled the rest of the inspection, flunking our platoon as soon as he saw the conditions of the jeeps. Our lieutenant was in big trouble for the failed inspection. It was a good thing for Randall, too, because before we left to go play hide-n-seek with the tanks, he had cleaned up his area of the room the night before by stuffing everything into his wall locker. His wall locker was an absolute mess and if they had inspected that, he would have caused us to flunk the inspection.

To flunk an inspection of this magnitude was a big thing, so our platoon was scheduled to be re-inspected in two weeks. So once again, we had to spend every moment cleaning the barracks and sprucing up the vehicles at the motor pool. I was back on patrol duty, working twelve-hour, night shifts and cleaning during the day. We were getting two hours of free time each day in which to eat and sleep. I harped on Randall to continue to keep his area of the room clean and warned him to organize his wall locker. Although he did keep his area of the room cleaned, he ignored my warning about organizing his wall locker. It was stressful, pulling double shifts and having little sleep. But at least Howard was not harassing me any longer because with a court-martial hanging over my head, he felt he had me over a barrel. They were not pairing me up to work with Sergeant Brown anymore either. Sometimes I was paired with Rogers, sometimes with Monroe, and other times Miller.

A few days before we were to be re-inspected for the failed GI inspection, we received word that a colonel from the 8th Infantry Division would be by a few days before to pre-inspect our barracks and the vehicles at the motor pool. We were all prepared. Randall had kept his area of our room cleaned, but despite my warnings he never cleaned out his wall locker. We were told to leave our wall lockers unlocked for the inspection as it would take place during the day while we were out painting vehicles at the motor pool. Randall locked his locker up, thinking that would be the end of it. On the contrary, the lock attracted more attention, making them wonder what he was hiding in it. I was at the motor pool when the actual inspection took place along with the rest of the squad, including Randall. Gibson, our squad leader, who was present during the inspection, told us what had happened. When they entered our room, they were pleased with the cleanliness. Also, in mock preparation for this inspection, instead of hanging a red tablecloth from my wall like I did for the inspection in BK, I hung a huge American Flag from my wall above my bunk. I thought it was important to show that even though facing a pending court martial, that I was patriotic. The colonel was impressed with seeing the flag. However, when they saw that Randall's locker was locked, the colonel was not happy and sent somebody to get a pair of bolt cutters. They cut the lock. One of the other squad leaders opened the locker door and stepped to the side as he opened the door. Upon doing so, a bunch of items, including dirty laundry, tumbled out of the wall locker on top of the colonel.

"Look out, sir," Specialist Moss said, "I think those are some soiled underwear on your shoulder." He then plucked the underwear off of the colonel's shoulder using the bolt cutters. Carrying the underwear to the window, he opened the window and flung them out the window.

"I'm embarrassed by this incident, sir," Top said, speaking up. "As far as I'm concerned, if this man, Randall, wants to live like a disgusting animal, then we will treat him like an animal. Gibson go down to the motor pool and bring Randall back here, now. Then I want to see you, Randall, and Sergeant Howard in my office immediately. Wherever his underwear landed outside, that is going to be his new home from now on. If he wants to live like an animal, then by God, he will sleep outside in a tent like an animal, and we will treat him like an animal."

When Gibson arrived at the motor pool, he told Randall to report back with him to the barracks. Meanwhile he dismissed the rest of us to go to lunch. I did not hear about any of the above details until arriving back at the barracks about ninety minutes later after lunch. Except for Randall's wall locker, the whole platoon passed the colonel's inspection. I was not shocked to hear that Randall's locker was a mess, nor that the colonel and everybody else were pissed about it. I was, however, shocked that Randall was behind the building in a tent. He was required to take his sleeping bag with him, but was not allowed to have any clothes except for what he was wearing. He was not allowed to come into the building to use the restroom but was to stay in his tent except to go to the bathroom, which he was required to do outside. When Top said he was going to treat Randall like an animal, he meant it. Needless to say, even though we had the afternoon off to prepare for our 12-hour night shift on patrol duty, I did not get much sleep that afternoon. I was disgusted with the Army and worried about my pending court-martial.

That night while out on patrol I was assigned to be Miller's partner. About midnight he asked me if I had ever been out at the dump. I told him, no, so he said I had to see it to believe it because wild boars were everywhere. When we arrived, it was pitch black. But everywhere the headlights shone, a wild boar could be seen.

"Hey, let's kill one of them," Miller said.

"Hey, let's not," I answered, looking at him like he was an idiot.

"Why not? It's fun."

"So you have killed them before?" I asked.

"All the time," he said. "

"I do not want any part of it," I told him and stayed in the patrol car while he got out and went around to the back of the car. I could hear a pig squealing as he beat it to death with his nightstick. Prior to that night, I respected Miller as a good policeman who could be counted on anytime back up was requested. He also seemed fair and reasonable when making arrests and would go out of his way to help protect another MP. But after this, I viewed him as a sick and disturbed human being because when he got back into the car, it was like he had finished riding a roller coaster. He was talking about how great it was beating the baby piglet to death and how I should give it a try. I was nauseated and told him I would rather not. I did not say a word to anybody about what happened and felt guilty for that, but did not know what could be done. It took a few weeks to put the sound of that poor pig squealing out of my mind.

I did not like killing. One time Rogers and I were patrolling in a jeep and a rabbit darted out in front of us and I hit it. We walked back to where it was laying in the road. I was about ready to burst into tears when it started twitching as we approached it. It was still alive.

"We should put it out of its misery," Rogers suggested.

"I think we should," I agreed, seeing how the rabbit seemed to be suffering, looking up at us with pleading eyes. "Do you want to shoot it?"

"No, do you?" he asked.

"Not really," I answered. Maybe we should club it." At that point, the rabbit jumped up and went running off a hundred miles an hour. I was never so relieved.

The next morning, I was surprised to see that Randall was still out in the tent. I suspected that by the end of the day, they would let him come back to the barracks since the Inspecting General was coming back in a few days. But that was not the case. The inspecting General came a few days later as was scheduled, and despite with Randall sleeping on the yard behind our barracks in a tent with a sign posted in front of the tent that said, "Do Not Feed The Animal," we passed the inspection. I was flabbergasted that the whole situation did not raise a flag with anybody as being wrong. Another week went by and they still had him living out in the tent. To make matters worse, they were encouraging – or at least allowing -- people to humiliate him. People from the other companies surrounding our barracks would throw food and garbage at him and call him a pig. Indeed, this man needed some sort of mental evaluation about his phobia of taking showers and his lack of cleanliness, but that was no reason to treat him like an animal. At least during the day they were now having him go down to the motor pool and work, so he was able to be out of his tent, but at night time he had to go right back into his tent and remain inside. For God's sake, the man was serving his country as best as he knew how and this is how they treated him.

Three weeks into living out in his tent, Carlson, a member of our platoon, came to my room and told me that some of the other member's of the platoon had been going into Randall's tent during the day and pissing and shitting all over his sleeping bag and pillow.

"What sick bastards," I said.

"What? It's funny," he said. "The pig deserves it."

"The guy needs mental help. I could see disciplining him because he fucked up the inspection, but to treat him like an animal is not right. For god's sake, order him to take a shower. If he does not' kick him out of the Army under a Section 8."

"A bunch of the guys gave him a shower that day of the inspection before he was sent out to the tent," Carlson said, looking at me like I should have known that already.

"What do you mean they gave him a shower?"

"They hauled him into the shower and stripped him naked and scrubbed him raw with toilet brushes," he said. I could not believe it.

"Instead of giving him a blanket party, they did that to him? That sucks." I left my room and stormed into Top's office.

"What the fuck are you doing bursting into here like this," Top demanded to know.

"I wanted to talk to you about Randall," I said, staring at him.

"Talk."

"This whole situation with Randall is going too far. Don't you think he's been punished enough?"

"I don't think you are in a position to make that decision," Top said. "How in the hell do you know what is best for him?"

"I know that being pissed and shit on isn't what is best for him. "

"This isn't anything you should be concerned about, Turner, so drop it," Top warned.

"So you think it is okay that people are throwing food and garbage at him and shitting and pissing in his tent?"

"I'm warning you, Turner. You're out of line."

"The man needs psychiatric help for god sake." I said almost shouting. "What good is it doing treating him like an animal?"

"So, you're a psychiatrist, now, is that it?" Top asked getting angry himself. "Perhaps you need a psychiatric evaluation yourself. I can arrange for that."

"No, I'm not a psychiatrist, but any idiot can see that what is happening to him is inhumane. It isn't right."

"Get the fuck out of my office, now. How dare you question my orders. When you have twenty-three years of experience in the service like I do, then maybe, I'll listen to your pea-brained ideas." I left his office with my tail between my legs, feeling helpless about Randall's situation and with my situation, too. This guy, along with Sergeant Howard, hated me. Together they were teaming up to burn me. *I'll probably wind up going to the Federal Prison in Leavenworth, Kansas*, I thought as I left Top's office.

Pissing Top off was not my intention, but that is what I did. I have no doubt that he was behind the event that happened two days later. I had taken a shower and was settling down, getting ready to take a nap about 2 pm in the afternoon prior to the start of the 12-hour patrol shift that started at 6 pm that evening. My door burst open. As I turned to see who it was, I was caught by surprise, as I saw several members of the platoon rushing into my room. The first guy ran up to me as fast as he could and slapped a handcuff on my wrist and yanked me towards my bed and locked the other end of the handcuff to the metal bed post. Another guy was right behind him, carrying another pair of cuffs. They had burst into my room to give me a blanket party. I did not fear the blanket party. Of course, I had never experienced one before. I knew it was their intention to beat the shit out of me. Once the beating was done, I feared not being released from the handcuffs more than the pain from the beating. I had claustrophobia issues. I have always had anxiety about being alone in an elevator or in a room by myself if any possibility existed of being locked in. The fear of not being released from the handcuffs kicked into high gear as soon as I realized I was cuffed and in somebody else's control. Fear can trigger strong reactions. That fear made me fight for survival, as in the back of my mind I feared being handcuffed to the bed and left there to starve to death. I used my one free arm to punch and elbow the first two people away, so I had freedom to stand and grab the bed frame with both hands. Picking up the bed in a violent surge, I twisted my whole body around, trying to use the bed as a bat, then slamming the bed down hard on the floor. This broke the bedpost frame away from the rest of the bed, and I was able to use the frame that I was cuffed to as a weapon and a shield. I went on the attack, swinging the bedpost at the closest person. He ducked and I missed hitting him. His back was to the window. I had to do something fast because, now, the rest of the people were in the room behind me trying to tackle me to the floor. I stayed on my feet pushing towards the first attacker, holding the bedpost up in front of me like it was a shield and pushed him up to the window. Meanwhile, four other guys were still trying to tackle me to the floor. I was enraged, figuring if they were going to beat me, then at least I was going to throw at least one of them out the window. I pushed as hard as I could. The window, which was not locked, swung open, and my first attacker fell backwards out the window opening. The weight of the other four guys pushed me forward and I fell towards the window opening with the bed frame still in front of me. The bed frame caught the boots of the guy I pushed out the window so that he was dangling upside down from my window from the second story of the building. He was pleading for me not to let him go.

"Talk to your buddies," I shouted back at him. "If they don't stop, I'm not going to have any choice but to drop you."

"No, don't let go," he cried out in a panic. "Please, don't let go." If I had let go, he would have fallen head first to the ground, perhaps breaking his neck. The other four guys tried to pull me back while grabbing the legs of the other guy, but I managed to stay between them and the guy dangling out the window.

"Don't let him go," one of the guys shouted.

"Then one of you better get the fuck over here and un-handcuff me, or, I swear to God, he's dead." One of them came over and unlocked the cuff on the bed frame. "Now, unlock my wrist, too," I demanded. He promptly obeyed. "Now, get the fuck out of here and shut the door behind you and I'll think about pulling him back in." Once they were out of the room, I pulled the other guy back in. His face was as red as an apple, probably from all the blood rushing to his head, and he looked like he had been crying.

"I'm sorry, man," he said. "This was not my idea."

"I don't care whose idea it was," I said, "but you pass the word, that if it happens again, they better plan on killing me because I will kill anybody who pulls a stunt like this again. In fact, I will kill anybody who barges in my room unannounced."

"I'm sorry, man."

"Get the hell out of here."

Things were getting dangerous. It seemed like I was on everybody's shit list. I made sure my door was locked every time I was in my room. When I went to sleep at night, I also put a chair in front of the door, figuring that if they unlocked the door with the master key and opened the door for another attempt at a blanket party, the noise of the chair scooting across the floor would wake me up in time to grab my baseball bat and damage a few skulls.

Two days later I was on night patrol when I noticed an ambulance pull up to the emergency room hospital across the street from the police station. I was leaving the police station after having made an arrest and was walking to my patrol car when the ambulance arrived. I had to look. It is human nature to stare at a tragedy. Randall was laying on the stretcher. I went over there to find out what had happened. I was told that he had overdosed and needed to have his stomach pumped. He was kept at the hospital for two days before being sent back to our unit at which time he was sent back out to live in his tent.

"What happened, Randall?" I asked him as he was lying in his tent trying to sleep. "Were you trying to kill yourself?"

"I do not want to talk about it?" he responded.

"What did you overdose on?"

"They said I overdosed on sleeping pills and alcohol."

"Where did you get those things from?" I asked. "Who gave them to you?"

"I did not try to kill myself," he said.

"Did you overdose by accident?"

"Like you or anybody even cares," he said. "I don't want to talk about it. Leave me alone."

"I care," I said. "I'd like to know who gave you the alcohol and pills. Did somebody give you alcohol laced with sleeping pills?"

"I told you I don't want to talk about it." I could tell, I was not going to get any information from him and went back about minding my own business." Prior to this incident and continually after the incident, I heard people yelling, "You should kill yourself you disgusting pig," from the barracks at all hours of the night. The yelling would be followed by something being thrown at

Randall's tent, like garbage or feces. Who could have blamed him if he did try to kill himself? However, I was not so sure that somebody did not try to kill him.

A week later I was working as dispatcher on the night shift. They often put me on as dispatcher because I had a strong ability of keeping track of each patrol car. I kept in radio contact with each unit, wanting to know their status and location every fifteen minutes. I wrote this information down on paper. That way when a call came in, I knew who was free to respond and who was not and who the closest patrol car in the area was. The desk sergeant was impressed as I could recall everything I had written down without referring to the paper. Also, even though I had been at Baumholder for a few months, I had the layout of the base memorized. Other MP's seemed to have a hard time with the dispatching duties. The desk sergeant started requesting me as his dispatch all the time. Of course, I wanted to be doing patrol duty and talked my way out of having to be dispatcher about half of the time. It was the last night of our month long patrol duty when half way through the shift, the desk sergeant told me to call all the patrol units back to the police station as the other MP company was going to take over the patrol duty that night, as we were all being relieved of duty. As each patrol unit returned back to the police station, they were all arrested by the Central Intelligence Division, CID, at Baumholder. The charges were cruelty to animals. The German Game Wardens were alerted to the fact that somebody was killing wild boars at the dump. They set up a sting operation, staking out the dump at nighttime to see who was involved. It turned out to be the majority of the people in our platoon were going out there at nighttime to kill boars for the sport of it. They were killing them and leaving their carcasses to rot in the dump. The boars were protected animals, and it was a felony offense to kill one. During the time of the stake out, fourteen boars had been killed. Even though I had not participated in the killing of a boar, I, too, was brought up on charges because I had been to the dump that one evening while on patrol when my partner killed a boar.

After being relieved of duty, we turned in our weapons and patrol cars and returned back to the barracks. We were told that the next day we would be brought down to the MP station for further questioning. It dawned on me that the Army cared more about those wild boars than they did about a man who had volunteered to join the military to serve his country. The killing of the boars was a serious matter; however, they gave more importance to the wild boars than they did to Randall, who was still living in a tent, being treated like an animal. An hour before they started questioning us at the station, Sanders, who was in the CID, came over to the barracks to see Rogers and me. He informed us of what was going to happen, stating they were going to try to get us to all confess to being responsible for killing all the boars found at the dump during the past year and to accept an Article 15. He said if we refused to talk to them, telling them we wanted a lawyer, the charges would have to be dropped because if they had to hold us all for a court martial to take place on such serious charges, we would all be relieved of duty while waiting for the court martial. Since they were so short of MP's, they would drop the charges. I for one did not feel that I should have been included in the charges in the first place. Second, I thought that what was done was disgusting and that those responsible should be court-martialed. I already was waiting to hear when my court martial for being disrespectful to Sergeant Brown was supposed to take place and did not need this one hanging over my head, too. The single fact I knew about the killing of the boars was that Miller had told me he killed them all the time. I had no proof and was ignorant about anybody else killing the boars. But the German Game Wardens had witnessed a bunch of people killing them during the month they staked out the dump. We were in the field, playing war games for a portion of the month, during which time no boars were killed. However, even though I had never killed any of the boars, I, too, was being charged. My choice in the matter was to take Sander's advice and not say anything and demand a lawyer and hope everybody else would do the same. Rogers informed everybody else of what Sanders had said. Before the day was over, they dropped the charges and we were all sent back to work. I guess they were hoping we would all confess and accept Article 15's. Nonetheless, the US Army had to pay the German Government for each dead boar. I was glad the bust took place and put an end to such a disturbing thing. It would have been one thing if the animals were eaten in a barbecue, but to kill them for some sort of demented fun and leave their carcasses to rot was sick.

A few days later, I was taking a shower and my glasses fell off of the ledge in the shower stall and the lenses shattered all over the floor. Other than a pair of prescription sunglasses, I had no other glasses and my vision was horrible without them. I had to have glasses for work that evening. Wearing the goggle inserts made for the inside of my gas mask was my solution. The Army had issued me these prescription goggles for my gas mask. I never used them because they did not stay in place inside the mask and they fogged up, making it impossible to see. They hooked onto the inside part of the mask and did not have arms on them to hook over the ears, but I figured until it got dark, I could wear my prescription sunglasses and then as I needed them, I could hold the goggle inserts up to my eyes to see for a short time. The next day I went down to the clinic to see if I could get another pair of glasses. They told me it would be about a month to get them and that I would have to pay for them. Money was something I was still short on, and I could not afford the new glasses until the next payday three weeks from then, and it would take about a month to receive them after that. A few days later Corporal Gibson called me aside and told me I was being unprofessional and looked ridiculous wearing sunglasses inside the barracks. I explained to him the situation and told him I phoned back to the States and asked my parents to send me a pair of my old glasses from high school as a temporary solution, but that it would take about two weeks before those arrived by mail. He told me that was not good enough and that I better have some glasses within a week.

We had been due a thirty-day break from patrol duty, but the other MP Company had other obligations, so our platoon was into our second straight month of patrol duty. I was working the night shift with Morgan as my patrol partner one night. We saw an ambulance with its lights and siren on, speeding down the road. I turned on our lights and siren and pulled in front of it to clear traffic and escort it into the hospital. Upon arriving at the hospital, once again, I saw that it was Randall who was on the stretcher. After they wheeled him into the hospital, I questioned the medics who had been in the ambulance, asking them what happened.

"A suicide attempt," the guy said.

"Did he overdose again?"

"No, he slit both his wrists," the medic said. "By the time we arrived, he was unconscious. He bled a lot. Did he overdose before?"

"A few weeks ago, he had to get his stomach pumped from an overdose of alcohol and sleeping pills. Is he going to make it?"

"He's going to live," the medic said. "We were bandaging his wrists in the ambulance on the way over here."

"Do you know who called for the ambulance?"

"No, we go where we are dispatched."

"I'm wondering who found him with slit wrists. Was he in a tent when you arrived?"

"Hell, yeah," he said, curling his nose up, "and did it ever stink. It smelled like a latrine."

His tent smelled like a latrine and so did all the facts. It seemed odd to me that people were encouraging Randall to kill himself, and once he attempts to do so, not once, but twice, somebody called for an ambulance, so that his life could be saved? Perhaps somebody else had compassion for Randall, too, but who?

Another scenario was that Randall did not try killing himself the first time. Perhaps somebody tried to overdose him by offering him alcohol laced with sleeping pills. Perhaps Randall himself called out for help and a passerby called for an ambulance, or perhaps a more improbable scenario was Randall made it into the barracks where he was able to call for the ambulance. When the overdose did not succeed, perhaps the same people who tried to harm Randall by giving him a blanket party, by scrubbing his nude body raw in the shower with toilet brushes, by throwing feces and garbage at him, by shitting and urinating inside his tent, and by encouraging him to kill himself, tried to harm him again by killing him and making it look like suicide. Perhaps the first time they laced alcohol with sleeping pills and called for an ambulance. If he died, so be it. If he lived then it would be precedence for a future fake suicide. Did somebody forcibly cut his wrists or force him to do it himself? If so, why then call the ambulance before he was dead?

I needed more details. I needed to find out who called for the ambulance each time. But how do I do that without raising suspicions and perhaps endangering myself? After all, I was in Top's doghouse. The last time I tried to stick up for Randall, I found myself in the middle of my own blanket party. My first thought was to go talk to Randall, but they had him sedated and were transferring him to Landstuhl Hospital. Plan B was to keep alert around the barracks and see if I could overhear some conversations.

A few days went by and I had not heard a thing. Then one day, I was called into Top's office regarding the earlier incident I had with the lieutenant out in the field and about my glasses.

"Turner, it seems like this is getting to be a regular habit of yours," Top said. "You must like being in trouble."

"I've been in more than my fair share of trouble since I transferred into this company."

"If I recall, the last time you were in here, I had to kick you out of my office as you were questioning my orders regarding Randall and were bordering on being disrespectful to me."

"I recall you kicking me out, Top, but I do not recall any disrespect. Funny how we see things differently."

"You're already waiting for a court martial date for being disrespectful to Sergeant Brown."

"Do you have any further news regarding the status of that, Top?"

"Not, yet," he said, "but I do have some further news on that incident out in the field with the lieutenant. I have to decide whether I'm going to bring you up on charges of being disrespectful to him."

"I hope you do, Top, as I want it to be known what a screwed up order he gave us that day in sending us to capture terrorists with blanks in our guns."

"I'll be getting back with you on my decision about that in a few days," Top said. "In the meantime, I want to talk to you about your glasses. Corporal Gibson tells me he ordered you to get a pair of new glasses a few weeks ago and you have ignored his order."

What a back-stabbing, kiss ass Gibson is, I thought. "No, I haven't ignored his order. I have made arrangements for a new pair of glasses and things beyond my control have prevented that from happening, yet, Top."

"I would like to believe you, but you have a history of being disrespectful," Top said. "So while I'm pondering whether or not to bring charges up against you for disrespect to the lieutenant, I'm going to bring charges of disobeying Gibson's direct order."

"If you can still look yourself in the mirror, then continue running this platoon anyway you see fit. That is not going to change anything I do."

"You're bordering on disrespect once again, Turner."

"I'm sorry if speaking my opinion makes you feel that way, Top."

"Unless you have any questions, I suggest when you leave here you get some Army issue glasses."

"I've already put that plan into motion, Top, but it will take them about a month before they arrive."

"A good soldier would have had an extra pair on hand as backup."

"I can't argue that, Top, but I have never claimed to be a good soldier. Speaking of which, Top, I do have a question about Randall." By this time my blood was boiling and my blood pressure was up from this whole conversation, so I figured I had nothing to lose by throwing more crap into the fire.

"Careful about what you say," Top warned.

"I was wondering if you know who called the ambulances each time Randall tried to commit suicide?" I asked.

"How the hell should I know or care who called the ambulance?" Top said, looking like he was ready to explode. "Why the fuck in God's name do you want to know that?"

"I find the circumstances odd that once Randall overdosed and later slashed his wrists that both times somebody coincidentally found him, I assume, alone in his tent."

"Why in the hell is that odd?"

"Take the first incident in which Randall overdosed on the sleeping pills. My guess is that if he was drunk and then overdosed on the sleeping pills that he passed out. If he passed out somewhere outside his tent, and somebody found him, then maybe I'm blowing this out of proportion, but if he passed out inside of his tent and somebody happened by his tent because they wanted to shit in his sleeping bag, but instead found him unconscious in his tent, how would they know to have called for an ambulance? I mean how did they know he was unconscious from having overdosed instead of being asleep?"

"Are you making accusations of foul play, Turner?" Top asked, glaring at me.

"Not at all, Top," I was curious as to what happened.

"It's not your damned business, so drop it," Top warned.

"I think otherwise, Top, as being room commander when all this trouble happened, I feel partially responsible for what has happened to Randall and feel obligated to find out what happened to him. I would like to catch the train to Landstuhl this weekend and visit him in the hospital to get his side of the story."

"Turner, both you and Rogers are scheduled to transfer out of Germany back to the States in a few months. I could easily put a stop to your transfer by having you committed to Landstuhl for a full psychological evaluation regarding these murder conspiracies and your inability to show respect for anybody of a higher rank. I'll have you permanently committed there. You and Randall could be good buddies. By the time you get out, if you aren't drooling all over yourself, you'll be too old to care about Randall and his fucking problems. I'm telling you right now to forget about this whole thing. If I hear that you've hopped a train to Landstuhl for any reason, I'll make sure you do not come back from there. I'll have them lock you up while you are there."

"I certainly don't want to endanger my transfer back to the States."

"With all these charges pending against you, you'll be lucky if your transfer out of here isn't straight to Leavenworth Federal Penitentiary. Now do you have any further questions?"

"No, Top, I don't."

"Then get the fuck out of my office."

I had been told when I transferred to Baumholder that it would be for six months and then I would be transferred back to the States, but that day was the first time I had heard anything about it, and I did not know Rogers was scheduled to transfer at the same time. When I requested to transfer from Miesau, my first choice was Fort Carson, Colorado. I was hoping that is where I would be transferred to. In the back of my mind, I wondered if Top was lying, trying to get me to drop my questioning about what happened to Randall. However, I could not drop the matter. In a couple of weeks, we were scheduled to have a few days off after pulling sixty days straight of nighttime patrol duty. I figured I would go to Landstuhl to see Randall. About a week before that happened, I was once again called into Top's office. By that time I had received an old pair of my glasses in the mail from my parents back in Colorado. They were not Army issue, but at least they were not sunglasses. When I went into Top's office, he told me that my orders to transfer back to the States had arrived. "Looks like you and Rogers both have orders to report to the 410th MP Company in Fort Hood, Texas on January 2nd, 1982."

"That's great," I replied. "When do we depart Germany?"

"I'm going to give you a packet with all the information in there, that tells you what you need to do to process out of Germany," Top said. "Your departure date is on December 21st. But don't get your hopes up. You have two court-martials to face first. I am going to recommend to Captain Taylor that you be court-martialed for your disrespect to the lieutenant. Plus you have the other court martial pending for your disrespect to Sergeant Brown. We should find out a date for that within a week. So, even though your transfer to Fort Hood is pending, that may change. However, go about your duties and start your out processing, making arrangements to have your belongings shipped back to the States, as either way, you will be going to Fort Hood, Texas, or to prison."

I left Top's office feeling rejuvenated about the fact that I would be getting out of Baumholder. I was not too thrilled about the idea of going to prison. However, I decided that if I was going to go to prison, I was going to take people down with me. I was going to find out the truth of what happened to Randall.

For the next few days, at the end of every twelve-hour night shift, I spent a few hours each morning taking care of items on the out-processing check list. I found out that the car I bought from Moran and later abandoned at the do-it-yourself, auto repair shop in Miesau was going to prevent me from leaving Germany, unless I signed the title over to somebody else. That meant at some point I was going to have to make a trip to Miesau to see if the car was even still at the repair shop. So, on my days off I decided to go to Miesau. I wanted to spend one of those days taking the train to Landstuhl to see Randall at the psychiatric ward at the Landstuhl Army Hospital. I had been there a few times in the past visiting people from Miesau who had been committed. However, Top warned me not to go to Landstuhl because I figured he was scared of what Randall might tell me. He threatened to have me committed to Landstuhl if he found out I had gone there. However, Top told me that if he found out I caught a train to Landstuhl to visit Randall, he would have me committed. So, I reasoned that I would not be violating Top's order if I rode my ten-speed bike to Miesau on my day off. It was a twenty-mile ride. I could take care of my business there by signing over the title to my car and then catch the Army bus from Miesau to Landstuhl.

I felt confident that if I rode off from the barracks on my ten-speed bike on our day off that I would not raise any eyebrows. People would think I was going for a bike ride. My plan worked great. On the first morning of two days off, instead of getting some sleep after working the twelve-hour night shift, I changed into some sweats, filled a bottle with water, and left the barracks with my ten speed. I was half way to Miesau, riding my bike down a big hill that – like many streets in Germany – was paved with cobblestones. My front tire caught in a rut between two cobblestones. The bike stopped, but I did not. I flew head first over the top of my handlebars, landing face first about ten feet in front of my bike. My clothes, face, hands, and knees were torn and bloody by the time I skidded to a stop. My bike was not damaged too badly. The steering wheel was a little crooked and I could not straighten it all the way, but I could still steer. However, I was sore from the fall and not able to move well, so the last half of the ride took double the time that I expected. By the time I arrived, it was late afternoon. I had hoped that I would be able to take care of the paperwork with the car, catch the bus to Landstuhl, visit Randall, catch the bus back to Miesau, and ride back to Baumholder all in one day. That plan was thwarted by my fall. I looked a mess and with my clothes all torn up, the Polish guard at the front gate of the base was reluctant to let me enter. When I used to be stationed there, they never asked anybody for ID. They were used to seeing drunk, and sometimes beat up soldiers coming back from a night of partying all the time. I looked horrible when I showed up at the front gate. They stopped me and asked what my business was on the base. I told them I was visiting friends. At first they denied me entry, but I showed them my military ID card and they let me enter.

I had friends at Miesau whom were still stationed there. I asked one of them, Robinson, if I could stay in the barracks. He said that would be no problem and made arrangements with two of the female MP's to let me stay the night with them in their room. Robinson was gay and he was close friends with them. I managed to go to the auto repair shop where my old car was still parked. I talked to the manager of the place and asked if I could sign the title over to the shop. He had no problem with letting me do that. The Motor Vehicle Department was right next door. It was the same place where I obtained my International Driver's License by cheating on the test. I did not have the title, but they had me in their computer system, so they had me fill out a sworn statement, stating I lost it and that I was granting ownership to the auto repair shop. That took two hours. I spent the rest of the day with Robinson and the two women. We sat around playing Monopoly and talking throughout most of the night. It was about 4 am by the time I slept. I left early to eat breakfast at the chow hall and caught the first bus from Miesau to Landstuhl.

I did not know what to expect or even what I was going to ask Randall when I arrived. I had brought him a Bible from the bookstore that was used by the church Weller attended. I went straight to the psychiatric ward and signed in as a guest. I then had to wait for a buzzer to sound that indicated that the security door could be opened from the outside. I went inside to find out the truth.

I went about the next few weeks laying low and keeping my nose clean and doing whatever I could during the day to make arrangements to transfer back to the States. The whole time I was worried about the pending court-martials and how they would affect my transfer and the rest of my life. Then one day, Top summoned me to his office. When I arrived, I was sweating bullets, as he looked pleased with himself, so I had a sinking feeling he was going to let me have it. I stood at parade rest in front of his desk waiting for him to acknowledge my presence.

"Turner," he said, smiling, "I want to update you on the status of your court-martials. I'm sure you are anxious to find out, so, I'm not going to beat around the bush."

"I'd appreciate that, Top," I said.

"The Captain has agreed with my recommendations to proceed with court-martials in both incidences. So, between now and the time of your court-martials, you are going to be restricted to the barracks." I felt doomed.

"Does this mean that my transfer to the States will be canceled?" I asked.

"I have not heard anything about that, yet, but I'm sure it will be," Top said, grinning from ear to ear. I hated that asshole and felt at that moment, I could kill him. I swallowed hard and decided to play the cards I had.

"I will be glad to get all this out in the open," I said. "I have no doubt in my mind that I will be cleared of any wrong doing. But while we are on the topic of court-martials, I would like to update you about the situation regarding Randall."

"Are you still trying to stir up trouble?" Top asked, as his smile faded away to a look of anger. "I told you to forget that whole thing."

"You ordered me not to catch a train from Baumholder to Landstuhl for the purpose of visiting Randall, but you did not say anything about catching a bus to Landstuhl from Miesau. I had an interesting conversation with Randall a couple of weeks ago and based on the additional information I have gathered this week, I plan on turning all the information I have over to CID. In fact I have already told them about the conversation I had with Randall."

"What the hell did you tell them?" Top demanded to know.

"I'm sure you will find that out in a few days after I tell them about the other information I have gathered during this past week. This new information combined with what Randall told me is enough to send several people to prison."

"And how do you propose you are going to get this information to CID if you are restricted to the barracks?" Top asked with a smug look on his face.

"I already have an appointment over at CID tomorrow. I have a friend who works at CID. We were stationed together at Miesau. I'm sure he would be quite happy to charge you with interference of a police investigation should you not let me keep my appointment."

"Okay, Turner," Top said. "You must have a reason for telling me this. Either you really do have something and you are trying to rub my nose in it, or you are full of shit. I think you are full of shit and you are trying to save your ass, but either way, I'm not willing to take that chance. I recommend we call this a draw. You drop your investigation and I'll drop these court-martial charges."

"I have nothing to fear from going forward with a court martial," I said. "I've always maintained that I would prefer a court-martial."

"Are you willing to gamble that things won't turn out like you hope?" Top asked.

"Up until this point, what choice have I had?" I asked. "If you are proposing that I drop my investigation into what happened to Randall in exchange for you dropping all court-martial charges, I might consider it?"

"You would be a fool not to accept the offer," Top said.

"I never claimed to be smart, but I do not trust you," I said. "I want something in writing."

"Of course," Top said. "If we drop the charges like promised, what's to stop you from once again taking up your investigation?"

"I will keep silent about everything I find out as long as my court-martials are dropped and my transfer to the States goes through as my orders state."

"I may call your bluff," Top said. "I don't think you have squat on us."

"Maybe I do. Maybe I don't. But by the way you are so eager to make a deal, you're worried that if I haven't found out what happened to Randall that I will. You want this deal much more than I do, Top."

"We are at a stand still," Top said, "Who knows, we may all end up sharing cells in Leavenworth."

"I did not say I'm not willing to deal," I said. "I am going to protect myself. I do not want any surprises. Right now you have me up for two court-martials; one for disrespect to Sergeant Brown; the other for disrespect to the lieutenant. Are you going to drop all charges in both cases?"

"I can make that happen," Top said. "Besides, the lieutenant has been asked to resign his commission due to how he fucked up the IG inspection where the jeeps were a wreck. His career is fucked. I could give a damn about his respect or lack of disrespect at this point. As far as Sergeant Brown goes, consider all charges dropped. I will talk to him and put it to rest."

"I also want Howard off my back," I said. "The guy is nuts and he is out to burn me."

"Consider it done," Top said.

"Alright, I will stop digging into what happened to Randall," I said, "and I will keep silent about what I know. Hell, the son-of-a bitch Randall brought all his troubles upon himself. I tried my best to help him out, but to no avail." Neither one of us trusting the other, we both agreed to drop everything. However, after leaving Top's office, I secretly continued to look for evidence regarding Randall's near death because I could not trust Top. The trouble was I did not know whom I could trust. Since moving out of the room he shared with Randall and I, Rogers seem to have distanced himself, and Weller's solution for everything was to pray, but that didn't seem to work for me.

After leaving Top's office, I worked on staying out of trouble, avoiding Howard, and also kept my ears open to see if I could find out anything new about Randall. But I was having no luck. I began to feel better about the agreement I made with Top because within a few days of leaving his office, Howard was arrested for Driving Under the Influence by another member of our platoon. Top had put out the order to have it done. Howard may or may not have been drunk. He had a reputation for drinking and driving in the past, but as a fellow MP, that was overlooked. Whether he was drunk when he was arrested made no difference. I knew Top was behind it and that he would use the DUI charges against Howard as a bargaining tool to get Howard off my back, as I demanded in exchange for my silence about what happened to Randall.

Before I knew it, December arrived and the Army shipped all of my personal belongings from Germany back to my parent's home in Colorado. I departed from Germany on December 21, 1981. I arrived back in Colorado two days later. My youngest brother picked me up at the airport and we drove to where my mother worked and surprised her, as I had not told her I would be able to make it home for Christmas that year, having not seen her or the rest of the family in over two years.

January 1, 1982 through June 2, 1982:

     I was able to spend two weeks at home before leaving for Fort Hood, Texas. While at home, I purchased a used Dodge Colt and drove down to Texas in humble style. I was scheduled to get out of the Army on July 11, 1982, so I had about six months left in the military. I was looking forward to doing my time and getting out of the Army, as while on vacation in Colorado, I contacted old friends and was anxious to get back to a normal life and to start college.

     At Fort Hood, I was assigned to the 410th MP Company. Rogers arrived a few days after I did. After leaving Baumholder, he, too, spent some time back home on vacation in Michigan and then drove his hot rod down to Texas. We were assigned to the same MP Company, which was understaffed, so people were being involuntarily extended to keep the company operating. Fort Hood is in Killeen, Texas and was the largest base in the United States. I did not care much for the non-mountainous, desert terrain of Texas and could not wait to leave, so I was hoping that my tour of duty would not be extended. I did not think my tour would be extended. *After all, why would they want to extend the tour of somebody they had already barred from re-enlisting?* Within the first week of arriving, we were thrown into police duties, working patrol, traffic control, guard duty at flooded intersections during heavy rainfalls, and even crossing guard duty at the elementary schools. They had us doing everything. On patrol duty, we worked alone most nights, as they were always short of MP's and could not partner us up with anybody. When we were not scheduled to work, we had time off to do what we wanted. They had us do monthly fitness tests, too. Once again, during the physical fitness tests, I had exceeded the top scores, doing 120 sit-ups in two minutes, 120 pushups in two minutes, and running two miles in under twelve minutes. After doing that two months in a row, our lieutenant approached me one night right before I started on patrol duty. He wanted to ride along with me as he had a proposition to discuss. An hour into the shift, he blurted out that he noticed my scores in the physical fitness tests and was impressed. "I put you in for a Presidential Fitness Award," he said. "However, they denied it. They said you have to pass the physical fitness test thirty-six times in a row in order to get the Presidential Award."

"Really?" I asked. "I did not know such an award existed."

"Absolutely, and if anybody deserves one, you do. I have never seen anybody get scores as high as yours, so I asked them to make an exception, but they would not."

"Well, thanks for trying," I said, feeling disappointed.

"That is not what I wanted to talk to you about though. I wanted to ask you if you are interested in re-enlisting for another tour of duty. I've signed up for Special Forces and I want you to consider signing up for Special Forces, too. I can make sure you get in."

"I appreciate the offer," I lied, "but the Army has barred me from re-enlisting."

"I read through your file and saw that they barred you for not taking the SQT test about a year ago. I also saw your sworn statement in your file as to why you did not take the SQT test. Frankly, I was outraged and reported it to my chain of command and an investigation is under way regarding the forgery of the training records at the 8th MP Company. Due to the circumstances, they are no longer barring you from re-enlisting. I know you can have quite a successful career in the military."

"No, way, you didn't, did you?" I asked, feeling betrayed, yet at the same time vindicated, having my record cleared from showing that I had been barred from re-enlisting. "I have no desire to re-enlist. I plan on returning back home to Colorado and starting college."

"I wish you would reconsider," he said, looking sad, "I think you would excel in the Special Forces."

Over the next few months, I might have considered enlisting in the Special Forces if I had been awarded that Presidential Fitness Award. So, in the end, I did not change my mind about re-enlisting. I stuck to my plans of going to college. I did receive a couple of job offers to join the Dade County Police Force in Florida and also the Houston Police force in Texas. They were not offers directed to me, but were general offers to all MP's leaving the service, letting them know that these two police departments were in high need of police officers. My dad was a retired policeman from the Denver Police and I often thought I would like to become a police officer and that was one reason why I joined the military police. Between working patrol duty at Bad Kreuznach, Baumholder, and Fort Hood, I worked about 14 months of patrol duty while in the Army – not a lot – but it was enough to determine that I did not want to stay in the military, and that I did not know if I wanted to be a police officer in civilian life. I wanted instead to go to college and explore other opportunities.

I had some interesting calls while at Fort Hood. For instance, one day I was dispatched to the Emergency Room of the hospital because of a disturbance. When I arrived, a nurse met me outside and said a woman in the emergency room had a snake around her neck.

"What do you want me to do?" I asked the nurse. "It sounds like she needs a doctor to remove it, not a policeman."

"No, I mean she has it draped around her neck." I went into the emergency room and saw this woman sitting in a chair with about a six-foot snake draped around her neck, sitting on one side of the Emergency room with all these empty chairs around her. Meanwhile on the other side of the room were ten other patients afraid to move. When I walked in, she stood up and started to walk towards me.

"Sit back down where you were," I ordered her as I unbuckled the snap on my holster, putting my hand on my forty-five, ready to draw it in case I needed to shoot her. "What the heck are you doing with that snake in here?"

"I came home from work," she said, "and when I went in the front door, the snake was lying all curled up in my living room, so I thought I would bring it here, so they could tell me if it is poisonous."

"You stay right there," I ordered her. "I'm going to radio for the game warden." The game warden came out, looked at the snake, and said it was a bull snake, stating they were non-poisonous and were good to have around because they eat rattlers.

"You can tell a non-poisonous snake from a poisonous snake by their eyes," the warden said. "Poisonous snakes have slanted eyes; whereas, non-poisonous snakes have round eyes."

"I don't plan on ever getting close enough to a snake to look to see whether or not their eyes are round or slanted," I said. "By the time you are that close, the damn thing will have bitten you already." I made the lady leave the hospital. She went home, deciding to keep the snake as a pet.

Yet another day, I was dispatched to the psychiatric ward of the hospital to assist staff with a combative patient who was trying to escape. I could not help but think of Randall back at the psychiatric ward at the Landstuhl, wondering what became of him. When I arrived at the hospital, I was required to lock my gun in a safe before being allowed to enter the psychiatric ward. I was briefed at the door by a doctor and an orderly who said this patient had made several long distance phone calls that day to Washington, D.C. trying to reach the CIA in an attempt to let them know he was being held against his will in the psychiatric ward. After warning him several times to stop making the calls, they attempted to restrain him and he resisted and they needed help to restrain him. Three of us went into the small office where the phone was located. The patient was on the phone, trying to talk the operator into connecting him to CIA headquarters. When he saw the three of us enter the room, he hung up and jumped to his feet shouting, "I'm being held here against my will. Contact the CIA and you will see this is all a big mistake." The three of us wrestled him to the ground and were able to put a restraining jacket on him. The sad part about it is that I believed his story may have been true, but I did not know how to help the guy. I had been threatened to be committed to the psychiatric ward by Top back in Baumholder when I was investigating what happened to Randall. On the other hand, maybe the guy was delusional.

Having made up my mind to leave the military and go to college, I was determined not to have my duty extended for any reason. I had 39 days of leave that I had not used up from the past two and a half years, so I decided that instead of waiting to get out of the military on July 11, 1982, I requested to use my last 39 days, so that I could leave Fort Hood on leave on Monday, June 2, 1982. I asked personnel if I could do that. They said it was okay to do, but that the paperwork was a hassle and that I would have to do it myself because they did not have the time to do it. So, I began gathering all the paperwork I needed to complete. Whenever I was not working, I was in the main office of our company clerk, using his typewriter to complete the forms. During any free time I had during the day, I was going from office to office at headquarters getting various signatures on the forms. Meanwhile, whenever I was working, I went to great lengths to make sure my name was not on any arrest reports. I accomplished this by not arresting anybody, if possible. When not possible, I had other MP's who still had a year or more to go in the military put their name on the arrest report as the arresting officer instead of me. One night I pulled over a drunken soldier who was riding his motorcycle back to his barracks. I pulled him over near the main gate and he still had several miles to go to get back to his barracks. All the other MP's were on calls. I could not let him drive off and kill himself or somebody else, so I verified who he was from his Military ID, and then I made him push his motorcycle all the way back to his barracks. I told him I would check throughout my shift to make sure he was pushing the motorcycle. I told him if I drove down the road at any time and did not see him pushing his motorcycle, I would go to his barracks and arrest him for DUI and for disobeying a lawful order from an on-duty MP. It took him three hours to push his motorcycle back to his barracks.

Despite all the efforts I made to avoid having my duty extended, one incident almost blew my whole efforts. One afternoon while on patrol, another MP, whom we called Hawk, radioed that he had made a traffic stop a few blocks from my location. To offer assistance, I pulled up to the corner adjacent to the street that he had made the stop on. So, my patrol car was parked behind his on the intersecting street because the layout of the roads would not allow me to pull in behind the other patrol car without blocking all traffic. I exited out of my car as Hawk was getting out of his car. I approached the stopped car from the passenger side and stood watching the driver, a female, from behind in her blind spot, so I could see her, but she could not see me. Meanwhile, Hawk went to the driver's window, obtained her license, registration, and proof of insurance, and issued her a ticket for speeding. The driver was an eighteen-year old woman. We found out later she was the daughter of a colonel on the base. After receiving the ticket, she drove away in a rage, stating her dad would have Hawk relieved of duty. An hour after the incident, I was radioed to return to the police station. The woman had gone to her father and told him that Hawk pulled her over and threatened to give her a ticket if she did not have sex with him. When she refused to have sex, she said Hawk gave her a ticket for speeding. It was a lie, but her lie did not hold up because for one, she said no other MP's were present other than Hawk, but the radio log books showed that I had called up and logged out at the scene, too, as a backup. Hawk had been called into the MP station to be relieved of duty while an investigation was conducted. Hawk, told the desk sergeant and the colonel that I was present and could corroborate his version of the events. When I arrived at the station, I was taken into a separate room and told to write a sworn statement regarding my version of the events without being told that Hawk was being accused of anything. In fact they did not tell me anything at all except to fill out a sworn statement. That way they could see if my version of the events matched Hawk's version of the events without the two of us being able to collaborate. I was told that an investigation could take a full year and that I might have my tour extended in the event I would be needed to testify at a court martial. However, I went about my business of getting all my documents signed as if I would be leaving the Army on extended leave. Two weeks later, the woman dropped her charges against Hawk. He was cleared of any wrongdoing. The rest of my time at Fort Hood was uneventful. Time went by slow. I felt like a kid in grade school with Spring Fever, waiting for summer to arrive. I started doing things in the community. Hookers hung outside the main gates of the base on paydays. However, I spent my free time either going to movies at the drive in or playing scrabble with a Baptist Minister and his family whom I met at a church revival they had on base one Sunday evening. This Baptist minister was a freaking genius. He had a PHD in Latin and Greek and could speak about any language. He was not a man to play against in Scrabble. If challenged on a word, he would cite the approximate page number where the word could be found in the dictionary. I attended his church services every once in a while on Sundays. I had him baptize me one Sunday during church services. Coming from a Catholic family, I was told I was baptized as a baby, but, hell, if I have any recollection of it. During my time in the Army, I came to believe a few things about the differences being religion and spirituality. I came to believe that religion is a bunch of baloney, while spirituality is a personal journey that can take place anywhere. I discovered during my many trips of skiing that you do not have to go to a church to commune with God or to find God. Often, I have stood on top of a snow-covered mountain and looked out over the horizon and knew God was real and felt I could talk and commune with God in the solitude of skiing down a mountain. I came to believe that religion, like the military, was run by hypocrites with politics, money, and power motivating them, leaving me feeling disillusioned abut both the military and religion.

As far as my Army career went, I was able to take my extended leave. I had my bags packed three days before that. The Friday before I left, I had to register for the draft before they would sign my last form to approve my leave. I was so excited about getting out that for three days leading up to my leave, I could not sleep.

At five minutes to midnight on June 1, 1982, I opened the window in my room on the second floor of the barracks, backed my car up next to the building right below the open window, opened the trunk to my car, went to our main office and asked the CQ to sign me out on leave as soon as the clock struck midnight. I then went back to my room and threw my entire luggage out the window into the trunk of my car and headed back to Colorado. My official three-year tour in the military ended July 11, 1982, the day my leave expired. By that time I was already back in Colorado, working as a security guard and pre-registered to start college that fall. I had left high school three years earlier and entered the Army feeling like the center of the Universe. I was now leaving the Army feeling cheated in that my experiences were nothing like I had imagined. It was not until years later, I was able to look back on some of the values I had learned in the Army and appreciate them for how those values have helped me out throughout the years – small things like getting up early and working hard to get work done whether at home or on the job, which helped me have the discipline to work full-time and go to college full-time and obtain my college degree. The discipline and values of hard work I learned in the military have also helped make me successful in my career, too. However, I also credit my parents for that, too, as all my life I have never known them not to work hard and hold down a steady job. Overall, although I was rebellious at times in the military, sometimes with reason, and other times from being a young kid who knew it all, I feel proud of how I served my country and fortunate that no war took place during my active duty. I devoted three years of my life to my country as a Military Policeman. I look back on my duty assignments and realize that if I had been sent to any other place than Miesau after basic training that I would not be the person I am today. I grew up at Miesau. Although being in the Army requires conformity, I became my own person there. I gained confidence in myself that later helped me through the tribulations I faced at my second duty assignment.

If I had stayed in Baumholder, I was doomed to be busted and court-martialed. I never did reveal to anybody what I learned from Randall from my visit to the mental institution. What I learned during my visit, I had to safeguard and not reveal to anybody. I remember visiting him that day, hoping I could help him and let him know he did have people trying to look out for him. I was risking another court-martial by visiting him when having been ordered not to do so. When I arrived at the hospital, it was an uncomfortable feeling. Every time I visited, I had a slight fear of being mistaken for a patient and not being able to leave and being held against my will. That is one reason why I feared Top's threat so much. When Top threatened to have me committed if I dared to catch the train to Landstuhl to visit Randall, it made me wonder if any other people were locked up in the psychiatric ward under false pretenses like the guy in Ft. Hood, Texas had claimed. It was not a place anybody would enjoy visiting, let alone enjoy being a patient there. In Landstuhl, all the patients were wearing Army Issue hospital pajamas and were in varying stages of consciousness, some more alert than others. Of those who were, some were more in control of their mentality than others. Most of the people were sitting around drooling on themselves. I found Randall sitting on a couch in front of a TV set with six other people, some sitting on the floor, and some sitting on the couch. I could tell right away that Randall was not alert. He was on medication and was staring at the TV. He was drooling on himself. When I talked to him, he acted as if he recognized me. If I asked him direct questions that required a yes or no answer, sometimes he would respond to my questions with a nod of his head, sometimes he would not. If I asked him an open-ended question, he stared at the TV with a blank look on his face.

By the time I left Landstuhl about an hour later, I knew nothing more about what happened to Randall than before I arrived. It was a lost battle. I caught the bus back to Miesau and thought, *screw it*. The day Top called me into his office to tell me that I would be facing two separate court-martials, I was at a loss and led him to believe that Randall had given me incriminating information. He bit into my bluff. My conversation with Randall turned up nothing. I turned up nothing new during my own investigation during the weeks after meeting with Randall. Least of all I had not spoken to anybody at CID about anything at any time. I was bluffing. I was playing a hunch that Top did have something to hide regarding what happened to Randall. Whether he did or not, my bluff worked. It saved my ass.

After getting out of the Army, I returned back to Colorado and over the next seven years, worked full-time at dead end jobs while fluctuating back and forth between going to college full-time and part-time. In 1989, I graduated from college. It was a dream I had since early childhood. I took a roundabout way to get that college education, but the things I learned about myself and life while in the military were far more valuable than anything I ever learned in college.